THE MULTI

Ashgate Studies in Human Factors for Flight Operations

Series Editors

R. Key Dismukes, Ph.D.
Chief Scientist for Human Factors at the NASA Ames Research Center, California, USA

Capt. Daniel E. Maurino
Coordinator of the Flight Safety and Human Factors Study Programme at the International Civil Aviation Organization (ICAO), Quebec, Canada

Sidney Dekker, Ph.D.
Professor of Human Factors and Flight Safety, and Director of Research at the School of Aviation, Lund University, Sweden

Ashgate Studies in Human Factors for Flight Operations is a series dedicated to publishing high-quality monographs and edited volumes which contribute to the objective of improving the safe and efficient operation of aircraft.

The series will achieve this by disseminating new theoretical and empirical research from specialists in all relevant fields of aviation human factors. Its foundation will be in applied psychology, presenting new developments and applications in such established fields as CRM, SA and decision-making. It will also encompass many other crucial areas such as fatigue and stress, the social environment, SMS, design, technology, communication and training.

Submitted work relevant to the objective of the series will be considered for publication by the board of editors. The series is intended for an international readership and so books with a broad geographical appeal are especially encouraged.

The Multitasking Myth
Handling Complexity in Real-World Operations

LOUKIA D. LOUKOPOULOS
NASA Ames Research Center
San José State University Research Foundation, USA

R. KEY DISMUKES
NASA Ames Research Center, USA

&

IMMANUEL BARSHI
NASA Ames Research Center, USA

ASHGATE

Published by
Ashgate Publishing Limited
Wey Court East
Union Road
Farnham
Surrey, GU9 7PT
England

Ashgate Publishing Company
Suite 420
101 Cherry Street
Burlington
VT 05401-4405
USA

www.ashgate.com

British Library Cataloguing in Publication Data
Loukopoulos, Loukia D.
  The multi-tasking myth : handling complexity in real-world
  operations – (Ashgate studies in human factors for flight operations)
  1. Aeronautics – Human factors 2. Flight crews 3. Time
  management 4. Distraction (Psychology)
  I. Title II. Dismukes, Key III. Barshi, Immanuel
  363.1'2414

  ISBN: 978-0-7546-7382-8

Library of Congress Cataloging-in-Publication Data
Loukopoulos, Loukia D.
  The multitasking myth : handling complexity in real-world operations / by Loukia D. Loukopoulos,
R. Key Dismukes, and Immanuel Barshi.
      p. cm. -- (Ashgate studies in human factors for flight operations)
  Includes bibliographical references and index.
  ISBN 978-0-7546-7382-8
  1. Burn out (Psychology) 2. Job stress. 3. Flight crews. I. Dismukes, Key. II. Barshi, Immanuel.
III. Title.

  BF481.L67 2008
  158.7'2--dc22
                                                                                    2008041949
ISBN: 978-0-7546-7382-8 (hbk)
       978-0-7546-7997-4 (pbk)
       978-0-7546-9412-0 (ebk)

Mixed Sources
Product group from well-managed
forests and other controlled sources
www.fsc.org Cert no. SA-COC-1565
© 1996 Forest Stewardship Council
FSC

Printed and bound in Great Britain by
MPG Books Ltd, Bodmin, Cornwall.

Contents

List of Figures

To airline pilots world-wide, who continuously prove that human skills are truly amazing, even in the face of enormous complexity.

To David Keeling whose footprints are visible between many of the lines in this book.

To Mrs. L. R. Towson, a fine teacher who believed in her students and first encouraged Key Dismukes to think of himself as a writer.

To Loukia's sister, Christina, a mother of three and an accomplished professional who is an authority at handling the complexity of her real world operations. To Joe R. and D.D., whose friendship is precious.

About the Authors

Loukia Loukopoulos has a PhD in Cognitive Psychology from the University of Massachusetts, Amherst and an Aerospace Experimental Psychology designation from the United States Navy. She served 6 years on active duty before becoming a Senior Research Associate at NASA Ames' Human Systems Integration Division. She currently resides in Athens, Greece where she is a human factors consultant to the Hellenic Air Accident Investigation and Aviation Safety Board and was a member of the team that investigated the Helios Airways accident in 2005. Dr. Loukopoulos is involved in a number of aviation human factors research and teaching activities, through the NASA Ames Research Center and the San Jose State University Research Foundation, the Hellenic Institute of Transport, and the Hellenic Air Force Safety School.

Key Dismukes is Chief Scientist for Aerospace Human Factors in the Human Systems Integration Division at NASA Ames Research Center. His research addresses cognitive issues involved in the skilled performance of pilots and other experts, their ability to manage challenging situations, and their vulnerability to error. Current research topics include prospective memory (remembering to perform deferred intentions), management of attention in concurrent task performance, pilots' use of checklists and monitoring, and training crews to analyze their own performance. Previously, Dr. Dismukes was Director of Life Sciences at the Air Force Office of Scientific Research. He received his PhD in biophysics from Pennsylvania State University and conducted postdoctoral research at the Johns Hopkins University School of Medicine and the National Institutes of Health. He has published several books and numerous scientific papers in basic and applied psychology and neuroscience, and has written on the implications of science and social policy for the public. He holds airline transport pilot, B737 and Citation type, and glider instructor ratings.

Immanuel Barshi is a Senior Principle Investigator in the Human Systems Integration Division at NASA Ames Research Center. His current research addresses cognitive issues involved in the skilled performance of astronauts, pilots, and flight/air traffic controllers, their ability to manage challenging situations, and their vulnerability to error. Among the topics investigated by his research group are spatial reasoning, decision making, risk assessment, communication, and skill acquisition and retention. The results of his work have been implemented in operational procedures and training programs in space, aviation, medicine, and nuclear facilities. Dr Barshi holds PhDs in Linguistics and in Cognitive Psychology. He has published papers in basic and applied psychology, linguistics, and aviation. He holds Airline Transport Pilot certificate with B737 and CE500 Type Ratings; he is also a certified flight instructor for airplanes and helicopters, with over 30 years of flight experience.

Acknowledgments

We express our gratitude to the real heroes of this book: the pilots, check pilots, and instructors who allowed us to observe them at work and enabled us to understand the real nature of cockpit operations. Our research would not have been possible without their generous help. We hope that this book will make it possible for the entire aviation community to benefit from their contributions.

We thank the two airlines that allowed us to observe their training and operations first hand and up close, and the procedures review team that enabled us to put some of our ideas into action.

We are indebted to those individuals who carefully reviewed drafts of this book and provided helpful suggestions for clarity and technical accuracy (in alphabetical order): Ben Berman, Barbara Burian, Jolene Feldman, Robert Mauro, Martin Nijhof, and John Rummel. Kim Jobe, as always, provided indispensable and expert assistance during both the research and the authoring stages.

This work was funded by the Federal Aviation Administration (Dr. Eleana Edens, program manager of the Human Factors Research and Engineering Group, and Dr. Tom Longridge, manager of the Voluntary Safety Programs Office) and by NASA's Aviation Safety Program. The U.S. Navy sponsored early work on this project by providing a billet for LCDR Loukopoulos to work at NASA Ames Research Center when she was on active duty.

Reviews for *The Multitasking Myth*

'The Multitasking Myth *brings the real world of airline flying to aviation psychology, and the insights of aviation psychology to airline flying. The authors show how to design operational procedures that fit both the ways pilots think and the actual demands the system places on them. Anyone who works in, or worries about, high-consequence operations needs these concrete suggestions. If you want to know what airline flying is all about—and how to make it more efficient and safer—read this book!'*

Benjamin A. Berman
Captain, Boeing 737
Former Chief, Major Investigations,
U.S. National Transportation Safety Board.

'*A delightful and insightful book! "Multitasking" is a much misunderstood myth, yet it represents a critical underlying topic in human factors: how can people safely pursue multiple concurrent goals in cognitively noisy environments? The distance between the two images of work can be huge. The "ideal" as laid down in written guidance makes generous assumptions about the cohesiveness, linearity and time-reversibility of tasks—which often has little to do with the messiness of "actual" event-paced practice. Loukopoulos, Dismukes and Barshi have put together the research in a way that is not only readable and enjoyable, but practically useful and relevant as well. This is the kind of book where the rubber of research meets the road of practice—in all kinds of safety-critical domains.*'

Sidney W. A. Dekker, Ph.D.
Professor, Director of Research,
Lund University School of Aviation, Sweden.

Preface

An airport tower controller clears an aircraft "into position and hold" on a runway to be ready to go as soon as she can get another aircraft to cross the far end of the runway. That other aircraft is on the wrong frequency, delaying communication, and the controller must manage several other aircraft during the delay. Visibility is poor because of twilight and smog. Forgetting that she has not yet cleared the aircraft holding on the runway to take off, or perhaps confusing it with a similar aircraft still on the taxiway, the controller clears an approaching aircraft to land on the same runway, which it does, destroying both aircraft, and killing several dozen people.

A nurse, preparing to inject a patient, notices that the drug he is drawing into the syringe is not the one he remembered being prescribed. He is about to check the physician's order when he is interrupted by an urgent call from another nurse. After helping the other nurse, he returns to do the injection but forgets his intention to check the drug order and injects the drug. The patient suffers a severe adverse reaction.

A driver, late for an appointment, uses her hands-free cell phone to call the person she is meeting to explain the delay. While talking, she belatedly realizes the car in front of her has suddenly stopped. She slams on her brakes too late to avoid smashing into the stopped car, which bursts into flames.

The father of an infant agrees to drop her off at the day care center on the way to work because the mother, who normally performs this task, is sick today. The infant falls asleep in the rear-seat carrier, and the father, preoccupied with heavy traffic, succumbs to the habit of driving straight to work. In the parking lot, the infant is still asleep in the carrier, the father does not see her, forgets she is there, and goes into his office. Two hours later the infant dies as the car heats up in the summer sun.

What these tragedies share in common is individuals performing several tasks concurrently and forgetting to do one of the essential tasks. Why do these accidents occur? How should we think about individuals who forget to perform tasks that are not in and of themselves especially difficult? Are they lacking in competence or conscientiousness? Or are these seemingly careless oversights actually manifestations of a natural human vulnerability to committing errors in situations that are subtly more complicated than is readily apparent?

Multitasking demands are deeply engrained in modern life, both professional and personal. Spurred by accidents such as those described above, scientists are beginning to study the cognitive processes involved when individuals attempt to juggle several tasks concurrently, and why those processes are vulnerable to failure. One of the most common forms of error occurring during multitasking is forgetting to perform some intended action. Research in the new field of prospective memory has begun to explore the cognitive mechanisms by which individuals remember to perform intended actions in the absence of an explicit prompt that the time has come to act, and the reasons they sometimes forget to perform at the intended time.

Although much remains to be learned, we are able to draw on recent research in prospective memory and on a much longer history of studies of the basic mechanisms of attention and memory, to give a general account of the cognitive challenges posed by multitasking and why it is error-prone. In this account we see that forgetting to perform a crucial task, with often disastrous consequences, is rarely explainable as a personal failure of the individual who forgets, rather it is the outcome of the interaction of task demands, individuals' experience, competing goals, and organizational factors with the intrinsic nature of human cognitive processes. Everyone, no matter how competent and conscientious, is vulnerable to lapses in prospective memory. Fortunately, armed with an understanding of human cognition, we can devise countermeasures to reduce vulnerability to these lapses.

Our own research focuses on the tasks performed by pilots. Forgetting to perform an intended essential task has figured in many aviation accidents. Airline cockpit operations offer a particularly useful setting for studying concurrent task management and prospective memory. These operations are highly scripted and standardized, thus it is easier than in most other settings for observers to know what the individual operator intends to do and to observe when actions deviate from intentions. In this book we characterize cockpit task demands, especially the ways in which those demands overlap in time, and the ways pilots must juggle competing tasks concurrently. We identify several prototypical situations and analyze the cognitive demands involved in attempting to manage those situations. We explore why and how such demands increase pilots' vulnerability to errors. With this foundation, in the final chapter we suggest specific measures both individual pilots and their companies can take to manage concurrent task demands and to reduce vulnerability to memory lapses.

Although we use cockpit operations for our examples and analysis, the lessons learned apply equally well to any arena in which individuals must juggle multiple tasks or must defer an intended action, that is, practically any professional setting. We take pains to explain technical aspects of aviation operations so that people outside this field can understand the examples and the conclusions, and apply this knowledge to making their own workplaces and their personal lives safer.

Loukia D. Loukopoulos,
R. Key Dismukes, and
Immanuel Barshi

Chapter 1

Introduction

On the evening of March 2, 1994, the crew of Continental Airlines flight 795 prepared for takeoff from La Guardia's runway 13. The taxiways and runways were covered with a thin layer of slush, conditions quite common for this airport at this time of year, and certainly nothing new for this crew of very experienced pilots. The captain had more than 6,000 hours in the particular aircraft type (MD-82) and 23,000 total flight hours; the first officer had 2,400 hours in type and 16,000 total flight hours. Beginning with their preflight inspection, and all the way up until taking the active runway, the pilots took appropriate precautions to prepare the aircraft for the prevailing icing conditions. Before departing the gate, they requested that the aircraft be sprayed with de-icing fluid and they visually inspected the wings from the cabin windows to insure that the de-icing was effective. They elected to taxi on one engine to save fuel, anticipating departure delays because of the weather, and kept the flaps retracted to prevent freezing slush from being thrown up onto the flaps during taxi. Before starting the second engine on the taxiway, they again visually inspected the wings from the cabin windows. Their takeoff briefing included a review of procedures for a rejected takeoff. At 1758 local time the flight was cleared for takeoff with the first officer at the controls. One minute later the captain commanded the first officer to abort the takeoff after noticing erratic readings on both airspeed indicators. But by this time the aircraft had reached 145 knots, considerably faster than shown on the airspeed indicators, and could no longer be brought to a safe stop within the confines of the runway. It was substantially damaged as it slid into a mud flat in Flushing Bay.

The National Transportation Safety Board (NTSB) investigation determined that the crew had failed to turn on the pitot-static heat system, which is normally done while the airplane is at the gate. Lacking heat, the pitot tubes[1] were blocked by ice or snow, which in turn caused the erroneous airspeed indications (NTSB, 1995). Also, just before takeoff the crew had failed to note an amber warning light on the annunciation panel indicating that the pitot-static heat was off.

Turning the pitot-static heat system on and verifying its status were actions highly familiar to the pilots of flight 795. Execution and timing of both steps were explicitly prescribed in the airline's standard operating procedures (SOP). Airline carriers use carefully scripted instructions, in the form of written procedures and checklists, to describe the exact actions that must be performed within each phase

---

1   The pitot tubes are external probes that provide air pressure information used to determine air speed. A cockpit switch turns on a heating system that prevents the accumulation of frozen precipitation from blocking the pitot tubes during freezing conditions.

of flight as well as the precise sequence in which those actions are to be executed. Pilots are trained to follow these instructions in a consistent manner. At the time of the accident, Continental Airlines used a Before Pushback/Before Start checklist that was to be performed with the airplane parked at the gate before starting the engines. The airline's procedure was for the captain to call for this checklist and for the first officer then to read out loud each item on the checklist, so that the captain could respond by stating the configuration or status of that item.[2] One item on the checklist called for the pitot-static system heat to be turned on and checked. To accomplish this in the MD-82, the captain was to rotate a switch on the overhead panel from the "OFF" to the "CAPT" position and verify that current was flowing by noting the indication on an ammeter next to the switch.

Beyond the checklist, which was the first layer of defense against inadvertent failure to turn on the pitot-static heat, crews in the MD-82 were provided further protection: an amber warning light illuminated on the annunciation panel to indicate that pitot-static heat was off. Checking the annunciation panel was an item on another checklist, the Before Takeoff checklist, yet another layer of defense, which the crew was expected to perform just before takeoff.

Even Skilled Experts Make Mistakes

Why, then, would a crew with so much experience and skill, who had performed the checklists to prepare this type of aircraft for flight thousands of times previously, make the errors that caused this accident? The answer to this question is complex. We have argued elsewhere that attributing potentially fatal errors made by highly-motivated expert pilots to "carelessness" or "complacency" is trivializing and misleading (Dismukes, Berman, and Loukopoulos, 2007; Dismukes and Tullo, 2000). Finding meaningful answers requires careful analysis of the nature of cockpit tasks and the operational environment in which they are performed, the demands those tasks place on human cognitive processes, and the inherent vulnerability of those processes to characteristic forms of error in particular situations.

Our review of airline accidents attributed to crew error (Dismukes et al., 2007) reveals that flight 795 shared critical features with other accidents in which crews inadvertently omitted procedural steps or failed to notice warning indicators. In another review, inadvertent omission of a normal procedural step by pilots played a central role in five of 27 major airline accidents that occurred in the United States between 1987 and 2001 and in which crew error was found to be a causal or contributing factor (Dismukes, 2007).

Flight crews are by no means the only human operators vulnerable to such errors. In 1991, an Air Traffic Control (ATC) Tower controller at Los Angeles

---

2   Some pilots at this airline used a "flow, then check" procedure in which they first set the cockpit switches to the desired positions from memory and then used a printed checklist to check that the settings are correct. The airline, however, did not require this procedure.

International airport cleared an airliner to land on runway 24L, not realizing that she had forgotten to release a commuter aircraft waiting on that runway to take off (NTSB, 1991). The resulting collision in twilight haze destroyed both aircraft and killed 34 people. Forgetting to perform a procedural step, such as removing all surgical instruments at the conclusion of an operation (Gawande, Studdert, Orav, Brennan, and Zinner, 2003), failing to remove a tourniquet after starting an IV line or drawing blood (Patient Safety Authority, 2005) or failing to accomplish medication reconciliation procedures in place to prevent administration of the wrong medication to patients (Joint Commission, 2006) are common forms of omissions in the health care setting. Indeed, omission of procedural steps is a form of human error with serious consequences in many complex work settings, such as that of aviation operations (Reason, 2002), aviation maintenance (Boeing 1993; Hobbs and Williamson, 2003; Reason, 1997), air traffic control (Eurocontrol, 2004), the pipeline industry (American Petroleum Institute, 2005), and nuclear power plant operations (Davey, 2003; Kastchiev, Kromp, Kurth, Lochbaum, Lyman, Sailer, et al., 2006; Rasmussen, 1980). According to Reason (2002), inadvertent omissions have been "… shown to constitute the largest class of human performance problems in various hazardous operations …"

The ubiquity of omissions during task performance in so many professional settings stems from the same underlying and contextual factors. Crews accomplish many tasks in the short time from the moment of preparing the aircraft for flight to the moment of takeoff, and most of these tasks involve multiple procedural steps. The high degree of familiarity with these tasks and the standardization of operating procedures usually keep the workload within human capabilities. This phase of flight is, however, often replete with interruptions, distractions, and unexpected task demands, even on routine flights (Loukopoulos, Dismukes, and Barshi, 2003, 2001). The crew of flight 795 experienced additional demands because of the weather conditions. They had to arrange for de-icing, and to check the wings for ice before and during taxi. They also had to defer setting the flaps to takeoff position and had to postpone starting the second engine until much later than usual, when approaching the departure runway. These demands disrupted the usual flow of procedures and delayed completion of checklists that included items associated with the flaps and engines. In fact, the first officer was still performing checklists when the captain positioned the aircraft on the runway and turned control over to the first officer to execute the takeoff.[3]

These additional demands, however, were not extraordinary, and experienced pilots would not have considered the workload on this flight to be excessive. Yet for reasons that will become apparent in this book, the nature of competing task

---

3   This sort of rushing to complete essential tasks just before takeoff further increases vulnerability to error. As we discuss in the last chapter, captains have a responsibility to be alert to other crewmembers' workload and control the pace of cockpit operations, and companies have the responsibility to structure the tasks and procedures, taking workload and pace of operations into account.

demands in the cockpit contributes directly to inadvertent errors of omission, such as those made by this crew and by other crews. The issue lies not so much in the total volume of work required as in the concurrent nature of task demands. Like other operators in complex environments, both pilots in the cockpit of a modern airliner must often manage multiple tasks concurrently, interleaving performance of several tasks, deferring or suspending some tasks while performing others, responding to unexpected interruptions and delays and unpredictable demands imposed by external agents, and keeping track of the status of all tasks during these events.

The issue of *concurrent task management* in the cockpit has only recently begun to receive attention from scientists and the operational community. Reviews of accident reports from the NTSB database and incident reports from the Aviation Safety Reporting System (ASRS) database (e.g., Chou, Madhavan, and Funk, 1996; Dismukes, Young, and Sumwalt, 1998; Sarter and Alexander, 2000) and simulation studies (e.g., Latorella, 1999; Raby and Wickens, 1994) reveal that pilots are prone to error when managing concurrent tasks—especially forgetting to perform an intended task (Dismukes, 2007). (Also see Damos, 1991, for an earlier review of multiple task performance, couched mainly in terms of workload). Problems stemming from concurrent task management demands are an issue in many workplace settings, such as the health care industry (e.g., among nurses —Institute of Medicine, 2007, 2004; Tucker and Spear, 2006), anesthesiologists (Cook, and Woods, 1994), operating room staff (Rogers, Cook, Bower, Molloy, and Render, 2004) and emergency department personnel (Gray-Eurom, 2006)) and the nuclear power industry (Theureau, Filippi, Saliou, Le Guilcher, and Vermersch, 2002).

A special case of forgetting to perform tasks is to become so preoccupied with one task that the individual inadvertently stops concurrent monitoring of the status of other tasks (Dismukes, et al., 1998). Even when monitoring does not drop out completely, the quality of monitoring may suffer (Wickens, 2005), and pilots may fail to notice changes in the status of the monitored system (Bellenkes, Wickens, and Kramer, 1997; Mumaw, Sarter, Wickens, Kimball, Nikolic, Marsh, et al., 2000). Preoccupation also makes pilots and operators of other complex systems vulnerable to "habit capture" errors in which they inadvertently take a highly practiced action instead of an intended action that is less common (Reason, 1990).

Another form of error occurs when pilots are interrupted and forget to resume the interrupted task (Degani and Wiener, 1990; Dismukes and Nowinski, 2006; Dodhia and Dismukes, 2008). Interruptions have been found to impair both individual and team performance engaged in diverse tasks involving detailed procedures: nurses administering medication (Hickam, Severance, Feldstein, et al., 2003; O'Shea, 1999; Pape, 2003); biomedical engineers providing space mission support (Rukab, Johnson-Throopa, Malinb, and Zhang, 2004); police dispatchers routing emergency calls (Kirmeyer, 1988a); physicians coordinating and communicating with nurses in the emergency department (Alvarez, Coiera, 2005; Chisholm, Collison, Nelson, and Cordell, 2000); and operators monitoring nuclear power plant operations (De Carvalho, Rixey, Shepley, Gomes, and Guerlain, 2006). Interruptions are also commonplace in routine office work. Not only are workers vulnerable to forgetting to resume interrupted tasks in a timely manner, when they do resume they must often struggle to mentally reconstruct the status of the interrupted task (implying a delay, aptly labeled "recovery time" by Tucker and Spear, 2006), and they are vulnerable to increased error rates (Gillie and Broadbent, 1989; Latorella, 1999; Monk, Boehm-Davis and Trafton, 2004; Speier, Valacich and Vessey, 2003; Trafton, Altmann, Brock and Mintz, 2003). Similarly, when pilots are forced by circumstances to defer a task that is normally performed at a certain point in a standard procedure to a later point in time, they are vulnerable to forgetting to execute the deferred task, especially when busy with other task demands (Dismukes, 2007; Dismukes and Nowinski, 2006).

One might argue that some of the situations described here do not involve concurrent task management because the tasks are performed sequentially rather than simultaneously. However, we use the term concurrent task management because the pilot is responsible for scheduling and executing multiple tasks whose status must at least be monitored concurrently. This is a dynamic process that must be continuously updated. The term concurrent task management does not imply that multiple tasks must be performed simultaneously, just managed concurrently. Another concern is that concurrent task management might be taken to imply deliberate, strategic efforts by pilots or other individuals to manage competing task demands, whereas in fact individuals sometimes react to competing task demands without an explicit overall strategy. In this book we use the term concurrent task management broadly to refer both to the challenge imposed by multiple task demands occurring within the same time frame, and to the ways in which individuals respond to those challenges, whether or not deliberate or well-thought out. This use of the term is consistent with how it is already being used in the research literature.

Aviation accident and incident report studies reveal that concurrent task management is challenging and vulnerable to error, but do not explain why these errors occur. That explanation requires a rigorous experimental investigation of the cognitive processes, particularly attention and memory, involved in responding to the demands of specific cockpit situations. Furthermore, the nature of concurrent task demands in the operational context, particularly in airline cockpit operations, has never before been analyzed in detail. To understand the issues underlying concurrent task management, we first need a thorough description of the types of tasks that must be performed concurrently, the demands posed by these tasks separately and together, the temporal structure of these demands, and the characteristic forms of error associated with typical combinations of tasks. This description can inform the operational community about cockpit situations vulnerable to error.

Another reason a detailed description of the real-world task demands of cockpit operations is required can be found in the FAA Advisory Circular (FAA, 2006a) on

Safety Management Systems. This Advisory Circular recommends that systems and task analysis, hazard identification, and risk analysis and assessment be performed as the first three steps of risk management. Further, to become eligible to participate in the FAA's Advanced Qualification Program (AQP) (FAA, 2006b), airlines must formally analyze the tasks performed by pilots and the skills required in the airline's particular operations. However, this analysis is typically performed on the basis of a formal description of pilot duties that in the next chapter we refer to as the "Ideal". As will become apparent in this book, this ideal description fails to capture crucial aspects of cockpit task demands and their complexity. A more realistic characterization of the full scope of cockpit task demands in actual flights (i.e., in "line operations") would provide better guidance for effective training under AQP. It would also provide a foundation for designing flight operating procedures to minimize vulnerability to error.

Still another benefit of characterizing concurrent task demands in line operations is that it can help the scientific community design experimental research to elucidate the cognitive processes that both enable concurrent task performance and make it vulnerable to error. This research can provide a rational basis for designing a wide range of countermeasures to reduce vulnerability to error. Our work aims to address these needs and to provide these benefits. Although our study uses cockpit operations as the domain for study, our analysis applies to many other domains in which humans must deal with concurrent task demands, ranging from hospital emergency rooms, to control rooms in nuclear power plants, to office work in the computer age.

Our Study

In the research presented in this book, we extend previous studies of concurrent task management in two important ways: (1) describing in some detail the various situations involving concurrent task management that challenge aircraft crews and (2) characterizing one of the most common forms of error associated with concurrent task demands—inadvertent omissions of intended actions. These inadvertent omissions constitute several forms of prospective memory error. *Prospective memory* refers to the cognitive processes involved in remembering or forgetting to perform actions intended to be performed at a later time (i.e., delayed intentions). As the example of flight 795 illustrates, human operators often do not recognize they have forgotten to perform a crucial action until it is too late to recover. Throughout this book, we link the real-world aspects of concurrent task management and prospective memory to the underlying cognitive processes. This linkage should provide a foundation for developing better ways of managing concurrent task demands and avoiding prospective memory errors.

We chose to study concurrent task management in the cockpit for several reasons: It is an unavoidable aspect of flight operations; the challenges of managing multiple tasks concurrently have contributed to many aviation accidents; and only recently have scientists begun to analyze the nature of these challenges. Further, the cockpit is a structured environment well-suited for observation, and our observations can serve as a model for analyzing concurrent task management in diverse other settings.

Our focus on inadvertent omission of intended actions as a consequence of difficulties with managing tasks concurrently was driven by four factors:

1. Omission of intended actions can have grave consequences, as illustrated by the example of Fight 795, discussed at the beginning of this chapter.
2. For the purposes of research, these omissions are easier to identify in accident and incident records than many other forms of error. Flight operating manuals (FOMs) specify in considerable detail the actions crews must perform during flight, thus omissions are fairly conspicuous. In contrast, crews are given a fair amount of latitude in judgment and decision-making; consequently, evaluating these aspects of crew performance tends to be more subjective.
3. A burgeoning new field of research on prospective memory is providing ways to understand the cognitive processes underlying vulnerability to inadvertent errors of omission (see, for example, McDaniel and Einstein, 2007).
4. We also suspect that inadvertent omissions of intended actions may underlie and contribute to more subtle forms of error. For example, preoccupied with one task, a pilot may inadvertently neglect to monitor the status of other tasks, thus undermining situation awareness, which in turn is likely to impair decision-making. Further, Dismukes et al. (2007) found that when crews become overloaded with multiple task demands they sometimes respond in a maladaptive fashion, inadvertently dropping strategic management in favor of a less demanding, but far less effective, style of reacting to events only as they occur, rather than anticipating and planning for events. This too is a kind of error of omission—omission of strategy.

Our Approach

We begin our analysis with a detailed description of the cockpit tasks of the two-person crew of a large airliner and then characterize the diverse types of situations in which tasks must be managed concurrently. This characterization provides a foundation for our analysis of the cognitive processes that enable humans to manage tasks concurrently, and the ways in which this management is vulnerable to error.

The study at the core of this book required a multi-faceted approach (described in detail in Appendix A). One component was an ethnographic approach in which we participated in airline flight training, analyzed FOMs and flight reference manuals (FRMs), and observed normal flight operations from the cockpit jumpseat at two major U.S. airlines. Another component involved analyzing incident reports describing errors associated with concurrent task situations, voluntarily submitted by airline pilots to NASA's Aviation System Reporting System (ASRS). The third component drew upon the existing research literatures in cognitive psychology and in human factors to organize our observational data into prototypical situations involving concurrent task demands, and to analyze the cognitive processes that are engaged when pilots attempt to manage those demands. From this analysis we have produced a cognitive account for why even highly skilled pilots are vulnerable to inadvertent errors of omission when performing familiar tasks.

Our ethnographic study focused on flight operations using the Boeing 737, which provides an excellent case study because it is the most widely used airliner, and it is operated by many air carriers around the world. We discuss specific examples from the B737 manuals of the two carriers that hosted our study because we analyzed these particular manuals in detail, participated in these carriers' training programs, and spent many hours observing their flight operations. However, from our experience with other air carriers and other types of aircraft, we are reasonably confident that our observations about concurrent task demands generalize to most, perhaps all, airline operations. What is more, our findings also generalize to other complex team operations, as in space flight, medical settings, military operations, and nuclear power plant operation, because such operations involve very similar cognitive demands and exhibit similar error patterns.

Cockpit tasks are highly proceduralized—the steps of each task are described in detail in the FOM, and pilots are expected to perform these tasks in a standard manner and sequence. This standardization accomplishes several things. It ensures that aircraft equipment systems are operated correctly, and it allows coordination of large numbers of aircraft moving through the airspace system. It facilitates learning how to operate an aircraft, minimizes the load on pilots' cognitive resources such as working memory and attention, and it allows pilots who have never flown together to coordinate their work effectively. (In large airlines, pilots are often paired with other pilots they have never met before.) However, as will become apparent in this book, the real world of flight operations is considerably more complex and dynamic than portrayed in FOMs.

We precede this analysis by putting the concurrent task management challenges in the cockpit in a larger context of "*multitasking*" in modern life (Chapter 2: What is Multitasking?). We address some common misconceptions about multitasking, showing that human ability to process two or more tasks in parallel without detriment is extremely limited. Then we provide an overview of the cognitive processes involved when individuals attempt to manage several tasks concurrently in typical situations. The remainder of the book focuses on cockpit tasks, starting with a detailed description of those tasks and characterization of the diverse situations in which tasks must be managed concurrently.

We present our findings in a layered approach, starting with a description of operating procedures as presented in FOMs (Chapter 3: The Ideal). Partly because of the constraints of language, the FOM presents the actions crews must take in each phase of flight as a linear sequence. The FOM gives no sense of parallel streams of activity, concurrent task demands, and dynamic changes in operating requirements in mid-task. Thus, perhaps unintentionally, FOMs convey cockpit operations as linear, predictable, and under the moment-to-moment control of the flight crew. We discuss the training pilots receive based on the FOM, and the implications of this training for the way pilots' knowledge structure of procedures is organized.

In Chapter 4 (The Real), we use cockpit jumpseat observations and discussions with pilots to characterize the actual demands of line operations and to compare these demands with the normative description found in FOMs. We find that the ideal execution of procedures is frequently perturbed, especially by demands of competing concurrent tasks, and these perturbations make pilots vulnerable to diverse forms of error, especially forgetting to perform intended actions. Next we provide examples of a wide range of errors pilots themselves report making in conjunction with concurrent task demands and analyze the cognitive processes involved in responding to these concurrent demands (Chapter 5: Analysis of Concurrent Task Demands). This analysis also examines the factors that make these processes vulnerable to characteristic forms of error. In the final chapter (Chapter 6: The Research Applied), we suggest techniques pilots can use to reduce their vulnerability to errors of omission, and we suggest ways airlines can redesign operating procedures and training to reduce this vulnerability. We illustrate these suggestions by describing how a major airline implemented our analysis to revise its flight operating procedures and reduced substantially its flight crews' vulnerability to errors associated with concurrent task demands. Given the fundamental nature of the cognitive processes underlying concurrent task management and hence the vulnerability to error, our suggested countermeasures are likely to benefit operators and organizations in high-risk industries outside of aviation, as well as individuals facing seemingly simple, everyday demands.

Our description of operations focuses especially on the stages of flight starting with preflight preparations at the gate and extending through taxi out to the runway until thrust is applied for takeoff. Concurrent task demands are especially heavy during this period, and the consequences of error often propagate into later phases of flight (as in the case of flight 795). However we do discuss later phases of flight to illustrate how the principles uncovered by our analysis extend throughout flight operations. Although much remains to be learned about concurrent task management and pilots' errors of omission, we feel our study provides the operational community with a strong framework for understanding concurrent task demands and with a vocabulary for discussing the issues and exploring solutions. We hope it will also stimulate the scientific community to develop new empirical methods to explore this domain.

Multitasking permeates almost every aspect of modern personal and professional life. Although our examples focus on aviation, this book is as much about doctors operating on patients, technicians running a control room at a power plant, cashiers tending to a line of shoppers, or parents picking up and dropping off their children at afternoon activities, as it is about airline pilots. It is written in a manner intended to be accessible to operators, researchers, academicians, designers, manufacturers, and regulators. We have strived to keep the language simple and have enriched the text with footnotes. The readers are also encouraged to refer to Appendix B, which describes critical aspects of air transport operations and to the glossary, which defines aviation and cognitive terms relevant to the text.

Chapter 2
What is Multitasking and How is it Accomplished?

In this chapter we present an overview of the influences of concurrent task demands in modern life, and we identify the cognitive issues that determine how well individuals are able to perform multiple tasks concurrently. This overview provides a context for understanding the issues discussed in more detail in later chapters in which we report our research. As will become apparent in these chapters, the challenges of managing cockpit tasks go far beyond the total volume of work involved; these challenges hinge on the character and timing of multiple task demands competing for pilots' attention and action. Further, having to manage multiple tasks concurrently is itself a task, one that increases individuals' subjective experience of workload (Kirmeyer, 1988a).

Multitasking in Modern Life

What we have been referring to as concurrent task management is more colloquially called "multitasking". Although multitasking seems a simple concept, it really covers a range of activities that, from a scientific perspective, involve diverse task demands and cognitive processes. The popular on-line encyclopedia, Wikipedia (selected because it captures current word usage), defines multitasking as "performance by an individual of appearing to handle more than one task *at the same time*" (3 August 2008, emphasis is ours). Yet, individuals sometimes also use the term multitasking to describe activities that are clearly not simultaneous but rather are executed by alternating back and forth among tasks. For example, a cook may alternate among steps required to prepare multiple dishes for completion at the same time. Presumably, the cook is well aware of alternating among tasks but, nevertheless, may use the term simultaneous rather loosely to describe what is being done. Even when tasks seem to be performed in a truly simultaneous fashion, that is generally not the case in reality.

In this book, we prefer to use the term concurrent task management because it is not laden with the assumptions and vague boundaries of the more commonly used term of multitasking. However, when discussing issues from the perspective of common parlance, we sometimes use the term multitasking to call attention to implicit and often-incorrect assumptions about how multiple tasks are accomplished concurrently.

Concurrent task demands are by no means confined to aviation operations, or to the professional world for that matter. Requirements to manage multiple tasks in the same time frame probably began to grow with the advent of the Industrial Age and have sky-rocketed in the Information Age in both the workplace and personal life. It is common for people to have several software programs running concurrently on their computers, while responding to email, instant messaging, telephone calls, and interacting with nearby colleagues in person. The sight and sound of individuals walking through airport terminals while consulting electronic devices, such as Personal Digital Assistants, has quickly gone from an oddity to the norm. Automobile drivers carry on cell phone conversations, obtain information from within-vehicle navigation devices such as GPS (Global Positioning System), and listen to the radio while driving. Young students do their homework while watching television and instant messaging their friends.

Obviously, humans have considerable ability to juggle multiple tasks in these fashions; indeed if early humans had not been able to monitor for predators while starting the camp fire our species would have not have gotten far. But there are severe limits to how much and how well one can juggle tasks, and this sort of juggling can cause accidents, as well as impose more subtle but pervasive costs. For example, a recent study found that nearly 80 percent of automobile crashes and 65 percent of near crashes occurred within three seconds of drivers' attempt to multitask in some fashion, such as using cell phones, eating breakfast, disciplining children, or putting on makeup (Klauer, Dingus, Neale, Sudweeks, and Ramsey, 2006) Cell phone use was the most common competing task. Another study showed that at any given moment six percent of U.S. drivers were holding phones to their ears (Glassbrenner, 2005). Alarmingly, many drivers apparently underestimate the extent to which cell phone use impairs their driving performance (Strayer, Drews,

---

May 28, 2002, early morning, Clarendon, Texas

A coal train with 116 cars was traveling eastward when it received an "after-arrival" warrant, an instruction to wait after arriving at a specific point coming up ahead for the arrival of another, westbound train before proceeding. At the time the warrant was issued, the coal train was 3.2 miles from the hold-short point and was traveling at about 48 mph. It was during that same time that the train engineer placed a call on his cell phone and was still on the phone as the train, 4 minutes later, passed the designated holding point.

During the time that the engineer remained distracted by his conversation, he made no apparent preparations to stop the train as instructed. Almost 10 minutes later, a little less than 8 miles past the designated hold-short point, the coal train collided with the westbound train. The collision resulted in fatalities and damages that exceeded $8 million.

(U.S. National Transportation Safety Board, 2003)

and Johnston, 2003), yet studies have shown that cell phone conversation increases the probability of being in an accident about four-fold, an impairment comparable to driving while legally intoxicated (Redelmeier, and Tibshirani, 1997; Strayer, Crouch, and Drews, 2004).

In contrast to communication patterns of a half-century ago, when letters were prepared on manual typewriters and required several days to reach their destinations, modern technology has both enabled multiple forms of "instant" messaging and created expectations that individuals should and will respond rapidly to communication. Corporations seeking to reduce costs have used automation to replace workers performing manual tasks, increasing the proportion of workers in office positions with multiple responsibilities and multiple streams of information flow. Although these changes are intended to increase worker efficiency, suspicion is growing that frequently jumping from one task to another in fact decreases effectiveness (Jett and George, 2003). And although humans generally like a certain amount of diversity and challenge in their work to counter boredom, evidence is mounting that prolonged high levels of multitasking cause stress, impairing both health and performance (Eyrolle and Cellier, 2000; Kirmeyer, 1988a, 1988b; Luong and Rogelberg, 2005; Zohar, 1999).

Beyond the workplace, pundits worry about the pervasive use of electronic devices (e.g., cell phones, personal computers, televisions, portable digital media players, video games) by children to engage in multiple activities concurrently. One study showed that a quarter of the time spent by children using non-school-related media (including print media), involved the use of two or more media simultaneously (Roberts, Foehr, and Rideout, 2005). Distraction, such as that caused by this type of multitasking, has been shown to impair learning (Foerde, Knowlton, and Poldrack, 2006). There is no empirical research, though, to address the issue of whether the resulting reduction in attention span of this "generation M" of media-multitaskers (Roberts et al., 2005) affects the ability to persevere in long-term tasks or social skills, as some speculate (Wallis, 2006).

Conversely, one might imagine that through media-multitasking these children develop skill at concurrent task management—in fact, experience in playing video games has been shown to enhance attention and task-switching skills (Andrews and Murphy, 2006; Green and Bavelier 2003). However, further research is required to determine the extent to which experience in attention and task switching generalizes to situations other than the ones practiced.

Beyond the issues of how young people are affected by extensive use of multi-media, some research does suggest that training in attention and task switching can generalize to situations beyond the original training. For example, student pilots given practice in a challenging video game requiring them to manage multiple tasks (manual tracking, visual monitoring, memory tasks, and decision making), performed better in initial pilot training than students without video-game training (Gopher, 1992; Shebilske, Goettl, and Regian, 1999).

How is Multitasking Really Accomplished?

As evinced by the Wikipedia definition, many individuals seem to think they can conduct multiple tasks in a truly simultaneous fashion, but to what extent is this really true? Many also clearly underestimate the hazards of attempting to multitask. Why and under what circumstances is multitasking problematic? Detailed answers to these questions require considerable research along several avenues, however we know enough now to provide a general outline. Juggling multiple tasks involves cognitive processes in ways that go considerably beyond the requirements for performing each task separately. The characteristics and limitations of concurrent task performance are determined by fundamental aspects of cognition, especially attention and working memory. In this section, we sketch the main cognitive issues to which we return in more depth in Chapter 5 (Analysis of Concurrent Task Demands).

In principle, individuals have a limited number of choices in attempting to perform multiple tasks competing for attention: simultaneous execution, interleaving steps of one task with steps of other tasks, reducing task demands by lowering criteria for quality, accuracy or completeness of performance, deferring one task entirely until another task is performed, or omitting one task altogether. All of these choices, except for the first, require scheduling tasks as well as performing them.

The manner in which individuals attempt to manage concurrent tasks and the degree to which they succeed depend on the interaction of the characteristics of the tasks performed, human information processing characteristics, and the experience, skill, and goals of the individual. Also, the approach individuals take to managing multiple tasks concurrently is not necessarily deliberate, much less well thought out; rather, individuals may simply initiate tasks as the thought occurs to them or react to task demands as they occur, an approach that increases vulnerability to error.

Simultaneous performance or task interleaving through switching?

Although individuals may think they are performing several tasks simultaneously, human ability to process more than one stream of information at a time and respond accordingly is severely limited. At a simple level, competing tasks may require visual gaze in different directions or require incompatible motor responses. At a more complex level, multiple tasks must compete for limited cognitive resources such as attention and working memory. Most work tasks require at least some degree of attentive processing, and challenging tasks demand focused attention ("attention" corresponds roughly to conscious awareness, although it actually involves a complex set of cognitive processes, many of which operate out of consciousness). Fully attentive processing is limited by a "bottleneck" to essentially serial processing—performing one task at a time—(Broadbent 1958; Welford 1967). And although humans can store almost unlimited amounts of information in long-term memory, the amount of information they can update and keep readily accessible for the task at hand (in what is called *working memory*) is limited to a few items, or chunks of information, at a time (Barshi and Healy, 2002). Various theoretical accounts of working memory have been proposed, but in general it consists of a set of cognitive processes that keep a very small subset of memory items readily available for immediate use when performing tasks, so that a slow, effortful search of long-term memory stores for task-relevant information is not required (Miyake and Shah 1999).

These constraints severely limit human ability to perform more than one cognitive task at a time. However, in certain situations, tasks can apparently be performed in parallel. For example, Allport, Antonis, and Reynolds (1972) found that with extensive practice skilled pianists could learn to simultaneously sight-read written music scores while verbally repeating back messages they heard (auditory shadowing), without degradation of performance of either task. However, performance was measured only in terms of errors made in music reading and errors made in shadowing, so it is possible that more subtle aspects of performance, such as quality of interpretation of the musical score or comprehension of the shadowed messages would have been impaired.

Simultaneous performance of this sort is only possible when tasks are highly practiced, practiced extensively together, and the responses to stimuli are always executed in the same way (Oberauer and Kliegl, 2004). Performance in this situation becomes largely automatic, making few demands on the brain's limited capacities for attention and working memory. In a similar fashion, with extensive practice, drivers and pilots learn to integrate many of the sensory-motor tasks of vehicle control in a way that seems largely automatic, drastically reducing the demand for deliberate, effortful thought. Most anyone can relate to this by thinking back to when they were first learning to drive a car. Initially, driving was a high workload situation that involved struggling to remember what to do next, to perform each action smoothly, and to integrate all the tasks and task components. But with extensive practice, driving in routine situations became possible without having to think explicitly about what to do or how to do it. Driving now seems automatic, allowing one to perform other tasks at the same time, whether or not it is appropriate to do so.

However, in contrast to simple laboratory tasks, the real-world tasks of driving and piloting are probably not fully automated, and some form of attentive processing is also required, if for no other reason than to supervise processes that have become largely automatic. Without attentive supervision of highly automated tasks, individuals are prone to errors such as driving past their intended exit from a freeway, especially if the intended exit is not the one usually taken (Barshi and Healy, 1993; Mycielska and Reason, 1982; Reason 1990).

Although automatization of highly practiced tasks allows individuals to perform additional tasks more or less simultaneously, it is not possible to simultaneously perform multiple tasks that involve novelty, planning, or overriding habits. These latter tasks require cognitive processing that is slow, effortful, and serial, because they depend heavily on limited resources such as attention and working memory. In these situations, individuals can fully attend only to one stream of information at any given moment.

July 1, 2002, late evening, near Überlingen, Germany

It was a quiet night and the little air traffic traveling in the airspace under ACC Zurich jurisdiction was routinely flowing through—or so the single controller on duty at the time thought. What was about to unfold over the next few minutes was the result of otherwise routine concurrent task demands being mishandled following a series of unexpected technical problems – a recipe for disaster.

When the crew of an Airbus contacted Air Traffic Control, the controller was working on that frequency while also providing air traffic control services on a second frequency to a Boeing and a Tupolev aircraft in the area. To handle the two frequencies, the controller had to switch his physical position and his attention back and forth between two work stations, to which he maneuvered by rolling his work chair. Until that time, the demands for concurrent task management would have been regarded as routine and benign (even though the controller was actually covering three radar controller positions, something that had become common practice at the Control Center).

Everything changed when the controller picked up the telephone to inform the airport of the arriving Airbus but was unable to make contact because of technical problems with the bypass telephone system (the main phone line was down for maintenance work). The controller became preoccupied with trying to contact the airport, at the expense of concurrent duties, namely that of monitoring the Boeing and the Tupolev aircraft, which he had failed to notice were actually on a collision course. Unbeknownst to him, the ground-based collision warning system had also been switched off for maintenance.

Before too long, concurrent demands for the controller's attention rose to a very high level: incoming and often overlapping radio calls on one frequency, outgoing calls on another frequency, communication via telephone, visual scanning of two radar screens projecting images at significantly different scales, the distraction of technicians in the room. He attempted to interleave tasks but in so doing failed to mentally update the continuously evolving "big picture" of the position of the two aircraft.

In this rapidly deteriorating situation, the two aircraft collided in mid air, 35,000 feet above the ground. Seventy one people lost their lives.

(German Federal Bureau of Aircraft Accidents Investigation, 2004)

Individuals may have the impression that they are performing two or more attention-requiring tasks simultaneously when in fact what they are actually doing is alternating among elements of each task. This misimpression is especially common when individuals are performing familiar tasks that are automated to some degree but which still require attention. For example, a driver using a cell phone is generally able to steer the car within acceptable limits under benign conditions and may think that he is driving and conversing simultaneously. But conversation makes substantial demands on attention, and while conversing the driver is far less likely to notice unexpected events that also require attention—for example, a pedestrian stepping into a crosswalk (Strayer et al., 2003). Conversely, if the driver notices the pedestrian, conversation will pause for a moment while the driver redirects the motion of the vehicle. Drivers may be deceived by the fact that one aspect of driving—steering along a well-defined road—is largely automated, but in fact performing other aspects, such as monitoring for pedestrians or even shifting gears (Groeger, and Clegg, 1997) requires switching back and forth with moments of conversation. This situation is dangerous because switching of attention is often not timely or reliable.

Earlier we used the example of a cook alternating among steps required to prepare multiple dishes for completion at the same time. In this sort of situation the individual is well aware that performance of multiple tasks is not simultaneous and deliberately switches among tasks at critical moments to keep each task moving along appropriately. This situation of interleaving is, in fact, much more realistic and common than the simultaneous performance of tasks. Keeping track of the status of each cooking task becomes a kind of meta-task, which must compete with the several cooking tasks for the limited cognitive resources of working memory and attention. As even experienced cooks can attest, this competition sometimes results in the cook losing track of the status of one of the dishes being prepared. One way in which experienced cooks reduce demands on working memory and attention is to rely on noticing visual and olfactory cues to update the status of each dish.[1] This strategy can work if salient cues are available to remind the cook of the current status of each task, but if cues are not salient (e.g., the chopping block is on a counter that requires facing away from the stove on which a salmon has been put to cook) or unexpected difficulties arise with one task (e.g., a jar cannot be opened), the cook may fail to switch attention in a timely fashion and the meal may burn.

Deferring execution of tasks

Given the severe limitations on simultaneous performance and the difficulties sometimes involved in task switching, individuals are often forced to defer one or more tasks while completing other tasks. This strategy requires reliance on the cognitive mechanism of prospective memory to remember to perform a deferred task at a later, more appropriate time. Interruptions also create prospective memory demands because the individual must remember to resume the interrupted task after the end of the interruption. (Or, if the individual chooses to complete the ongoing task first, he or she must remember to turn attention to the cause of the interruption later.)

---

1   In more technical terms, two different cognitive strategies are involved here. One, a "top-down" approach, is to keep the meta-task of concurrent task management in the forefront of awareness, constantly updating it, and deliberately scanning all the dishes being prepared periodically. The other approach is "bottom-up", relying on noticing cues or being reminded of one task by the actions of another task.

An order for an IV bag to contain, among other things, sodium chloride was put through to the pharmacy. The technician started preparing the bag but was asked to assist another technician as she was about to add sodium from a multi-dose vial from which some amount of sodium had already been removed. She responded to the unexpected interruption by stepping away from her primary task of preparing the solution for the IV bag. When she returned, she saw the partially empty sodium chloride vial next to the bag she had been preparing before being interrupted and assumed she had already completed the task of adding the substance to the solution. The IV was administered to the patient whose condition, after 5 hours of infusion, indicated severe hyponatremia because of the lack of sodium in the infused IV solution. The situation was immediately corrected but the patient's hospitalization was prolonged because of the error.

(United States Pharmacopeia, Patient Safety CAPSLink, September 2003)

Unfortunately, deferring tasks creates considerable risk that the individual will forget to perform the deferred task when the opportunity later arises. For example, a nurse in the process of administering medication to a patient using an IV line is required to set up the line, and then turn the infusion pump on to start infusion of the prescribed volume of medication. But if the nurse is called away from the patient's side to respond to an audible alarm from another patient's monitor, he is vulnerable to forgetting to return to turn the pump on at the first patient's bedside. Apparently, the human brain does not have any special mechanism to remember to perform deferred tasks. Human memory has been studied extensively for over a century, but usually under retrospective conditions—the individual is prompted to search for information previously stored in memory. But under prospective conditions, the individual is not explicitly prompted to search memory for the deferred intention when the appropriate moment arrives, thus she must somehow "remember to remember" (see reviews in Kliegel, Martin, and McDaniel, 2004 and McDaniel and Einstein, 2007 for more detail). We argue that interleaving tasks, like deferring tasks, also requires prospective memory, because the individual must remember without prompting to switch attention between tasks at the appropriate time.

Reducing task demands

Individuals may respond to overwhelming concurrent task demands by lowering criteria for quality, accuracy or completeness of some task elements or by eliminating some tasks altogether. If this is done strategically rather than reactively, it can be an effective approach to dealing with the overall situation by focusing on the most critical aspects of the situation. Individuals skilled in a work domain usually do not simply react to each task demand as it arises, but rather try to manage the combination of task demands to achieve overarching goals (Huey and Wickens, 1993; Raby and Wickens, 1994). Skilled human operators assess the relative importance and urgency of task demands and adjust their strategy accordingly. For example, emergency room

On an early weekend evening, an anesthesiology team of four physicians was called to attend to five separate surgical procedures- all of which were characterized as emergencies. The anesthesiologist in charge had to make a critical decision about how to divide the multiple, concurrent demands among the team members, by managing a variety of factors. Given the staffing, only two operating rooms could be run simultaneously. Anesthesia procedures would have to be interwoven, so that one case would be starting as another was finishing, thus making the most efficient use of time and available resources.

The surgeons responsible for each of the procedures were putting pressure to have their case attended to since the urgency of each case increased with the passage of time. To complicate an already challenging situation, delays were being experienced with the pre-operative preparations of some patients. The nurses and technicians in one of the operating rooms were insisting they be given priority since this was their last shift for the day and they would be able to go home only after it had been completed.

The fact that the hospital was a designated major trauma center meant that the anesthesiology team had to be in a state of readiness at all times, in case it was called to attend to an emergency situation demanding immediate surgery. If all members of the anesthesiology team were assigned to surgery, the team would not be in the required readiness state.

The anesthesiologist in charge weighed in all factors, and ultimately decided that the team was not going to be able to fulfill all task demands. She gave priority to the existing surgical procedures, betting on her experience that most major trauma cases occur late in the evening or in the early morning hours. The team's readiness for a potential large trauma case was thus temporarily "shed." Luck was on the team's side that evening. All scheduled surgeries were successfully accomplished and following that, the team returned to the expected readiness level.

(Bogner, S. (Ed.), *Human Error in Medicine*, 1994)

personnel treating a patient with multiple injuries often must defer working on some injuries while dealing with those that are life-threatening. Operators may choose to defer or omit altogether less important tasks, they may seek to engage other individuals to help with the workload, or they may change their course of action to buy additional time (e.g., a flight crew may enter a holding pattern to buy time to set up a challenging approach). Further, skilled operators may alter their normal criteria for quality of performance of some tasks in order to accomplish all essential tasks. As an illustration of these strategies, the crew of an aircraft on fire might declare an emergency to receive priority handling from ATC, request a discrete ATC communication frequency to eliminate the need for radio frequency changes later, omit non-essential procedural steps, set up a steeper than normal descent, accept a firm landing, and stop the aircraft on the runway in order to expedite getting on the ground and evacuating the aircraft.

Although all of the above strategic adaptations can be very effective, implementing them is itself a task that also makes demands on limited cognitive resources. One of the ironic manifestations of high workload is that as individuals find themselves getting overwhelmed and seek to reduce cognitive demands they often do this, perhaps unwittingly, by abandoning strategic management of their situation and simply react to each new task demand as it is presented (Dismukes, et al., 2007). Although this response reduces workload, it eliminates prioritization and prevents the individual from planning ahead and maintaining control of the situation. Inadvertent omission of crucial task elements is often the result, along with loss of situation awareness and with poor decision-making.

Some studies of pilots managing the concurrent task demands of cockpit operations have compared pilots' performance to that of an optimal scheduler and found skilled pilot performance to be considerably less than optimal, although other researchers have found performance in some situations to reflect adequate priorities fairly accurately (Wickens, 2000; Shakeri and Funk, 2007). What is optimal for a general-purpose computer may not be optimal for a human operator, whose cognitive processes operate quite differently. For example, it seems to be difficult for humans to maintain multiple goals in working memory unless attention is frequently returned to each goal to keep it active. This switching of attention among goals is especially difficult if the environment does not provide strong cueing of the status of the task associated with each goal. How individuals maintain and switch among multiple goals is a topic still in its infancy and requires much research.

Having developed a sense of multitasking and concurrent task management in everyday life, and using the description of some cognitive limitations given in this chapter as a foundation, we now turn to look in detail at the nature of cockpit tasks and their demands.

Chapter 3
The Ideal: Flight Operations as Depicted by Flight Operations Manuals

When pilots begin working for a major airline, or when they transfer to a different type of airplane within the company, they are assigned to a training course for the airplane they will be flying.[1] In this course pilots learn about the airplane's systems and operating characteristics through classroom and computer-based training. They also learn the large number of cockpit tasks required to operate the aircraft in accordance with its design characteristics and the management policies and philosophy of operations of their particular airline.

Cockpit tasks, organized in the form of procedures, are originally described in Operations Manuals (OMs) provided by the airplane manufacturer for each specific type of aircraft. Procedures described in the OM are derived from the system design features and performance characteristics and limitations of the specific airplane type. The OM lays out the best way to operate the airplane safely and efficiently, but of necessity it describes cockpit tasks with little regard to the actual operational environment and the particular kinds of operation conducted by individual airlines.

Air carriers differ greatly in the type of operations they conduct: the locations to which they fly, the lengths of flights, the types of weather encountered, whether they use hubs, the numbers of pilots employed, the sizes of fleets, the numbers of variants of airplanes within a fleet, and the level of cockpit automation. These factors in turn affect other aspects of operation, such as the number of flights crews typically fly on a given day, the time on the ground between flights, and the number of days for which a crew is paired on a multi-day trip. To address the specifics of its own operations and to promulgate its own management policies, each carrier adapts and expands the manufacturer's OM into a more detailed Flight Operations Manual (FOM).

To perform their jobs in accordance with their employers' operating and safety standards, pilots are required to follow the standardized operating procedures

---

1 In the U.S. airline industry, pilots hired by major airlines typically already have substantial flight experience, either from having flown for smaller airlines or for the military. In general, they are familiar with airplane systems and with standardized operating procedures, but usually have not operated the type of airplane they will now be flying, and in some cases have not flown large airliners before. In contrast to the U.S. industry, pilots in some airlines in other countries are hired without previous aviation experience, in which case the company provides ab initio (initial) training that prepares them to fly an airliner.

closely, so training is heavily based on FOMs, and rote memorization of the procedures therein. During the training course, pilots repeatedly practice executing these procedures in flight simulators. At the end of the course, qualification in the airplane requires pilots to demonstrate not just that they can fly the airplane but also that they can execute the large volume of detailed procedures quickly, accurately, and mostly from memory.

In this chapter, we describe cockpit tasks as they are presented in FOMs (and therefore also in training), and conclude that FOMs implicitly portray cockpit work as having three central characteristics. It is linear, predictable, and under the moment to moment control of the cockpit crew. This portrayal results both from the explicit description of cockpit tasks in the FOMs and from aspects of real-world operations not described in FOMs. We describe this ideal perspective in some detail to give readers who are not airline pilots a sense of the nature of cockpit work and to lay a foundation for contrast with the much more complicated and dynamic world of actual flight operations described in the next chapter (Chapter 4: The Real).

Our analysis of FOMs is primarily based on a detailed review of the Boeing 737 manuals used by two major airlines at the time of our study, but is also informed by a more casual perusal of manuals for several types of aircraft used at other airlines. Although the details of FOMs differ among companies and aircraft types, the basic structure of procedures and the way procedures are described are quite similar. While we were writing this book, Boeing revised its OM for the 737, and one of the airlines from which we collected data substantially overhauled its flight operating procedures guided in part by our analysis (see Chapter 6: Research Applied). Thus, some of the details of our description of procedures may no longer be current. However, our goal is to give readers a general sense of the way procedures are characterized by FOMs regardless of the details of any particular FOM.

Normal flight procedures (procedures used in normal situations not involving malfunctions or emergencies) are grouped and described in the FOM in the sequence in which they are used in the conduct of a flight: Pretakeoff, Takeoff, Climb and Cruise, Descent, Approach, and Landing. (Procedures for abnormal situations and emergencies are provided in a separate chapter of the FOM and are not discussed here.) Normal procedures both prescribe how the airplane is to be operated during each phase of flight and help the crew prepare the aircraft and themselves for the ensuing phase of flight. Different phases involve different types of procedures, and the different types of procedures are described in FOMs in differing levels of detail. For our purposes the main types of procedures are:

1. initial configuration and testing of aircraft systems before flight,[2]
2. engine starting and shutdown,
3. programming of the Flight Management Computer (FMC),

---

2   Performance considerations (e.g. takeoff weight, runway length, weather) appear in both configuration procedures and in control of aircraft movement procedures.

4. control of aircraft movement through space by manipulation of flight control surfaces and engines,
5. navigation, using onboard electronic systems and signals from external sources, and
6. checklists, used in conjunction with the other types of procedures, to ensure that crews do not omit or incorrectly perform items, especially those critical to safety or effective performance.

We do not discuss all of the many procedures required to operate a large transport aircraft, but give examples of different procedures in several phases of flight. We discuss the Pretakeoff phase in much greater detail than other phases because four of the six types of procedures are used in this phase and because the issues we address are similar among the several phases of flight. Also, the contrast between the ideal and the real is especially striking in this phase, and pretakeoff errors often have adverse consequences, some of which are not manifested until later phases of flight. Airline pilots will note that we do not discuss a great deal of explanatory and supplementary material all FOMs contain. This is deliberate as we want to focus on the procedures per se.

The B737 and almost all large civil transport aircraft developed since the 1970s use a two-person flight crew, the captain and the first officer. During ground operations (before takeoff, and after landing, when the aircraft is on the ground but still under crew control) the captain and first officer perform many tasks separately, though a few tasks are conducted together. During flight, from takeoff to landing, the division of responsibilities changes, with one pilot taking the role of the flying pilot and the other the role of the monitoring pilot (sometimes called the pilot not flying) to reflect the fact that one pilot has active control of the aircraft (whether flying manually or on autopilot), while the other is responsible for monitoring the flight (aircraft track, systems, radios) and supporting the flying pilot. Regardless of whether the captain is the flying or the monitoring pilot, he or she has overall command responsibility for the flight, and the first officer is responsible for supporting the captain in that role. For both ground and flight operations, formal procedures describe, with varying levels of detail, how each task is to be executed.

Phases of Flight

Pretakeoff (or Preflight)

This phase of flight begins with the aircraft at the gate before the engines are started and ends when it is positioned on the runway for takeoff. The crew must configure and test the aircraft's systems before starting the engines. (The major systems are electrical, hydraulic, flight controls, engines, fuel, pressurization and air conditioning, fire protection, displays and instruments, automation, communication, and navigation.) For the first flight of the day (or when one crew replaces a previous crew after a flight) the FOM lists a hundred or more actions the crew must perform before starting the engines, and some actions require multiple steps, grouped in a procedure (e.g., Pretakeoff procedure).[3] However, on subsequent flights the number of actions to be performed is reduced substantially, provided the same crew remains on the airplane. Typically, depending on the type of aircraft and type of operation, crews may need as much as 30-45 minutes to prepare the airplane for the first flight of the day, and about 20-35 minutes for subsequent flights. (These figures include briefing flight attendants and interacting with gate agents. Under time pressure, flight crews may compress these tasks.)

The Pretakeoff procedure typically requires each pilot to separately perform a long sequence of actions, configuring and testing items silently from memory as a "flow." (This is referred to as a flow because the hands of an experienced pilot "flow" over the switches and controls in a smooth choreographed fashion while performing the sequence of procedural actions.) Performing the flow always in the same order enables pilots to learn the sequence more readily during training and to execute the actions quickly without losing track of what has been done. It also helps reduce vulnerability to inadvertently omitting actions or steps within actions. In the FOM, actions in procedures are generally presented as a long list of items for each pilot. For example, in the Pretakeoff procedure, each line in the list specifies the physical component (switches, levers, or gauges), the action to be performed on the component, and the specific setting:

>   e.g., Probe Heat switches ....OFF
> or general outcome desired at the end of the action:
>   e.g., VHF Navigation radios ....Set for departure.

Items differ vastly in complexity. Some items are relatively simple and require either:

- physical positioning of a single switch (or lever)
    - to a position standard and consistent for the particular phase of flight (e.g., turning the autobrake switch to the position labeled "RTO," for Rejected Take Off, before every departure),
    or
    - to a position appropriate for the particular flight, in which the action is labeled "as required" (e.g., setting the stabilizer trim to the appropriate number of units determined by the weight and balance data computed for a particular takeoff),

---

3   The content, names and number of procedures and checklists (see later in the text) vary among airlines, reflecting each organization's approach to operations. We try to be as generic as possible in our descriptions and simply provide examples of names that we have found in different airline FOMs.

or

- visual verification of a single switch (or lever) position (e.g., the nose wheel steering switch is by default in the NORM position and the procedure simply directs the pilot to verify it).

Other items are more complex and require combinations of actions, such as:

- physical positioning or verification of a switch (or lever) *and* visual verification of accompanying indication(s) (e.g., setting the flaps to a particular setting requires physically positioning the lever in the required position, verifying that the needle on the corresponding gauge correctly indicates the flap position commanded, and looking at the relevant indicator to ensure complete transit of the flaps to the commanded position.

Still other items are even more complex, involving:

- combination of actions on an entire section of an instrument panel (dedicated to an aircraft system) to values:
  - standard and consistent for the particular phase of flight (e.g., configuring the air conditioning and pressurization system panel after engine start requires positioning the two pack switches, the isolation valve switch, and verifying the indication of two needles on the pneumatic duct pressure gauge, three bleed switches, and eight illuminating annunciations),

or
  - appropriate for the particular flight and which require the pilot to have pre-determined the appropriate response before accomplishing the procedure (e.g., the single procedural item for the fuel system before flight involves checking that two engine valve and two spar valve lights are illuminated; two filter bypass, one cross-feed valve, and six low pressure lights are extinguished; the cross-feed selector switch is closed; three fuel quantity gauges indicate the expected fuel quantity; and six fuel pumps switches are in the on or off position depending on the quantity in each corresponding set of fuel tanks). The pilot's response is then of the form "xx lbs released, xx lbs on board, pumps on" implying that the fuel quantity on board is xx lbs as stated on the flight dispatch release form and that the fuel pumps are on, as required for flight,

  or involving
- complex, time-consuming, attention-demanding activities (e.g., the single procedural step of "programming" the FMC involves entering data (numbers and letters) derived from communication with air traffic control (ATC) as well as from various pieces of paperwork into nine different "screens" (electronic pages) using the FMC keyboard and may also require

consulting performance charts in a binder or on a separate, hand-held computer),

or

- waiting for the effects of certain actions when testing a system (e.g., checking the ground proximity warning system requires momentarily pushing the appropriate switch and then waiting for proper verification of the four resulting aural sounds and their corresponding illuminated alerts— this test takes about ten seconds to complete).

The sequence in which items are to be set or checked is determined mainly by spatial location and by equipment design features. Most cockpit switches, dials, and gauges are located in four places: the forward and aft overhead panels above the windshield; the mode control panel on the glare shield immediately below the windshield; the main instrument panels vertically oriented beneath the windshield and running most of the width of the cockpit; and a center console on the floor between the pilots. Control levers for engine throttles, flaps, and spoilers and a control wheel for elevator trim are on the forward portion of the console, and trim knobs for rudder and ailerons are on the aft portion of the console.

Most items of the procedure flow are performed by moving through a sequence of adjacent locations, following a left to right and top to bottom pattern. In general, items are assigned to the pilot closest to the switch or gauge, to avoid having the pilots reaching across each other, however, this assignment also depends on the other duties of the pilots. Some instruments and displays are duplicated on the two sides of the cockpit, and these are set and checked by each pilot on his or her respective side. Typical captain and first officer flow patterns when performing the Pretakeoff procedure are shown in Figure 3.1.

Despite this orderly arrangement, the procedure cannot always be executed entirely in the sequence of physical proximity of switches and gauges because of equipment operating features. For example, before starting the engines, an Auxiliary Power Unit (APU) is used to provide electrical power and air conditioning. The APU start switch and the battery power switch are located on the forward overhead panel, above the captain's head. However, before the APU can be started, the fire detection system, located on the console between the pilots, must be checked. Thus, starting the APU requires turning on the battery switch on the overhead panel, reaching down to the console to test the fire detection system, and then reaching back up for the APU switch on the overhead panel.

In the course of preparing the aircraft for flight, the crew requires certain sets of information in order to execute several of the procedural items. In particular, the crew must have:

- a load sheet (with aircraft weight and balance data used for programming the FMC),

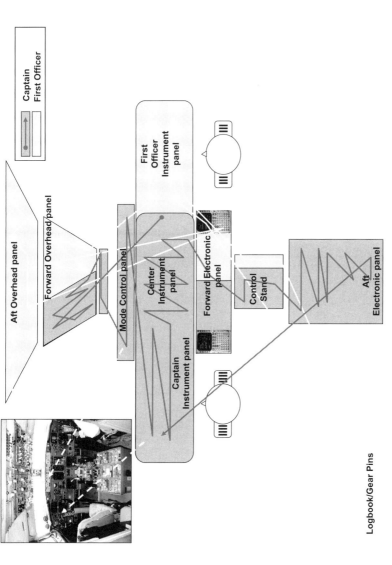

Figure 3.1   Flow of activities during the pretakeoff phase of flight

Inset: with permission from www.b737.org.uk

- the flight plan, flight release, and ATC clearance (necessary for setting the Mode Control (MCP) and the pressurization panels, as well as for programming the FMC),
- the aircraft logbook, which contains aircraft maintenance information (to review, sign, and ensure it is on board prior to departure from the gate),
- airport information (Air Terminal Information Service, ATIS) (to input ambient temperature when programming the FMC, to adjust the altimeters to the current setting, and to determine the current runways in use), and
- a fuel slip indicating the amount of fuel that has been pumped into the aircraft fuel tanks (to ensure the planned-for fuel is indeed available, and to use when entering data into the FMC).

The required information is provided by human agents from outside the cockpit (e.g., load sheet from the gate agent; logbook from the Maintenance; weather information, flight plan, flight release from the Flight Dispatch office). One might assume from the FOM that the required information will always be available when needed. However, the FOM provides little discussion of where this information will come from or when it will arrive, and does not mention the possibility that the information will not be available when the crew reaches a procedural item requiring information from outside sources. Nor does the FOM mention that when this information does arrive it often does so in a way that impinges upon other ongoing activities.

According to the FOM, the captain and first officer complete their cockpit preparation tasks independently of each other, and then first interact to conduct a takeoff briefing before starting the engines. The purpose of this briefing is to ensure that both pilots are prepared for and in agreement about the execution of the impending departure, and normally includes relevant ATC instructions and aircraft performance and configuration settings, as well as environmental, aircraft system, and other factors that may affect the departure. The FOM lists mandatory items to be discussed in the briefing, but does not mention the possibility that some of the necessary information may not be available when the briefing is normally given, that the crew will sometimes be operating under time pressure to take off or risk losing their departure slot, or that changes in clearances may require re-programming new routing and necessitate a revised briefing after the airplane has started to taxi.

Because the FOM does not mention that interactions with outside agents often interrupt execution of procedural flows and checklists, that information will not always be available when needed to complete tasks, or that external events will sometimes require revising previously accomplished tasks, the linear description of task steps in the FOM makes cockpit work appear to be quite predictable and completely under the moment-to-moment control of the crew.

After the takeoff briefing, the crew must ensure that various conditions are met before having the airplane pushed back from the gate and starting the engines. All cabin and cargo doors must be closed, passengers must be seated, and the ground crew must be in position and must give approval for engine start. This requires coordination with the gate crew, the cabin crew, the ground crew, and, at very busy airports, Ground or Ramp Control. The FOM describes in detail interaction with the ground crew (see below), but does not address the ways in which interaction with the other human agents affects timing of cockpit tasks and frequently imposes additional task demands on the cockpit crew.

Once the pilots determine that all prescribed conditions are met, they perform two separate checklists. The first (sometimes called the Receiving Aircraft checklist or the Before Start checklist) is designed to ensure the pilots have accomplished items from the preceding Pretakeoff procedure with special emphasis on those items critical for the upcoming flight (e.g., setting the aircraft pressurization). The second checklist (sometimes called the Before Start checklist) is designed to ensure that items critical for a safe engine start and for having the aircraft pushed back (if the aircraft is parked at a gate) have also been accomplished. The first checklist, referring to the lengthy aircraft preparations, may contain a dozen or more items, while the one that is accomplished just prior to engine start typically contains only three or four items. Both checklists are meant to be performed without interruption, using a printed, laminated card available on-board the aircraft that lists all of the checklists.[4]

In general, airlines vary in the number of items included in these checklists and in the manner in which the checklists are to be executed. Most commonly, checklists for normal procedures are of the "read-and-verify" type and are intended, as the name suggests, to help the crew verify actions they have already accomplished using a memorized flow. When performed on the ground, the first officer (or monitoring pilot for a checklist performed in flight) reads each checklist item (the "challenge") aloud and the captain (or flying pilot for a checklist performed in flight) verifies that the item has been accomplished and states so verbally (the "response"). The challenging pilot monitors the responding pilot's verification and announces the checklist complete when all actions have been performed properly.[5]

To save time, airlines typically start the engines while the airplane is being pushed back by a tug operated by the ground crew. Pushing back requires close coordination between the captain and the ground crew, and their interaction is explicitly scripted in the FOM, which describes the sequence of actions and communications between the two. Starting the engines is a multi-step process that also requires very close coordination between the captain and the first officer

---

4   The air carriers we worked with used checklist cards at the time we conducted our study. Performance of electronic checklists that are available on some aircraft at other airlines is somewhat different.

5   Another type of checklist is "silent," in which the monitoring pilot sets and checks items silently without involving the flying pilot. Still another type is the "read and do" checklist, often used for emergency procedures, in which each item to be accomplished is first read aloud and then accomplished by whichever pilot is designated.

to ensure that the engines start properly. (Turbine engines are vulnerable to "hot starts" and "hung starts," which require quick response to prevent engine damage. The most recent generation of airliners use automation to reduce the number of steps that must be performed by pilots during the engine start sequence.) The procedure for engine starting is also closely scripted in the FOM, which specifies the actions and callouts for each pilot and the sequence for execution. Thus, the captain is often coordinating engine start with the first officer at the same time they are coordinating the aircraft pushback with the ground crew.

Unless the distance is very long, pushback is completed before both engines are started. The ground crew uses an interphone connected to the airplane to tell the captain that the pushback is complete and to request that the parking brake be set. Once the captain responds that the parking brake has been set, the ground crew disconnects the towbar and so informs the captain. FOMs typically describe the pushback and engine start procedures separately, and do not call attention to the fact that the timing and interleaving of the two processes will vary and that the captain must divide attention between the two processes.

After both engines are started, the captain signals the ground crew to disconnect the interphone and the tug and to clear the immediate area, and the two pilots perform another procedure (commonly called the After Start procedure), consisting of about twelve items specified in the FOM, followed by the respective checklist (e.g., After Start checklist). After the captain receives an all-clear salute from the ground crew and as soon as the first officer announces that the checklist is complete, the captain directs him to set the flaps to the takeoff position and to call Ground control for permission to taxi (taxi clearance). A few variations to this flow are observed among different airlines. The exact point at which flaps are set to takeoff position varies (e.g., before calling for taxi clearance or before beginning to taxi), and is often a function of weather conditions—for example, flaps may be kept retracted until just prior to takeoff in freezing conditions. In addition, some airlines require crews to start only one engine during pushback (and the second engine when approaching the runway) when the taxiing distance to the runway or the queue of aircraft headed to the runway is too long, as a way to reduce fuel costs.

The Ground controller assigns a specific taxi route that the crew must follow to reach the departure runway. Depending on the airport and prevailing conditions, the route may be short or long, simple or complicated. Low visibility weather conditions, furthermore, can make navigation challenging. The captain controls the airplane's movement with a nosewheel steering tiller,[6] engine thrust levers, and brakes. Both pilots are expected to have airport layout charts available for consultation, and both pilots are responsible for following the assigned taxi route and avoiding runway incursions and collisions. The first officer handles radio communications, but both pilots must monitor the frequency.

---

6   Some types of aircraft and indeed some versions of the Boeing 737 have two tillers, one for each pilot. In these, the first officer sometimes does the taxi instead of the captain.

Perhaps because most system configuration tasks have already been accomplished by this point, the FOM description of the procedure to be accomplished while taxiing (e.g., Taxi procedure) is shorter than that conducted during the preflight preparations. Depending on the airline, a dozen or more items are listed for the pilots to perform separately or together. Some of these items, such as checking the flight controls and the stabilizer trim, are simple and take only a few seconds to complete. Other items involve multiple steps. For example, the first officer may be required to use the final weight information to perform performance calculations (from performance cards or using a special, portable computer, if available) to finish programming the FMC and to set the airspeed "bugs" (reminders of critical airspeeds on the airspeed indicators). The captain is then expected to check the first officer's data entries in the FMC. After all the taxi procedural items are completed the captain calls for the associated checklist (e.g., Taxi checklist), the first officer challenges each item, and, depending on the item, either the captain or the first officer responds (for a few critical items, both pilots respond). This checklist is typically completed while the aircraft is still taxiing.

If starting the second engine has been delayed until near the end of the taxi, the FOM directs crews to use the normal Engine Start procedures and checklists, preferably with the aircraft stationary and the parking brake set. However, the FOM makes no mention of the fact that the crew may be forced to interpose the procedures for starting the second engine during other taxi or pretakeoff tasks.

Although typically not discussed in FOMs, the tasks performed during taxi require each pilot to divide attention among concurrent task demands. For example, while performing other tasks, the first officer is expected to monitor the progress of the taxi to help the captain conform to the assigned route and avoid obstacles or errors. Both pilots must monitor the radio concurrently with other tasks. Concurrent task demands increase substantially at unfamiliar airports and in adverse weather conditions; for example, the crew may have to take the airplane to a de-icing pad, which will require reconfiguring some of the airplane's systems and controls, or the crew may have to defer setting flaps to takeoff position to avoid having freezing slush thrown up on the flaps during taxi. Although FOMs describe procedures for de-icing, they say little about how this is to be integrated into the normal flow of tasks.

As the airplane approaches the departure runway, the crew completes a final list of procedural items (e.g., Before Takeoff procedure) specified in the FOM. When the Tower controller clears the airplane to move onto the departure runway, the captain calls for the associated checklist (same name as the procedure). Some FOMs are vague about the exact timing and manner of execution of this procedure and its checklist. While checklists are meant to verify actions already accomplished using the procedure, first officers sometimes must perform the last checklist items as the captain taxies onto the runway, blurring the distinction between performing actions during the procedure and verifying them during the checklist, thus increasing concurrent task demands.

Figures 3.2, 3.3, and 3.4 provide high-level graphic summaries of crew tasks during the before start, pushback, and the taxi portions of the Pretakeoff phase, as characterized by FOMs. Each of these figures is a time-activity graph, with the time axis running from top to bottom. Tasks explicitly assigned to the captain or first officer individually are listed on the left and right, respectively. They include both specific procedures depicted in text boxes (e.g., in Figure 3.2, left side: "Pretakeoff procedure"), and more general monitoring requirements—which are also necessary but not specified in written procedures—depicted in cloud-shapes (e.g., in Figure 3.2, top: "Monitor interphone"). Checklists that require the joint effort of both pilots are shown in the middle (e.g., in Figure 3.2: "Before Start checklist"). External agents and required pieces of information are also listed (e.g., Figure 3.2: "Passenger count" delivered by the cabin crew). Horizontal lines with arrows depict points of interaction among individuals (e.g., in Figure 3.2, the line indicating the interaction between captain and first officer in accomplishing the Before Start checklist, beginning with the captain's request "Ask for checklist" and the first officer's response "Begin checklist"). Figures 3.2, 3.3, and 3.4, as well as all other time-activity figures referred to in this chapter are labeled "Ideal" because they represent the theoretical, ideal manner in which cockpit tasks are to be accomplished, as described in the FOM.

Takeoff, Climb, and Cruise

FOM descriptions of tasks and procedures for phases of flight following the takeoff are qualitatively different from pretakeoff descriptions, reflecting substantial differences in the nature of crew work. For example, instead of tasks described step-wise as procedures, the FOM text describes how flight controls are to be operated to control the takeoff roll. Since the pilots already know how to fly the airplane, the goal here is presumably to standardize the techniques used by crews. A diagram of the takeoff flight profile up to 3,000 feet provides an integrated perspective of speeds to be flown as a function of altitude and a flap retraction schedule—this too ensures that crews use standardized techniques that have been worked out for safe, efficient operation during this crucial phase. The FOM also prescribes standard callouts for both pilots (e.g., pilot flying: "Set takeoff thrust") and directs when and how critical actions are to be taken (e.g.: "At V_R, initiate a smooth, continuous rotation using 2–3 degrees per second rotation rate toward initially 15 degrees of pitch attitude"). Modifications of normal procedures are also presented for special conditions, such as unpressurized takeoffs, crosswind conditions, and noise abatement takeoff profiles.

Because the takeoff roll and initial climb are critical periods in which anomalies would threaten safety, crews must focus carefully on controlling the airplane and on critical decision points at which the crew would have to respond to any engine or other system malfunctions. FOMs typically say little about the overall tasks of the crew during this phase: to fly the airplane along the assigned departure route, monitor the radio for ATC instructions, and, in some cases, to

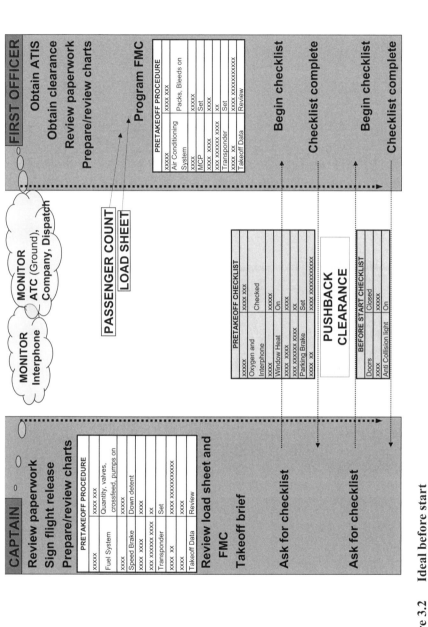

Figure 3.2   Ideal before start

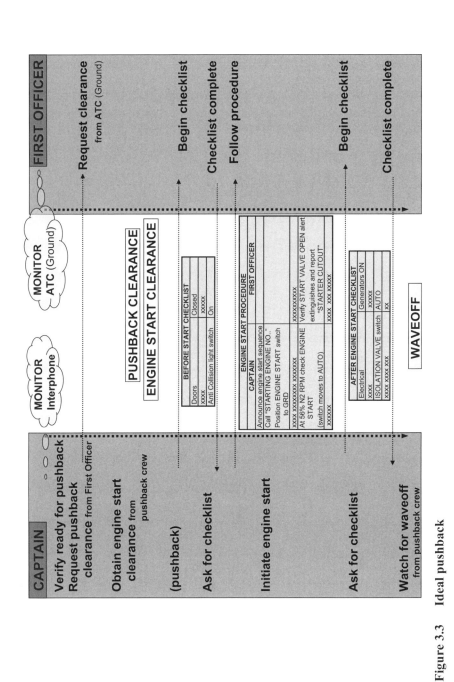

Figure 3.3   Ideal pushback

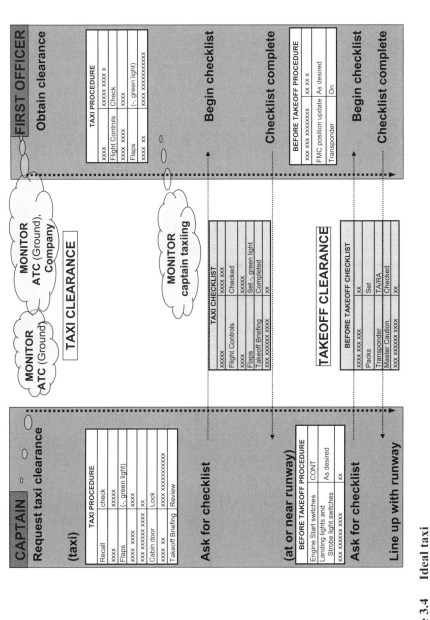

CAPTAIN

Request taxi clearance

(taxi)

TAXI PROCEDURE	
Recall	check
xxxx	xxxxx
Flaps	(-, green light)
xxxx xxxx	xxxx
xxx xxxxxx xxxx	xx
Cabin door	Lock
xxxx xx	xxxx xxxxxxxxxx
Takeoff Briefing	Review

Ask for checklist

(at or near runway)

BEFORE TAKEOFF PROCEDURE	
Engine Start switches	CONT
Landing lights and Strobe light switches	As desired
xxx xxxxxx xxxx	xx

Ask for checklist

Line up with runway

MONITOR
ATC (Ground)

MONITOR
ATC (Ground), Company

TAXI CLEARANCE

MONITOR
captain taxiing

TAXI CHECKLIST	
xxxxx	xxxx xxx
Flight Controls	Checked
xxxx	xxxxx
Flaps	Set -, green light
Takeoff Briefing	Completed
xxx xxxxxxx xxxx	xx

TAKEOFF CLEARANCE

BEFORE TAKEOFF CHECKLIST	
xxxx xxx xxx	xx
Packs	Set
Transponder	TA/RA
Master Caution	Checked
xxx xxxxxx xxxx	xx

FIRST OFFICER

Obtain clearance

TAXI PROCEDURE	
xxxx	xxxxx xxxx x
Flight Controls	Check
xxxx xxxx	xxxx
Flaps	(-, green light)
xxxx xx	xxxx xxxxxxxxxx

Begin checklist

Checklist complete

BEFORE TAKEOFF PROCEDURE	
xxx xxx xxxxxxxx	xx xx x
FMC position update	As desired
Transponder	On

Begin checklist

Checklist complete

Figure 3.4   Ideal taxi

monitor for adverse weather that would require course deviations. Also, in visual meteorological conditions (VMC), both pilots are expected to monitor outside the cockpit until reaching 18,000 feet for airplanes on potentially conflicting courses, and to monitor system and navigation displays. Integrating these diverse tasks requires both pilots to systematically shift attention among various displays and controls and the visual environment outside the cockpit. However, management of attention switching among tasks is apparently considered a skill acquired through experience and is usually not discussed in FOMs.

Several procedural actions and checks are accomplished immediately after takeoff, once the crew has retracted the aircraft flaps and gear, and these checks are prescribed by a short checklist (e.g., After Takeoff checklist) with no more than 6 items. Once the aircraft has attained an altitude of 10,000 feet, the end of the "Sterile Cockpit" period,[7] another set of checks (e.g., altimeter, cabin pressurization and temperature) is accomplished. Similarly, a few more procedural items are performed at 18,000 feet (the altitude at which (in the U.S.) the altimeter setting is changed to the standard sea-level atmospheric pressure of 29.92 inHg).

At this point, the FOMs typically say little more about how the flight unfolds, as it reaches and then travels at its assigned cruise altitude, until it is time for the aircraft to start a descent. For the benefit of continuity, and particularly for the sake of our non-pilot readers, suffice it to say that Air Traffic Control (ATC) may during this period give instructions temporarily diverting the flight away from the course planned and programmed, and may assign intermediate level-offs during climb before clearing the flight to its cruise altitude. After reaching the intended cruise altitude, unless the flight is very short or adverse weather threatens the planned operation, crew workload is reduced substantially, consisting largely of monitoring the airplane's system indications, flight plan progress, autopilot operation, and FMC operation (if so equipped); monitoring for ATC instructions; and making course changes as necessary. Fuel remaining on board the aircraft and the balance of fuel among tanks must be monitored, and sometimes the engines must be fed fuel from only one tank to rebalance the fuel load if the engines have drawn from the tanks unevenly. Procedures and checklists are not usually required during this period, and the FOM mainly addresses techniques and considerations for efficient cruise performance.

Figure 3.5 is an abbreviated time-activity graph for takeoff, climb, and cruise. Similar to the previous figures, this graph depicts all tasks assigned to the captain or first officer individually, on the left and right sides, respectively. Tasks include both specific procedures in text-boxes (e.g., After Takeoff procedure), checklists that require joint effort (e.g., After Takeoff checklist), and general monitoring

---

7   The "Sterile Cockpit" rule, enacted by the FAA in 1981 dictates that the crew shall restrict all communications to only those pertinent to safety of flight below 10,000 feet of altitude. This rule was designed to protect the crew from unnecessary distractions, in recognition of the criticality of the period of initial aircraft climb following takeoff as well as the time during approach for landing.

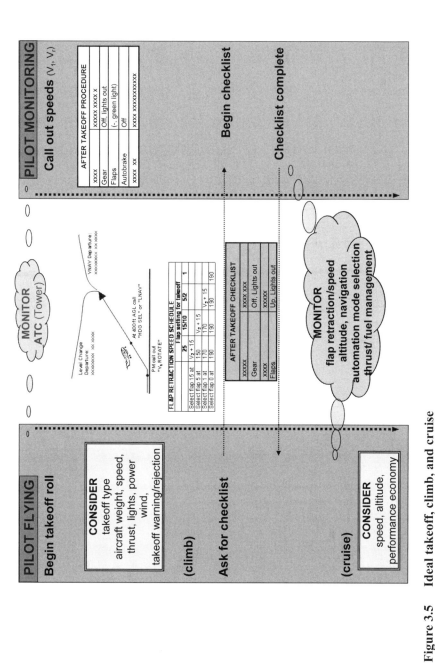

Figure 3.5 Ideal takeoff, climb, and cruise

requirements (e.g., "Monitor flap retraction"). Horizontal arrows again depict points of interaction between the crew members. This figure is also labeled "Ideal" because it represents the manner in which cockpit tasks are to be accomplished in an ideal world without perturbations.

Descent and Approach

As the flight approaches the top of descent, typically around 150 nautical miles from its destination, the crew begins a series of tasks prescribed in the FOM to prepare for arrival, including obtaining weather information, communicating with the airline's arrival station, making a call to the cabin crew (flight attendant notification), evaluating landing performance considerations (e.g., runway length and condition and wind), setting approach speed and altimeter reference markers, and conducting an approach briefing that articulates the central aspects of the situation and the crew's plan for conducting the approach. Here, too, the FOM provides guidance of issues for crews to consider, rather than describing procedural tasks step-wise. A descent profile chart is provided describing speeds and descent rates.

Although it is clear from the FOMs that the crew must consider weather in their planning, the extent and ways in which adverse weather may complicate the approach and increase crew workload is not mentioned. Supplementary text provides guidance on holding patterns, diversion procedures (when the crew elects to fly to the alternate destination because of weather or other reasons), and fuel considerations.

As the descending aircraft approaches 18,000 feet, the crew performs a flow of several procedural items (e.g., Approach/Descent procedure) and a short checklist (with the same name). A few more procedural items to be performed at 10,000 feet are specified in the FOM, following by a timely notification of the cabin crew to secure the cabin (when the aircraft is at an altitude of around 2,500 feet.

Below 10,000 feet, flights are typically instructed by ATC to set up a specific instrument or visual approach, and crews may choose among several levels of automation, ranging from none (manual flight) to full automation. (During instrument approaches the aircraft's flight path is controlled solely by reference to cockpit instruments, whereas during visual approaches the crew uses the outside visual scene to control path, supplemented by instrument indications). FOMs typically provide a fair amount of text discussion of issues to consider (e.g., visibility, workload) when conducting either visual or instrument approaches. Airline pilots are highly experienced in the techniques used to fly both instrument approaches and visual approaches, so these techniques are, understandably, not described in detail in FOMs. However, most airlines now provide criteria and required callouts to make for deviations from normal airspeed, sink rate, localizer position, or glideslope to ensure that the pilots detect and respond to deviations quickly and maintain the proper path all the way down to the runway (known as flying a stable approach). FOMs typically provide graphic profiles for both visual

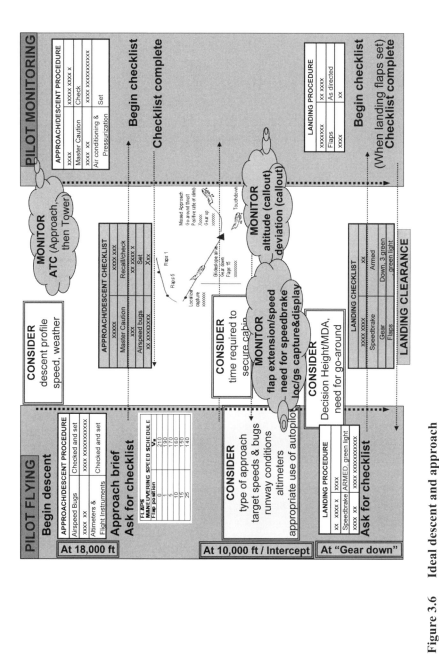

Figure 3.6   Ideal descent and approach

and instrument approaches, and list a series of standard callouts to be made during each type of approach (e.g. pilot flying: "Landing gear down, flaps 15"). After the flaps are set to the final position for landing, the monitoring pilot executes a short checklist (e.g., Landing checklist).

Like the Takeoff, the Approach phase requires careful focus by crews because threats and undetected errors can have profound consequences and require quick response. Depending on air traffic and weather conditions, workload can range from moderate to heavy. FOMs typically do not discuss managing this workload or dealing with weather issues, presumably because these skills are acquired through experience, and it would not be useful to try to guide execution of these skills through written procedural steps. Figure 3.6 is an abbreviated time-activity depiction of descent, approach, and landing as it emerges from the FOMs.

Landing, Taxi-in, and Shutdown

FOMs provide text descriptions to standardize the techniques to be used in landing the airplane. Text material also describes general considerations for exiting the runway and taxiing to the gate. Taxiing-in involves managing several tasks concurrently, similar to taxiing-out for departure. The FOM prescribes procedural flows (e.g., After Landing or Taxi-In procedure) to be conducted by both pilots, on the captain's command, after the airplane exits the runway and another set of procedural flows (e.g., Engine Shutdown and/or Parking procedure) for shutting down the engines and other systems after the aircraft has come to a stop (at the gate or its designated parking spot). These are followed by associated checklists (with the same names), typically composed of ten or so items. Figure 3.7 is an abbreviated time-activity depiction of landing, taxi-in, and shutdown. Like the previous figures, it is also labeled "Ideal", for the same reason.

Characteristics of the ideal operating environment

FOMs portray operations in a pristine, idealized environment free of interruptions, distractions, contingencies, and unexpected events. Reading an FOM, one would not suspect that pilots may be called to manage multiple tasks concurrently. The crew's work appears to have three central characteristics: it is linear, predictable, and controllable.

Linear: Tasks always follow a prescribed order in a fixed sequence.

FOMs describe procedures that exactly specify the successive order in which tasks are to be accomplished. The implication is that each item is to be accomplished after the previous one is completely finished. For three tasks A, B, and C, for example, a procedure directs the pilot to start with Task A, finish it before moving on to task B, and upon completion of task B, move on to handle task C.

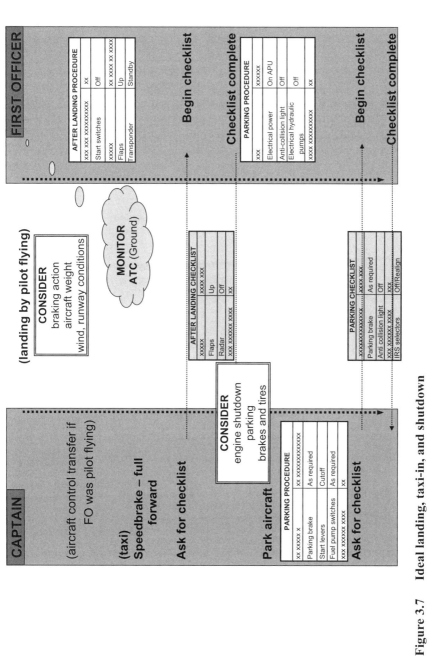

CAPTAIN

(aircraft control transfer if FO was pilot flying)

(taxi)
Speedbrake – full forward

Ask for checklist

CONSIDER
engine shutdown
parking
brakes and tires

Park aircraft

PARKING PROCEDURE	
xx xxxxx x	xx xxxxxxxxxxxxx
Parking brake	As required
Start levers	Cutoff
Fuel pump switches	As required
xxx xxxxxx xxxx	xx

Ask for checklist

(landing by pilot flying)

CONSIDER
braking action
aircraft weight
wind, runway conditions

MONITOR
ATC (Ground)

AFTER LANDING CHECKLIST	
xxxxx	xxxx xxx
Flaps	Up
Radar	Off
xxx xxxxxxx xxxx	xx

PARKING CHECKLIST	
xxxxxxxxxxxx	xxxx xxx
Parking brake	As required
Anti collision light	Off
xxx xxxxxx xxxx	xxx
IRS selectors	Off/Realign

FIRST OFFICER

AFTER LANDING PROCEDURE	
xxx xxx xxxxxxxxxx	xx
Start switches	Off
xxxxx	xx xxxx xx xxxx
Flaps	Up
Transponder	Standby

Begin checklist

Checklist complete

PARKING PROCEDURE	
xxx	xxxxxx
Electrical power	On APU
Anti-collision light	Off
Electrical hydraulic pumps	Off
xxx xxxxxxxxx	xx

Begin checklist

Checklist complete

Figure 3.7   Ideal landing, taxi-in, and shutdown

In this fashion, the three tasks are always completed in this prescribed order. The possibility of changing the order of tasks is mentioned only in passing.[8]

Linearity is implied by the description, both among items within procedural flows and checklists (e.g., the flaps are always verified after completion of the flight controls check), and from the overall scheme of activities (e.g., the FMC is always programmed after the final passenger count and load data have been delivered to the cockpit).

Describing tasks in a linear fashion has two important implications. First, completion of one task implies that all preceding tasks have also been completed. If a pilot completes task C, this must mean that both preceding tasks A and B have been accomplished. Second, linearity suggests seriality; that is, only one activity is performed at a time. If a pilot is involved in one task, he or she does not have to handle any other task in parallel.

Predictable: Tasks and events can all be exactly anticipated, both in nature and timing.

FOMs describe activities in a way that makes them seem completely predictable. Predictability is conveyed because the possibility that operating circumstances might force changes in the timing or sequence in which tasks are performed is not discussed. The disruptive effect of interruptions is not mentioned, nor is the possibility that unexpected tasks will arise that must be interleaved with normal tasks in an ad hoc manner. The ideal world assures pilots that when they complete task B, they should next execute task C, not task A. Further, in the ideal world, whenever a pilot requires certain information to conduct a task, that information is complete and immediately available. For example, the first officer can assume that, when programming the FMC comes up in the prescribed sequence of tasks, the final passenger count, which is necessary to complete this task, will be available. And the captain can assume that when he or she is ready to run a checklist, the first officer will be free of other duties to conduct that task together with the captain.

Controllable: Execution of tasks is under the moment-to-moment control of the crew.

Partly because of the predictability attribute, crews appear to have complete control over the timing, pace, and manner of execution of their tasks. Sufficient time is apparently available to complete all tasks, and crews can pace their activities in a way that is safe and efficient. Crews can formulate plans at a time when they can devote full attention to this critical task, and they can execute those plans in the manner anticipated. In normal operations, crews will not have to

---

8   Carriers note that "minor variations in order are acceptable" but do not say how such variations might be accomplished. The manufacturer also acknowledges that "certain items may be handled in the most logical sequence for existing conditions" but is quite vague as to the handling, the sequence, or the conditions (Boeing, Normal Procedures, NP.10.2).

balance competing goals (e.g., weather avoidance vs. on-time arrival) and make choices with uncertain outcomes. The volume of work is manageable. Pilots are not affected by cognitive limitations, especially working memory and attention limitations, which might cause them to fail to notice critical information or forget to perform an intended action.

So what? One might argue that the purpose of the FOM is only to prescribe the tasks that crews must perform and to describe the actions crews must take to execute those tasks. The most effective way to describe flight procedures is in the sequence in which they are normally conducted, and the nature of language forces the description to be linear. FOMs are not intended to portray the complexity of real-world operations, which pilots are expected to learn to manage on their own through experience.

All of this is true, but it does not address two major problems with the way procedures are developed, described, and taught. First, procedures in both OMs and FOMs are typically developed without considering the many ways in which the complexity of real-world operations perturbs and disrupts their execution. Procedures developed from the perspective of an ideal operating environment tend to be brittle; they do not provide the flexibility needed to manage the many perturbations of the ideal that occur in actual line operations. Second, although pilots do learn to manage concurrent task demands and other complexities of real-world operations, they tend to underestimate their vulnerability to error in certain situations. Furthermore, the techniques they learn to use to manage concurrent task may not be effective. Several studies have found that failure to follow procedures is a common theme in accidents (see, for example, NTSB, 1994a) and in everyday flight operations not resulting in accidents (Helmreich, Klinect, Merritt, 2004), but until recently the causes of deviations from procedures have not been examined in depth (Dismukes, Berman, and Loukopoulos, 2005; Dismukes et al., 2007).

It is not our purpose to criticize the design of FOMs, or to suggest that FOMs should be written to prescribe solutions for every single possible eventuality during a flight. It is well understood that FOMs are but the backbone of operations, written with the intention to provide basic guidance about how to operate the aircraft in a manner that conforms to the carrier's operational, financial, and safety goals. However, to the extent that training is exclusively based on FOMs, and in the absence of a separate Training Manual to address the complexity of real-world operations, our description here lays the foundation for an argument later in the book that the design and training of procedures are not sufficiently robust to deal with the complexities of real-world operations and to minimize vulnerability to error.

In the next chapter we describe some of the many ways in which the pristine operations of the ideal world are perturbed in the real world, and conclude that real operations are not entirely linear, predictable, or under the complete control of the flight crew. In the chapter after that we describe a wide range of errors resulting from the divergence of the real from the ideal. The manner in which FOMs are currently written may be sufficient for their main purpose of standardizing cockpit procedures, but the errors associated with the real nature of actual flight operations suggest that the design and training of procedures must explicitly address the demands and challenges of real world operations. In the final chapter we suggest some ways in which this can be done.

Chapter 4
The Real: Flight Operations
Add Complexity and Variability

In the previous chapter we summarized the tasks of the flight crew as described in FOMs and concluded that those manuals and the associated training convey cockpit work as linear, predictable, and controllable. In this chapter we examine the degree to which that characterization accurately captures the real world of routine flight operations. Our discussion of this real world is based on an ethnographic study in which we observed a substantial number of scheduled, passenger-carrying flights from the cockpit jumpseat at two airlines. In this study we took detailed notes of events and crew actions throughout the course of these flights and, whenever possible during cruise or after the flight, we asked the pilots to comment on these events and actions. (See Appendix A for methodological details.) We have also conducted a large number of less formal observations from the jumpseat of diverse aircraft at several other airlines; these observations helped inform the formal study and provided a broader context for our formal observations.

Our jumpseat observations focused on perturbations that forced the crew to alter the sequence of execution of tasks described in the FOM, disrupted the flow of work, or increased the complexity of work. From these observations we constructed a realistic portrait of crew work in actual flight operations. It is not surprising that the real world is far more complex and dynamic than the simplified portrayal of the FOM, but by comparing the real with the ideal of the previous chapter we lay a foundation for understanding the vulnerability to error of skilled pilots when performing routine tasks. This in turn makes it possible to redesign operating procedures and training to address the demands of actual flight operations more effectively.

Although all of the observed flights followed the general schema of the FOM, no two flights were the same, varying dynamically with unscripted task demands and because of differences in pilots' responses to these demands. The real operating environment is far more interactive than indicated by the FOM. In each phase of flight, the cockpit crew must interact with a wide range of human agents on the ground and in the air; these agents provide critical information to the crew, require information from the crew, and impose demands that affect the structure and timing of the crew's other tasks. (See Appendix B for a list of these agents and their responsibilities.) Weather conditions and air traffic conditions also greatly increase the dynamic complexity of the crew's work.

How crews responded to perturbations hinged on subtle variations in the timing and the nature of competing task demands, and their responses were also undoubtedly influenced by personal preferences, experience, and work habits. Consider, for example, the frequently-occurring situation in which the first officer attempted to contact the Ground controller to obtain the required departure clearance but found the frequency occupied and had to monitor the radio for an opportunity to break in and make the request. We observed one instance in which the captain asked the first officer to request departure clearance while the first officer was still entering data into the FMC. This first officer chose to continue entering data while simultaneously monitoring the radio for an opportunity to make the request. In a very similar situation another first officer chose to suspend entering data until she was able to contact the Ground controller and receive the clearance. In still another instance the first officer had finished entering data before the captain asked him to obtain the clearance.

One might be tempted to interpret the perturbations we describe in this chapter simply as increased workload for the crews. Indeed they do increase workload, but on most flights the crews' workload, as we shall see, was clearly within their capabilities, was easily managed by experienced crews, and rarely did they seem rushed. In this book we develop a new perspective, going beyond traditional concepts of workload, to argue that these commonplace perturbations have a larger and more subtle significance than the simple volume of work. These perturbations, which permeate pilots' work, require both pilots to manage

---

Mr. and Mrs. M, a married couple, were brought into the emergency department for medical care after their vehicle was struck by a truck. The two patients were placed in the same trauma bay, next to each other. They were both going to be requiring blood so samples were typed and cross-checked for each, separately. This process involves drawing blood samples from each individual, identifying the blood group, and running a quick cross-check to determine compatibility. Mrs. M was quickly assessed to be less stable than her husband and therefore more urgently in need of a transfusion.

The emergency department is a crowded, noisy, stressful work place that increases the risk of errors. Personnel have to be sensitive to, yet not allow themselves to be distracted by, the concurrent demands that suddenly arise with the arrival of a new patient. The situation becomes ever more complex with the simultaneous arrival and urgent need for stabilization and assessment of more than one patient. The commotion that forms in the trauma bay may lead to labeling blood tubes away from the patients. Patients with the same surname (as in this case) further add to the potential for error. In the hubbub following the arrival of Mr. and Mrs. M., the blood typing tube for Mrs. M was confused with that of her husband, and therefore inadvertently mislabeled. Fortunately for Mrs. M, a blood bank technologist happened to notice the discrepancy, after checking with records of a previous admission of Mrs. M. to the hospital. The error was corrected and the potentially fatal incompatible transfusion was narrowly averted.

(Agency for Healthcare Research and Quality, 2004)

multiple tasks concurrently, interleaving performance of some tasks, deferring or suspending other tasks, responding to unexpected delays and unpredictable demands imposed by external agents, and keeping track of the status of all tasks. The cognitive demands imposed by managing concurrent tasks in this fashion, play a central role in pilot's vulnerability to error, especially errors of inadvertent omission, as discussed in the next chapter.

Appendix C lists a large number of perturbations observed in these flights. Rather than discuss each perturbation in detail, we have selected seven examples from the complete set. The examples do not represent distinct categories of perturbation situations—rather, they illustrate the wide continuum of perturbations and provide a representative cross-section of the sum of our observations. For each example we discuss the context of the perturbation, the source, and the consequences for the crew and the flight. We explore each example to illustrate the large range of perturbations observed, their diverse nature, the varied contexts in which they occur, their diverse sources, and the many ways in which they influence the flow of work, increase the complexity of the flight operation and require crews to manage multiple tasks concurrently. After presenting these examples, we contrast the real characteristics of actual flight operations with the ideal characteristics portrayed by FOMs.

In each of the seven examples, the crews dealt with perturbations successfully, without error, which was generally the case in our jumpseat observations. Crews are able to manage diverse perturbations effectively in the great majority of instances. Still, perturbations increase vulnerability to error, as is illustrated later when we contrast these seven examples with similar perturbations pilots themselves reported to have occurred on other flights, and which were *not* dealt with as successfully.

We have taken a small journalistic liberty in discussing the selected examples: We describe pilots' thoughts in response to the situations they encountered. Of course, we do not know, in a rigorous scientific sense, what the pilots were thinking in these specific instances, but from many observations, later discussions with the pilots observed, discussions with many other pilots, as well as our own personal experience as pilots (K.D. and I.B.), we feel comfortable characterizing how pilots typically understand these types of situations.

"Chain of mounting pressure"

Context: The aircraft was at the airport gate and the crew was busy preparing for the next flight. A load sheet containing the latest figures on weight (passengers, fuel, and luggage) on board had already been delivered by the gate agent to the first officer, who had entered the data in the FMC, as required. This enabled him to determine that the aircraft weight and balance were within limits and to compute critical takeoff data (rejected takeoff speed, rotation speed, etc.). The captain, having verified the first officer's actions and calculations, requested the Pretakeoff checklist, which the crew proceeded to perform in the standard challenge and response fashion. Just as the two pilots were completing the final two items of the Pretakeoff checklist, the gate agent re-appeared at the cockpit door holding a revised load sheet. Additional luggage, which previously was assumed would not arrive from a connecting flight on time, had just been loaded in the aircraft cargo hold. The first officer used the new load sheet to begin revising the data he had previously entered into the FMC. To expedite the programming task and to guard against inadvertent mistakes, the two pilots spent the next few minutes bent over their respective computer screens, making keyboard inputs and talking to each other. A radio call from the company dispatcher, however, interrupted the crew right as they were about to compute and enter in the FMC the new operating speeds. The dispatcher informed the crew that another aircraft from the same company had just arrived at the ramp area and was now waiting to pull into the gate their aircraft was currently occupying.

Perturbation sources: The arrival of new data having a direct influence on aircraft takeoff performance is not an uncommon occurrence. This perturbation requires re-computing and re-entering the data into the flight computer, and the crew, knowing this to be a time-consuming, head-down activity, realized this was best accomplished before pushing back. The crew collaborated to respond to this new task demand when it was notified of the company aircraft waiting to pull into the occupied gate. The captain realized they needed to expedite preflight preparations so he could signal the ground crew to push the aircraft away from the gate. Once that was accomplished the crew could start the engines, obtain taxi clearance, and taxi their aircraft away from the ramp area to allow the company aircraft to move in and de-plane its passengers. The captain wanted to support the company's goals for on-time departures and arrivals and wanted to accommodate the passengers of both his aircraft and of the other company aircraft. From his experience with the tempo of operations at this busy airport, he had grown accustomed to this type of situation, and had often initiated pushback before completing FMC programming to expedite operations, resuming programming after his aircraft had cleared the gate. Today he made a conscious decision to repeat this strategy; he established contact with the ground crew, interrupted the first officer's programming, and directed him to assist in the engine start sequence.

Consequences: Ideally, as portrayed in the FOM and described in the previous chapter, the first officer would have completed all pretakeoff tasks by the time the captain directed initiation of the pushback and engine start sequence. However, like the captain, the first officer had flown in and out of this busy airport many times, and was not surprised by this situation or the captain's request to proceed with pushback before completing re-programming.

Interrupting his programming meant that the first officer would have to remember to return to it and resume where he had left off, as soon as possible after pushback and engine start. Should this not be possible until after the captain had already started taxiing, he would have to make sure to complete the programming task no later than when the captain called for the Taxi checklist because that checklist required verifying that the necessary data had been entered into the FMC. In such a case, the first officer would also have to interleave his monitoring of the taxi progress with his programming of the FMC.

The first officer may have subconsciously counted on a number of things to help him remember to resume the suspended task. He kept open in front of him the laptop performance computer used to calculate critical operating speeds and other takeoff data, and left the display on the screen with the takeoff speeds. He also left the FMC on the screen that displayed the fields into which he would later copy the new speed data. Of course, both computer screens still displayed the previously-entered speeds, but the first officer still may have hoped that the screens could serve as reminders of the need to compute and enter the new speeds. Further, he knew that the captain would later be reviewing all the relevant FMC pages as part of his own duties, and that would perhaps serve as another reminder. If all else failed, the Taxi checklist would provide a final layer of protection against forgetting because one of the challenge items required verification that all programming had been completed

After pushback and engine start, the captain directed the first officer to request taxi clearance and, upon receipt of the clearance, started taxiing the aircraft to the departure runway. The first officer resumed re-programming as soon as he confirmed that the captain had acknowledged the taxi instructions and had started moving in the right direction. He looked back down at the performance computer still in his lap, and, keeping a watchful eye and ear to monitor taxi progress, resumed re-programming.

The crew on this flight successfully dealt with the perturbation caused by the nearly simultaneous arrival of new load data and a company aircraft waiting to pull into the gate their own aircraft was occupying. The programming task was suspended, and later re-initiated in time to complete all takeoff preparations. The captain's strategy to expedite preparations accommodated the desires of the company's passengers and helped maintain a good on-time departure and arrival record for the company. Thus the outcome of this strategy seems entirely positive, yet this strategy has a hidden downside, for it increased the crew's vulnerability to error to some degree.

Interrupting a habitual task for an appreciable period exposes pilots to the risk of forgetting to return to the interrupted task, especially when the pilots are later caught up in other attention-demanding tasks. In this case, the first officer suspended re-programming the FMC to complete not just one, but several other tasks before returning his attention to the FMC. Checklists are, of course, a safeguard against errors of omission, but checklists are themselves sometimes forgotten or imperfectly executed, so the risk is not negligible. Still another risk was engendered when the crew started taxiing before completing programming: the first officer's attention was directed down to the FMC, making it more difficult for him to monitor outside the aircraft during taxi, which is one of his responsibilities and an important safeguard against costly collisions. Unfortunately, it is difficult to quantify the increase in risk in these situations.

Some pilots and airline managers may feel that re-arranging the normal sequence of tasks to expedite operations does not increase risk as long as workload remains within manageable limits. However, the risk is not necessarily a matter of workload but of disrupting the processes of attention and memory that enable correct performance. Several major airline accidents have resulted from such disruptions (Dismukes et al., 2007).

Our comments here are not meant as criticism of this crew. Nor do we argue that airlines must never allow these sorts of procedural deviations. Deciding whether to allow procedural deviations to expedite operations should be a matter of management policy based on explicit cost-benefit and risk analyses. This book is meant to inform management in the conduct of such analyses.

"Visitor"

Context: The crew had executed a normal takeoff, retracting the flaps and landing gear on schedule. After takeoff, the air traffic controller had instructed the crew to climb to and maintain a cruise altitude of 22,000 feet. This was exactly what the crew had expected from their experience with this particular airport, the airspace surrounding it, and the traffic patterns usually flown in the area. The cruise altitude assignment matched that of the departure clearance given the crew during preflight preparations. The crew had used this cruise altitude to compute flight-relevant data and to program the flight profile in the FMC.

During the initial portion of the climb, the flying pilot had selected the appropriate autopilot mode, per company procedures, and the aircraft was now in a normal climb, tracking the FMC-programmed route (speed, altitude, and waypoints) on the way to the assigned cruise altitude. The crew was monitoring the altimeters and the aircraft's progress as it followed the autopilot's commands, and the cockpit was quiet as the two pilots put away their charts and other paperwork.

Perturbation source: The sound of a chime in the cockpit interrupted the silence. The first officer recognized the chime as the cockpit "doorbell", which meant that the flight attendant was requesting permission to enter the cockpit. She knew to expect the flight attendant at about this time—per company procedures, he would be checking to see whether the pilots needed anything before starting the passenger cabin food and beverage service. The first officer pushed the cockpit door button to unlock the door to let the flight attendant in.[1]

---

1   Cockpit doors, although variable in other design features, remain locked during flight for security purposes. Non-emergency access to the cockpit can only be gained by "requesting" permission to enter (i.e., notifying the crew via interphone (a chime sounds in the cockpit)). The cockpit crew can either grant or deny access by controlling the door lock from the inside.

Just then, the air traffic controller issued a new instruction to "climb and maintain flight level two-seven-zero [27,000 feet]." This was not an unusual instruction, and the higher altitude would save fuel, but it required the crew to take several actions to set up the climb to the new altitude. The flight attendant entered the cockpit, unaware of the just-received communication from air traffic control, and began to ask the pilots whether he could be of service.

Consequences: Normally, pilots would have welcomed the flight attendant's arrival to inquire how things were going in the passenger cabin and perhaps to ask for something to eat or drink. However, in this case, the flight crew did not respond to the flight attendant, remaining focused on the new task demands posed by the controller's call for a higher cruise altitude. The first officer acknowledged the air traffic control instruction by "reading it back" to let the controller know that the instruction was correctly understood and would be followed. The captain, with his hands on the yoke and the thrust levers, asked the first officer to replace the previously-entered altitude (22,000) in the Mode Control Panel (MCP) with the new altitude (27,000), which she did, verbally verifying the entry by announcing "27,000" while pointing to the altitude window on the panel. The first officer then turned around to face and greet the flight attendant.

Normally, social conventions and neurobiological orienting mechanisms cause people to immediately turn their attention to an individual who comes into their presence and addresses them. Consequently, although distractions such as a flight attendant coming into the flight deck do not involve essential flight duties, they are likely to divert attention in much the same way as more flight-relevant interruptions. Both interruptions and distractions can cause pilots to lose their place in an ongoing task, overlook a required action, or forget to resume a suspended task.

Perhaps recognizing the danger of distraction from previous experience, the crew kept their attention focused on responding to the controller's instructions, deferring interacting with the flight attendant until a break occurred in the demands of their flight duties. Correctly interpreting the situation, the flight attendant waited quietly until the pilots completed their ongoing tasks.

Although the crew managed this situation optimally, one should note that distraction was inevitable, at least momentarily, when the flight attendant entered and made his query. Salient intrusions such as this automatically divert individuals' attention, and attention is further required to assess the situation and re-direct attention to the more important task. It is difficult to assess the degree of distraction involved when crews such as this one are well-disciplined in maintaining their focus, but it is reasonable to assume that vulnerability to error increases slightly, albeit momentarily. A far greater risk occurs if crews are not so disciplined, and allow their attention to be diverted for longer periods by distractions that are not critical to flight duties.

"Flaps to go!"

Context: The crew was on an instrument approach to their destination airport. Visibility was poor and the pilots could not yet see the airfield, but the aircraft was steady on a descent path that would bring it to the runway. To begin the process of configuring the aircraft for landing, the flying pilot asked the monitoring pilot to set the flaps to 5 and to initiate the Landing checklist. The flaps extension would begin the process of slowing the aircraft, and the Landing checklist would ensure that items critical for the impending landing (e.g., landing gear extended, speedbrakes armed) were accomplished before reaching about 1,000 feet above the ground.

Perturbation source: The monitoring pilot directed his attention away from his ongoing task of monitoring the aircraft and its progress along the approach path and began the actions directed by the flying pilot. He remained on the Approach controller frequency, continuing to monitor for radio calls. While setting the flap lever to 5 and tracking the corresponding gauge to confirm that the flaps had been set in motion, he also reached up to the glareshield to pull out the checklist card, which he now kept in his hands. As soon as the flap gauge indicated the flaps had reached the commanded position, he turned his attention to the Landing checklist. He challenged each item in turn by reading it off the checklist card and verified the correct setting of the item before responding, as required by the FOM. In this manner he performed the first four checklist items. When he reached the fifth item, which called for ensuring the flaps are in the desired setting for landing, he recalled that, during the approach briefing the crew conducted before starting descent, they had decided this landing would be executed with flaps set to 30. This decision was based on performance data, computations, and company guidance.

The monitoring pilot knew that several minutes would pass before the flaps could be extended to their final setting of 30.[2] Specifically, he anticipated two more calls from the flying pilot for intervening flap extension settings (flaps 15 and flaps 25) as the aircraft was gradually slowed for landing. He could not complete the checklist until the flaps were at the final setting, however this was not at all an unusual situation—it occurs on almost every flight involving 737s and many other airliners. The Landing checklist procedure is written in a way that requires the monitoring pilot to complete the first part of the checklist (typically three or four items), then suspend the checklist until the flaps can be set to the final position for landing. Then the monitoring pilot must remember to resume the checklist to complete one or two additional items before announcing completion of the checklist.

---

2   Aircraft flaps must be extended and retracted according to a manufacturer-prescribed schedule that defines safe flap surface exposure as a function of aircraft speed. Abrupt extension of flaps into excessive wind stream can damage the flaps and severely impair handling of the aircraft.

Consequences: Normally, after completing a checklist and announcing it complete, the monitoring pilot returns the checklist card to its storage slot on the glareshield, an action signifying that the checklist has been accomplished and no longer requires attention. However, in this situation the monitoring pilot returned the card to its slot but left it sticking out partially to indicate that the Landing checklist was not yet complete and would have to be resumed. Also, at this time he announced "flaps to go" as a way of reminding himself and the flying pilot that further action was required.

The monitoring pilot resumed his role, focusing on attending to the aircraft flight progress by alternately checking the instruments and the view out the window, and monitoring the radio for further instructions from the Approach controller. When the flying pilot called for the intervening flaps settings as expected (flaps 25, and a few seconds later, flaps 30), the monitoring pilot moved the flap lever to the appropriate position and reached for the checklist card still protruding from its slot. He challenged the last two items on the checklist (final flap setting and autopilot set as desired for landing) and announced "Landing checklist complete" to indicate that the sequence was complete. He then immediately stowed the checklist card, this time pushing it all the way in its slot to indicate that all checklist items had been addressed and the aircraft was properly configured for landing.

Deferring an action step from a habitual task exposes crews to the risk of forgetting to perform the deferred action later when they are busy with other tasks. Further, landing flaps are typically set at a time when both pilots are busy with other duties such as monitoring aircraft speed and altitude and making required callouts, looking outside the aircraft for the runway or for conflicting traffic, responding to radio calls from ATC, and being prepared to respond to TCAS (Traffic Collision Avoidance System) alerts. These competing task demands increase crews' vulnerability to forgetting to resume the suspended Landing checklist.

This crew did remember to resume the suspended Landing checklist, and in fact, crews remember to do this in the great majority of flights. Two actions taken by the monitoring pilot—positioning the checklist to stick part way out of its slot and calling "flaps to go"—probably helped the crew remember to resume the checklist. Also the flying pilot's commands for further flap extensions served as indirect reminders because flap extension, through experience, is associated in memory with execution of the Landing checklist. It is fairly common for pilots to develop personal techniques to help remember deferred items such as suspended checklists; although these can be quite helpful, they do not eliminate vulnerability to errors of omission, especially in high workload situations. In fact, several major accidents have occurred in which crews forgot to complete a suspended or interrupted task in the face of multiple, concurrent task demands. For example, one of the factors in the 1999 landing accident of an MD-80 at Little Rock, Arkansas was the crew's failure to resume an interrupted Landing checklist during a very busy approach (NTSB, 2001; see also, Dismukes et al., 2007).

"Please call back later"

Context: The aircraft was parked at the gate as the crew prepared for departure. The first officer was in the process of performing his Pretakeoff procedure actions, as prescribed by the company FOM. The captain, having already finished his own pretakeoff tasks, was ready for the Pretakeoff checklist, which would verify that both pilots had performed all actions critical for this Pretakeoff phase of flight.

Perturbation source: Turning to the first officer to request that he initiate the Pretakeoff checklist, the captain found him still busy verifying the numbers on the load sheet and typing the data in the FMC. He saw that the first officer had not yet finished his own Pretakeoff procedure actions.

Consequences: The captain recognized that interrupting the first officer to ask for the checklist could be problematic for several reasons. First, the crew would be unable to complete the checklist anyway, as that would depend on completion of programming of the FMC; further, interrupting the programming task would risk their forgetting to resume programming or making other types of error. Pushback was not scheduled for 12 more minutes, so there was no immediate time pressure.

The captain decided to give the first officer time to finish programming. He looked around his own area and saw the papers he had been handed when descending the jetway to the aircraft. He remembered that the weather report contained information about winds aloft that could potentially affect later stages of the flight. He had already reviewed the weather while waiting for the incoming aircraft to pull in, but now took the opportunity to look over the papers again and refresh his memory. This would come in handy when he later conducted the departure brief before pushback. The captain made no attempt to create any special reminder to call for the deferred checklist, apparently assuming he would automatically remember when the first officer finished programming. Indeed, once the first officer looked up from the FMC and put the load sheet on the control panel for the captain to review, the captain called for the Pretakeoff checklist, which the crew accomplished together.

The captain adapted to this situation, as he undoubtedly had many times before, by momentarily deferring a task when the conditions for its execution were not agreeable. In this instance, time pressure was not an issue, but that is not always the case—contrast this situation with the one encountered in the first example— ("chain of mounting pressure") in which there was immediate pressure to vacate the gate area, leading the captain to interrupt the first officer. As previously discussed, deferring a task with the intention of completing it later exposes crews to the risk of forgetting to perform the deferred task at the appropriate time, especially if they are busy with other tasks at that time. In the current example, the captain remembered to execute his intention to call for the checklist when the first officer finished programming, but in similar situations crews under time pressure have on occasion forgotten to conduct deferred checklists. This example illustrates one of the many reasons pilots cannot completely control the sequence and timing of their own tasks, a notion we explore more extensively at the end of this chapter.

"Eavesdropping"

Context: The aircraft was parked at the gate prior to departure. The captain of the observed flight (which we will call FictionAir flight 123) monitored the Company frequency while performing his preflight duties. Listening to that frequency is required by the carrier's standard operating procedures and serves to ensure that crews are informed of modifications to flight plans caused by changes such as in weather, airport traffic, delays in loading or unloading, or other factors.

Perturbation source: A number of communication exchanges occurred between the company dispatcher and another aircraft of the same company (FictionAir flight 456), which was at that time parked at a neighboring gate and was also preparing for departure. All communications were appropriately prefaced with the flight number so the crews could identify which aircraft was being addressed. Flight 456 was experiencing some potential departure delays because of weather, as became evident by the dispatcher's call: "FictionAir 456, anticipate you will have to wait for the Albuquerque flight. They have 3 of your passengers and are running 14 minutes late." The captain of flight 123 monitored all of these exchanges. The captain's primary task at this point was to finish performing his pretakeoff flow. With only three more minutes before his flight was scheduled to push back from the gate, the captain had to press on with the flow and to execute the Pretakeoff checklist before pushback.

Consequences: Normally, monitoring the radio frequency to identify calls addressed to his aircraft, although performed in parallel with other tasks, required very little of the captain's attention because experienced pilots develop a skill in monitoring for and detecting their own call signs automatically. However on this day the captain found himself having to pay particular attention to the content of communications with the other company aircraft in order to continue updating his mental picture of the overall situation in the ramp area. With only one pushback tug available at the four neighboring gates at this ramp, any changes to other flights' pushback time could directly affect his own flight, especially since flight 456 was scheduled to push first. Paying attention to the content of these communications, rather than simply screening for his own call sign increased demands on inherently limited cognitive resources (attention and working memory). Thus the captain was forced to continuously switch attention between performing the pretakeoff flow and monitoring communications to update his awareness of the situation.

In this instance, the situation was resolved when the Company controller decided to re-sequence the order of departure of the two aircraft and issued a command for flight 123 to proceed first. The captain asked the first officer for the

Pretakeoff checklist and prepared for pushback and engine start, and the flight proceeded without difficulty. Although this crew managed the situation effectively, switching attention between tasks for sustained periods exposes pilots to the risk of becoming preoccupied with one of the tasks to the neglect of the other task and in some cases forgetting to switch attention back to the other task at all. This happened in an accident at Guantanamo Bay in 1993, in which the captain, who was flying the approach, became preoccupied with trying to find a strobe light on the ground to avoid Cuban airspace and failed to control the airplane's turn to final appropriately (NTSB, 1994b). Then, preoccupied with regaining control of the turn, he failed to recognize the need to abort the approach and go around. Fatigue apparently exacerbated the captain's vulnerability to preoccupation. (The crew had been on duty for nearly 18 hours, and the captain had been awake for more than 23 hours.)

"No can do!"

Context: The flight was in the beginning stages of its approach to its destination airport. The crew anticipated landing on runway 17R, which was the most commonly used runway at this airport at this time of the year. The first officer, who was the monitoring pilot, announced "going off"[3] to acquire ATIS information, which she partially transcribed on paper.

Perturbation source: After reviewing the ATIS information, the first officer realized that the airfield was now directing aircraft to land on runway 17L. This change was probably made to accommodate the high volume of traffic arriving at the airport at this time of the day. Before saying anything to the captain, who was the flying pilot, she quickly checked the performance numbers and found runway 17L was not an acceptable option for their aircraft because this runway was too short to accommodate their aircraft with its landing weight on that day. She informed the captain and waited for his assessment.

Consequences: The captain responded that they would need to request a landing on the originally planned runway, 17R, which was long enough for the weight of their aircraft. The first officer was aware that the Enroute controller would very soon be directing them to contact the Approach controller who was the controller to whom the crew would have to make their request. She therefore deferred making the request, intending to make it immediately upon establishing contact with the Approach controller who would be able to coordinate this type of request with the airport. A short while later, when the Enroute controller directed the flight crew to

---

3   When a pilot announces "going off" he or she is indicating that they are going to stop monitoring the air traffic control frequency while they divert their attention to another task. This prompts the other pilot to take sole responsibility for monitoring and communicating with air traffic control, in addition to their other tasks.

switch to the Approach frequency the first officer happened to be glancing at the ATIS information she had previously transcribed on paper, and remembered to make the intended request for runway 17R.

Runway changes are certainly not unusual in today's flight operational environment. In fact, they are quite common, and pilots learn to expect them at certain busy airports. Changes in flight plans during descent, however, create additional tasks that pilots must integrate with their usual, expected tasks. This integration can be challenging, increases workload, and exposes crews to the risk of errors, especially errors of omission. Crews are particularly vulnerable when one of the tasks to be integrated inadvertently drops out of the focus of attention, and the surrounding environment does not provide effective cues to remind pilots of the unattended task. The observed pilot was fortunate in that a happenstance event (looking at the ATIS information at the moment the Enroute controller communicated with the crew) reminded her of the deferred intention, but that was merely coincidence. The haphazard noticing of a cue cannot be relied on to guard against inadvertent omissions. The risk of forgetting is further increased when the workload in the cockpit is already high, as it often is during an approach to a landing. A runway change was one of the factors contributing to the runway overrun accident at Burbank, California in 2000 in which the crew became preoccupied and overloaded trying to salvage an unstabilized approach (NTSB, 2002; see also, Dismukes et al., 2007) and this factor has been implicated in many incidents (ASRS, 2007).

"Everything changes"

Context: The crew was halfway down their assigned taxi route on the way to the planned departure runway (runway 7). They had set the flaps to the takeoff position before getting underway, and were just about to initiate the Taxi checklist. The captain was at the controls and the first officer was monitoring his actions and the traffic on the taxiways, as per standard operating procedures.

Perturbation source: The winds had shifted since the original flight plan had been approved, and the airport was now using another runway for departures. The Ground controller issued an instruction directing the crew to taxi to and depart from runway 14 instead. She also issued new taxi instructions that would get the aircraft from its current position to the new departure runway for takeoff.

Consequences: With more than half the distance to the runway already behind them, the crew would normally already have performed the Taxi checklist at this point. On that day, the crew realized they would have to give precedence to the task demands generated by the unexpected change in the departure runway while underway. The checklist would therefore have to be performed later than usual (but of course no later than reaching the runway). Instead of performing the checklist, the first officer started responding to the new task demands. He first acknowledged the instructions (repeating them back to the controller) and next, based on his familiarity with the airport layout, mentally assessed how immediate a response was required to comply with the new taxi route instructions. The new route showed they would need to turn at taxiway D, and he estimated they would reach that intersection within a minute. He realized that they would barely have enough time to perform the calculations necessary to verify that the aircraft takeoff weight was within acceptable limits to take off from the new runway. At the same time, he knew he must not neglect his normal duty to monitor the taxi in progress and to conduct the Taxi checklist before the aircraft arrived at the departure runway.

The first officer advised the captain of the imminent change in routing, and the captain directed him to take care of the necessary calculations and preparations. Because these were all activities with which the first officer was quite familiar, he probably did not regard it as difficult to concurrently monitor the captain, switching attention back and forth between the head-down calculation task, and the head-up monitoring task. He was able to perform both these tasks that required his primary attention before reaching the runway by interleaving them, continuously switching attention from one task to the other. At the same time, he also monitored the radio frequency for additional changes that might require further action.

The change in departure plan before the aircraft reached the takeoff runway was certainly not an unusual occurrence, as airport conditions (e.g., weather and traffic) often change dynamically, necessitating runway changes for both landing and departing aircraft. When the operational situation changes and new tasks arise, crews have to find ways to integrate the new task demands with their normal tasks, and sometimes this requires interleaving steps of the new tasks with steps of the normal tasks. Thus, at a time when pilots would usually be able to devote full attention to a single task, they now must switch attention among tasks and execute tasks more rapidly.

Pilots usually accomplish this interleaving effectively; however, the cognitive demands of interleaving different types of tasks (in this case, monitoring someone else's actions, monitoring aural messages, entering data in a computer, engaging in simple mathematical calculations) are not at all trivial. This situation increases vulnerability to error, probably more than most pilots realize. Pilots may choose to reduce task demands to manageable levels by deferring or omitting lower priority tasks, which can be effective, but only if done in a deliberate, strategic fashion.

This handful of examples selected from the much larger set of events observed during routine flight operations (see Appendix C for a longer list) reveals the general flavor and the manner in which routine flight operations are actually conducted. The sources and effects of perturbations in pilots' formally prescribed tasks are numerous and variable. Some perturbations are momentary interruptions that can be acted upon quickly ("visitor"), but other perturbations require time-consuming actions to reach resolution ("everything changes"). Some come in the form of requests that can be dealt with by briefly suspending an ongoing activity ("flaps to go"), whereas other requests must be deferred until later ("no can do"). Perturbations may be single events ("please call back later"), or they may be compound strings of events, each incrementally imposing additional demands on the crew ("eavesdropping"). The source of perturbations is often external to the cockpit and can generally be traced to one of the many human agents who function within the same operational environment, or to ambient situational factors (e.g., weather changes). The timing and pattern of perturbations are unpredictable, and multiple perturbations sometimes occur simultaneously or in rapid succession.

Notably, all of the perturbations we observed occurred in the context of normal, routine operations—they did not arise out of an emergency or abnormal situation that required extraordinary attention or special handling by the pilots. Also notable is that perturbations were typically dealt with swiftly and effectively. Discussions with crews confirmed our impression that such events are considered part of "doing business" and are not normally cause for concern. Pilots generally feel confident that they are skilled at handling routine perturbations. (However, the next two chapters suggest that pilots may underestimate their own vulnerability to error in these situations.)

Simply listing perturbing events is not sufficient to convey the manner and extent to which they disturb the ideal execution of procedural steps listed in FOMs. Beyond analyzing the selected examples above, and in order to better convey the consequences of perturbations we turn again to time-and-activity figures. We now present a new set of figures, labeled "Real," for each phase of flight. These are essentially revised or "populated" versions of their ideal counterparts because, in addition to the normative activities, they also depict perturbing events noted during our jumpseat observations.

Figure 4.1 is a populated version of Figure 3.2. We began with the ideal Pretakeoff phase, listing all the FOM-specified activities in the prescribed sequence and with the appropriate timing. On it, we have overlaid observations

---

Early in the morning a maintenance technician performed an engine vibration evaluation on a Boeing 757 aircraft. This test involved running the engine on high power for a few minutes and testing for unwanted vibrations. When engines are operated while the aircraft is on the ground and not properly configured for takeoff (as is the case when an engine is powered up for a maintenance procedure and not in preparation for taxi and/or for takeoff), the takeoff configuration warning horn sounds. To avoid becoming distracted by the loud horn during the vibration run, and to ensure the clarity of communication in the cockpit, the engineer pulled the circuit breakers for the warning horn. This was common practice for this type of a test. The technician would be re-setting the breakers at the completion of the test.

When the engine was shut down, the technician became preoccupied with having to find the engineer who had some documents necessary for the completion of the required paperwork. This distraction led the technician to forget his intention to re-set the warning horn circuit breakers. The flight crew discovered the omission during their preflight check.

(U.S. Aviation Safety Reporting System, Report # 687309)

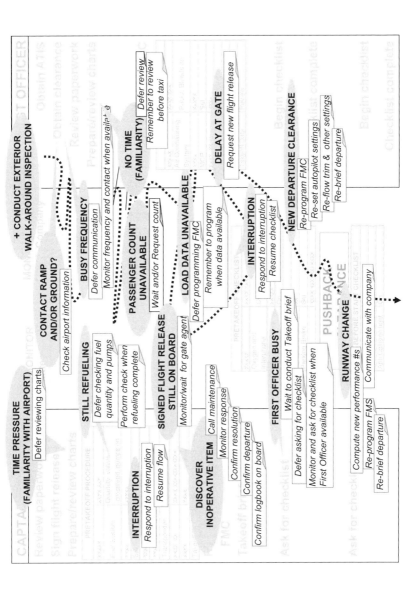

Figure 4.1   Real before start

of perturbing events from different flights. Each perturbing event is denoted by an oval-shaped text box (call-out box) describing the source and nature of the event and placed on the vertical axis to indicate the approximate time of occurrence. The cognitive demands associated with each perturbation are indicated in rectangular boxes below each call-out box. For example, the perturbation caused by a "busy frequency" when the FO requested pushback clearance forced the FO to keep trying until the frequency became free (Figure 4.1, top, center).

Figure 4.1 represents the entire data set collected during the Pretakeoff phase. It is important to note that the events depicted on this figure did not all occur on any one flight—they are the aggregate of many events noted in all the flights observed. (Similar events are collapsed into a single call-out box, even though they may have occurred at different times with somewhat differing repercussions.) Thus, the figure resembles a worst case scenario with perturbations along every step of the way. In reality, on most flights we observed only a few perturbations. However, the constraints of observing and note-taking undoubtedly prevented noting all perturbations that occurred on a flight. Also, perturbations surely show up in more forms than observed in our sample of about 60 flights, however, we feel this sample is large enough to be representative of routine flight operations nationwide. Using the same populating process, Figures 4.2, 4.3, 4.4, 4.5, and 4.6 show observed events for the other phases of flight and depict them superimposed on the corresponding ideal illustrations of Figures 3.3, 3.4, 3.5, 3.6, and 3.7.

Characteristics of the real operating environment

Comparing the two sets of figures (ideal and real), it becomes apparent that the real flow of activities is much more convoluted than its ideal counterpart and this observation is applicable to every phase of flight. Perturbations are generally not anticipated and are mostly acted upon as they appear, disrupting the habitual, practiced, flow of anticipated activities based on written manuals. Each perturbation entails additional cognitive demands that must be integrated with the demands of anticipated tasks. Graphically, the end result is that linear flow of events and actions depicted in the figures by straight arrows morphs into a winding path in the real figures.

The divergence between the real and the ideal time-activity graphs suggests that the picture of cockpit operations as pilot-driven, which emerged from analyzing FOMs in the previous chapter, is rather misleading. Rather than linear, predictable, and controllable, real operations are better described as:

Dynamic: Tasks do not always follow a prescribed order.

Pilots must often deviate from the linear flow of actions, A → B → C..., prescribed in FOMs. When A is completed the situation sometimes makes performing B impractical, and the pilot must move on to C with the intention of returning to B when the situation permits. Also, pilots must often respond to

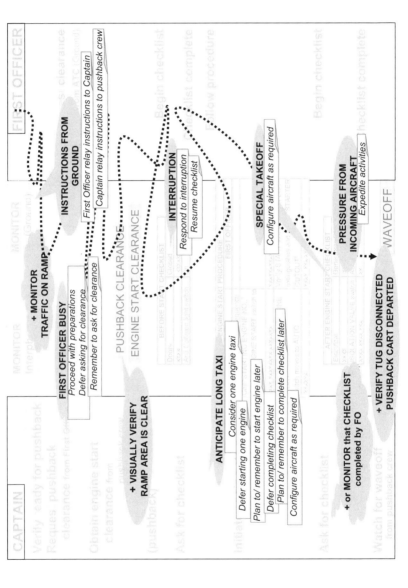

Figure 4.2   Real pushback

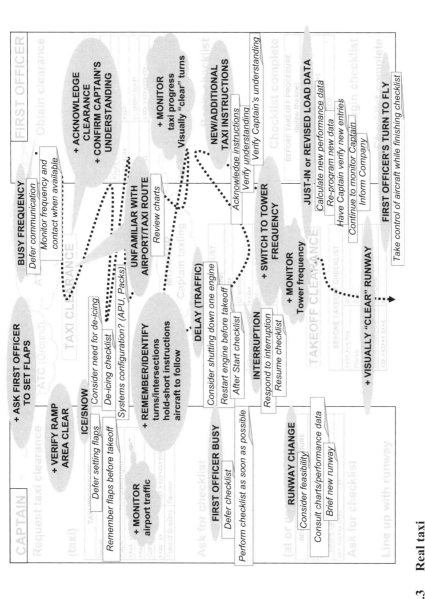

Figure 4.3   Real taxi

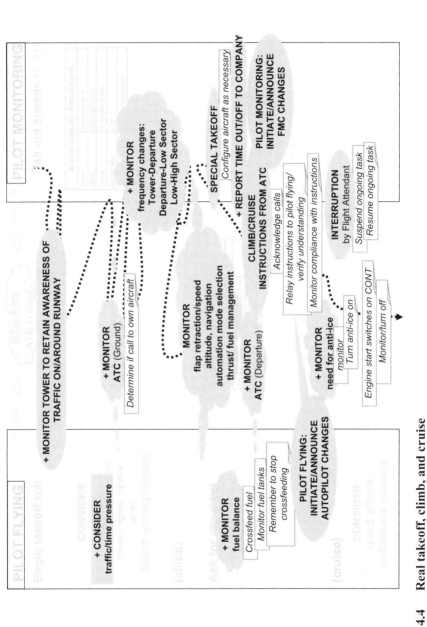

Figure 4.4   Real takeoff, climb, and cruise

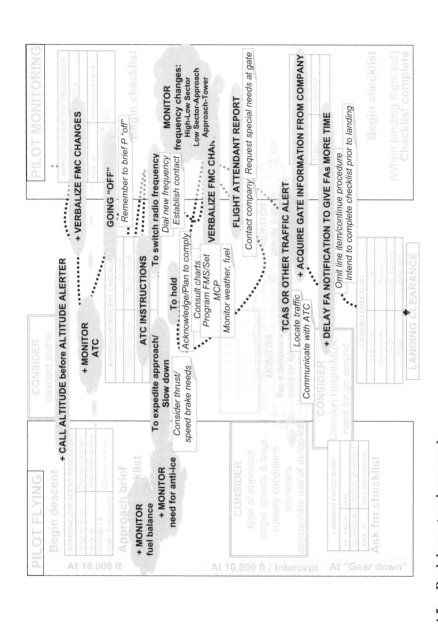

Figure 4.5   Real descent and approach

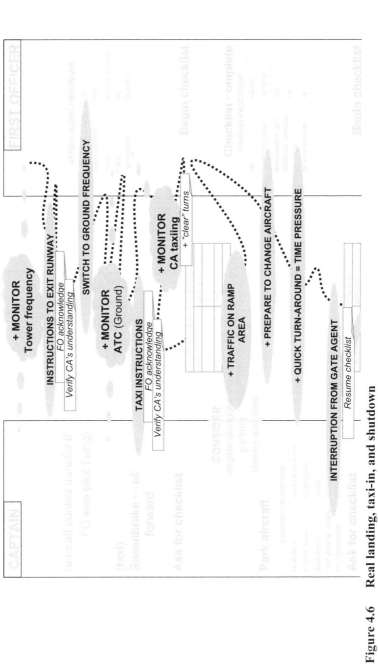

Figure 4.6   **Real landing, taxi-in, and shutdown**

The Real   67

unplanned demands, inserting new tasks, e.g.: A → B → X → C... Finally, tasks often must be performed concurrently, so the real sequence consists of alternating between elements, more like: part of A → part of B → part of A → part of B → part of C → part of D → part of C → part of D... Because of these variations, the flow of activities is dynamic rather than linear. Further, these situational-dependent deviations vary from flight to flight and even from moment to moment, which undercuts the automatic execution of habitual tasks; this increases vulnerability to error.

Semi-predictable: Tasks and events can not all be exactly anticipated (neither their nature nor their timing).

Predictability hinges upon the absence of unexpected events. Our field observations make it clear that real-life flights are inundated with unpredictable demands that generate unscheduled tasks for crews. Note that most of these events are unpredictable, but not truly unexpected. Because these events occur with some frequency in the course of operations, pilots have moderate to extensive experience handling them. However, pilots do not know when a given perturbation will occur or what tasks they will be performing when it happens, and thus cannot plan ahead how to manage it.

The availability of information necessary to perform specific crew tasks is also semi-predictable. Lacking required information disrupts the ideal flow of execution of tasks (e.g., lacking final weight and balance information, the first officer cannot complete FMC programming). Further, because each of the two pilots must juggle task demands that are not entirely predictable, they are not always immediately available to each other when they come to tasks that require them to collaborate.

Semi-controllable: Initiation of tasks is not entirely under pilot control.

Ideally, a pilot should be able to initiate a task when ready to devote full attention to it. In reality, it is often the case that circumstances or external agents require tasks to be initiated earlier or later than planned, at a time when other activities might be in progress. This pressure pushes crews from a role that is ideally proactive toward a more problematic, reactive mode of operating.

Because the timing and execution of activities is not entirely under crew control, the time available for executing tasks is sometimes less than desired or expected. The combination of lack of scheduling control and unanticipated additional task demands increases time pressure and workload, especially in critical phases of flight in which the crew is already quite busy. Further, FOMs portray the two pilots performing most of their tasks separately; however, unanticipated perturbations often require the attention of both pilots, increasing both workload and the need for collaboration.

In sum, situational constraints and unscheduled demands drive cockpit work to a significant degree, reducing the extent to which it is under crew control. This has important implications for captains' responsibilities. In his or her role as pilot in command, the captain is the one with whom most agents outside the cockpit interact, and the one who must make final decisions on handling all situations. To complicate matters, each group of agents acts in response to its own operating needs and pressures, communicates using its own language, and works with its own, often incomplete, mental picture of the overall situation. The ground crew, the cabin crew, the air traffic controllers, for example, all have their own agendas. In pursuing their own operational goals and needs, they often create time pressure and impose operational demands on the flight crew. The captain (as pilot in command) must decide how to address these externally generated demands while also meeting the flight crew's own goals. At the ramp, for example, the ground crew might be under a tight schedule and anxious to push the aircraft back so it can report at another gate where another aircraft is waiting to be pushed. At the same time, the cabin crew may need more time to carry out a final passenger count because of a delay in boarding, while the Ground controller may be anxious to get the aircraft away from the ramp to accommodate other incoming aircraft. In the air, the Approach controller may push the crew to keep their speed up in order to maintain separation among airplanes in the busy airspace; the flying pilot may question whether this higher speed will allow enough time to slow down closer to the runway, while the lead flight attendant might still be anxiously waiting for the monitoring pilot to verify that her request for a wheelchair at the destination gate has been received by the gate agent on the ground. Quite often, groups of human agents are not in direct communication with one another and must rely on the captain to coordinate their respective demands.

There is danger that these pressures can push crews into a reactive mode in which the crew responds to each demand as it arrives, losing control of the situation and compromising safety. In principle, the captain is responsible for controlling the situation to ensure that the crew can manage the workload and have time to perform all tasks effectively. For example, the captain is empowered to respond "unable" to ATC instructions, if necessary, though this may not endear him to controllers. But strong organizational and self-imposed pressures work against crews' attempts to maintain control of the pacing and structure of their tasks. On-time performance and fuel costs are strong drivers in the hyper-competitive airline industry. Thus we suggest in the final chapter that airlines should explicitly train pilots to recognize the danger posed when they allow themselves to be pushed into a reactive mode, should provide realistic training in managing workload and competing task demands, and should emphatically support captains' efforts to maintain a proactive stance.

In closing the previous chapter, we argued that operating procedures designed solely from the ideal perspective are likely to be brittle and conducive to error in real-world situations. We also argue that training should help pilots develop effective ways of managing dynamic real-world task demands. Our visits to airline training centers (more than just the two that supported this study) led us to conclude that airlines provide very little training and guidance to help pilots manage these situations. Crew Resource Management (CRM) classes that focus on making efficient use of available resources (human, equipment, information) sometimes provide general guidance on workload management but rarely address the specific manifestations of real-world demands depicted in this chapter. Apparently, managing these manifestations is something that pilots are supposed to learn on their own during line operations, which they do, although it is far from clear that all pilots develop effective techniques.

In the next chapter we examine the consequences of the divergence of real-world cockpit operations from the ideal of the FOM and from pilot training. We describe pilot errors associated with real-world perturbations, analyze the cognitive processes that come into play when pilots respond to concurrent task demands, and develop a perspective on vulnerability to errors of omission.

Chapter 5
Analysis of Concurrent Task Demands and Crew Responses

It is clear from the last chapter that actual flight operations are much more complex than portrayed by FOMs. The ideal flow of procedures is constantly perturbed by events and task demands; consequently, cockpit work is in reality dynamic, semi-predictable, and only semi-controllable. Even routine flights require pilots to deal with multiple task demands concurrently by improvising, rearranging, and interleaving planned tasks with unexpected tasks. But so what? In the 60 flights that we formally observed, the crews dealt with many diverse perturbations effectively and with aplomb. Questioned during the Cruise phase or after the end of the flight, pilots reported not having found the perturbations to be in any way extraordinary or threatening. Some were consciously aware of having experienced and addressed multiple perturbations but casually regarded this as "business as usual." Others were so inured to concurrent task demands that they seemed not to recognize that perturbations had occurred and, knowing the purpose of our presence in the cockpit, expressed disappointment that "nothing interesting" had happened.

Consider, however, the following report submitted to NASA's Aviation Safety Reporting System (ASRS) database by the captain of a Boeing 737:

"As we pushed back, I noticed a lengthy line of aircraft waiting for takeoff at our anticipated runway, which was just a short distance behind us. I made a decision to just taxi the short distance on one engine [engine #2]. This break in our normal flow was distractive enough that I didn't call for flaps. Ground Control then assigned us a different, distant runway with more complicated than normal instructions… Still anticipating a wait at the end, I continued taxiing on one engine. During the taxi, we continually evaluated the heavy rain showers we would encounter on our departure… We stopped at the end of the parallel [taxiway] and Ground sent us to Tower. Tower told us to pull up [#1 in line]. We started the second engine and with rollback [of engine indications], I started moving immediately fearing delay might make ATC change their mind about us being next. Again, the break in flow resulted in not calling for takeoff flaps. We continued scanning the weather as we moved ahead and turned, running the checklist. The combination of doing these things resulted in passing through the flaps item on the checklist without confirming their position. We were cleared for departure and as I pushed the throttle up we got 2 chirps from the takeoff [configuration] warning horn."

(ASRS report # 519061)

(Note: all ASRS narratives have been edited and text in brackets has been added for clarification. ASRS reports can be accessed online at http://asrs.arc.nasa.gov/.)

The takeoff configuration warning horn sounds if the throttles are advanced when the aircraft is on the ground and not properly configured for takeoff.[1] In this incident, the flaps had not been extended as required for safe takeoff, but the flight was saved from disaster by the warning system. In at least one other case, however, the same warning failed to sound and the crew attempted to take off, crashing shortly after starting to climb (NTSB, 1988).

Pilots reporting close calls such as in the ASRS report above are usually shocked that they could have made such a potentially catastrophic mistake, but typically attribute the oversight to a momentary loss of vigilance and resolve to "be more careful" in the future. However, we argue that pilots underestimate their own vulnerability to errors of omission and that checklists and other safeguards against inadvertent omissions are themselves vulnerable to error. In this chapter, we discuss the kinds of error associated with typical concurrent task situations arising from the types of perturbations we described in the previous chapter and analyze the task demands and cognitive processes underlying the vulnerability to errors of omission. This analysis lays a foundation for developing countermeasures to reduce this vulnerability, discussed in the final chapter.

Between 1987 and 2001, 27 major airline accidents occurred in the United States in which crew error was found to be a causal or contributing factor (Dismukes, 2006). In five of these accidents, inadvertent omission of a normal procedural step by pilots played a central role (NTSB 1988, 1989, 1995, 1997, 2001). Two accidents involved failing to set flaps and slats to takeoff position. The other three involved: failing to set hydraulic boost pumps to the "high" position before landing, causing the landing gear to not extend on command; failing to turn on the pitot heat, causing erroneous airspeed indications on takeoff (Flight 795, mentioned at the beginning of this book); and failing to arm the spoilers before landing, which combined with other errors and a wet runway to prevent the airplane from stopping before the end of the runway. A striking feature of each of these accidents is that, not only did the crew forget to execute a normal procedural action they had performed on thousands of previous flights, they also failed to catch the omission when later performing the checklist designed to ensure completion of this and other crucial procedural actions.

In a detailed analysis of the 19 major U.S. airline accidents attributed primarily to crew error in the decade between 1990–2001, Dismukes and his colleagues (2007) found that concurrent task and workload issues appeared explicitly or implicitly in the great majority of those accidents. In some, workload and time constraints were quite high in the final stages of the accident sequence, but in many others adequate time was available to perform all required tasks. In this

---

1   In older versions of the Boeing 737, the takeoff configuration warning horn sounds as a function of flaps not having been set for takeoff and EPR (exhaust pressure ratio) reaching a certain setting.

latter group of accidents, it appears that crew performance was undercut by the cognitive difficulties inherent in reliably switching attention back and forth among concurrent tasks and in remembering to perform tasks that must be deferred out of normal sequence. This analysis found no evidence that the errors in these accidents could be attributed to deficiencies in the skills of the pilots—they were all highly experienced and appeared to be representative of the general population of airline pilots.[2] Thus, it appears that errors of omission largely associated with diverse aspects of concurrent task management, when not detected and corrected, are a major threat to aviation safety (also, see Dismukes et al., 1998).

Considering the intrinsic threats posed by frequent perturbations and concurrent task demands, why were the crews we observed so nonchalant about managing these situations? The first explanation is probably that pilots develop considerable skill responding to routine perturbations, and become adept at juggling concurrent tasks, integrating unplanned new tasks, and rescheduling tasks. Judging from the outcome of the flights observed, pilots appear to handle these situations without error most of the time, and when errors occur they are usually caught before propagating into an accident or even a frightening incident.[3] Second, many of the cockpit tasks experienced pilots perform are highly practiced and over time

---

On an early afternoon in January, an EMB145 aircraft had been flown with the pressurization system in the manual mode after a suspected leak of the service door. The necessary maintenance work was deferred, as per procedures, until the aircraft got to an airport where the necessary repairs could be performed. In the meantime, the aircraft outflow valves were secured in the open position. When the aircraft arrived at its maintenance base, the technician proceeded with the necessary repair tasks that included resealing the rubber door trim and the lower service kick plate. He logged the accomplished tasks and noted that the pressurization system had been restored. The aircraft was dispatched for flight. In flight, the flight crew discovered that the aircraft could not be pressurized in either the automatic or the manual system modes. Once safely on the ground again, an investigation to determine the cause of the failure of the pressurization system showed the outflow valves still open, in the position they had been secured prior to the maintenance work. At the completion of the earlier maintenance work to restore the system, the technician had forgotten to remove the tool that had been used to keep the valves open.

(U.S. Aviation Safety Reporting System, Report # 687117)

---

2   See Dekker's (2002) criticism of the "bad apple" theory of aviation accidents according to which it is assumed that a complex system would be safe if not for the erratic behavior of unreliable operators—that is, accident pilots are considered deficient and not representative of airline pilots.

3   Data from the last decade show around 15 million aircraft departures are carried out per year worldwide. Yet the 10-year accident rate (fatal accident or hull loss) in scheduled passenger flight operations is less than 1.0 accident per million departures (Boeing, 2007).

become largely automatic and seem not to require substantial mental effort. (This is discussed in depth later in this chapter). Thus, managing several familiar tasks concurrently may not seem challenging. Finally, pilots (not to mention airline instructors, procedures designers, and managers) may be overconfident in the reliability of measures designed to catch errors of omission, in particular when executing checklists and performing monitoring tasks. But execution of checklists is vulnerable to errors of omission for many of the same reasons that steps in procedures are inadvertently omitted. Monitoring also requires clearly-defined processes, discipline, and well-established habits to be effective. (See Dismukes et al., 2007, and Sumwalt, Thomas, and Dismukes, 2002, 2003, for detailed discussion of these issues.)

Still, if the great majority of errors do not propagate into accidents, why should we be especially concerned with them? The main reason is that accident rates are at best an incomplete measure of the level of safety of a system. Accident rates are, thankfully, very low; thus analyzing accidents, though useful, only gives insight into what has happened in the past. And because accidents result from the somewhat random interaction of multiple factors, the small sample available from the history of accidents only partially captures latent vulnerabilities lurking in the system that may interact to produce new accidents.

Collecting data on errors provides a much larger and more representative sample of latent vulnerabilities. Error data can be obtained from several sources, for example:

1. Direct observation of flight crews performing in line operations, as we have done in this study, and in LOSA (Line Operations Safety Audits),
2. Flight simulation, in which direct observations can be supplemented by video, audio, and flight data recordings, and extensive de-briefings of pilots, and
3. Incident reports from pilots and other personnel, as provided to the ASRS and to similar report databases that are kept by individual airlines as part of their Aviation Safety Action Programs (ASAP).

LOSA data indicate that even on completely routine flights most crews make at least one error (FSF, 2005; Helmreich, Klinect, and Merritt, 2004). But it is not sufficient to just identify and perhaps categorize errors. To determine how errors affect the safety of the aviation system, one must examine the circumstances in which errors occur (including task demands, events, and organizational factors), the cognitive processes underlying each type of error, and the ways in which pilots typically respond or fail to respond to various types of error—which is what we attempt to do in this book. This type of analysis lays a foundation for devising practical ways to reduce system vulnerabilities.

Our ASRS Study

To explore how the kinds of perturbations observed in our jumpseat study might affect pilots' vulnerability to error, we conducted a search of the ASRS database.[4] This database consists of several hundred thousand reports voluntarily submitted by pilots and other aviation personnel about incidents in which safety was potentially compromised. These reports, many of which identify errors made by the reporting individual, briefly describe an incident, the surrounding circumstances, and any insight the reporter may have to offer on why the errors were made. We used a guided search technique to identify reports describing errors associated with the kinds of perturbations we observed from the cockpit jumpseat, using the events and the surrounding circumstances as search terms. (See Appendix A for more details on our study methods.) For example we found that runway changes during taxi often presented crews with multiple additional task demands that had to be integrated with normal tasks, so we used "runway change" as one of the search terms. In this fashion, we identified reports of pilot errors associated with perturbations similar to those we observed from the cockpit jumpseat. Appendix D briefly summarizes the perturbation ("Perturbation source") and the resulting error ("Consequence") reported in each incident. Although this list is far from exhaustive, it is representative of the reality of line operations, and the perturbations are quite similar to those we personally observed.

Scanning this list, it is clear that the nature and timing of the perturbing events was quite variable, ranging from a momentary interruption while the crew was performing a checklist to the attention-consuming demand of maintaining visual contact with traffic while making final landing preparations. The consequences of these perturbations also varied in nature and severity, mostly leading to errors of omission, some of which were noticed immediately, before generating an undesired situation, and others only after the error caused a subsequent problem. The amount of time before these problems became apparent varied greatly (e.g., one pretakeoff error had immediate consequences, while another did not become apparent until the flight reached cruise).

We have selected four of these incidents to illustrate how perturbations can increase pilots' vulnerability to error. Multiple factors undoubtedly played a role in each of these incidents, but clearly the perturbation was a central factor.

"After takeoff from ATL [Atlanta airport] and climbing through 16,000–17,000 ft, the flight attendant called and inquired as to seat belt, rough ride, thunderstorms, etc. This got us both occupied and I forgot to do the Climb checklist, thus

---

4   De-identified ASRS data are publicly available in a form that can be readily searched, which is one reason we used this source of error data. LOSA data and ASAP data, which provide a rich and complementary source of data, are unfortunately not available to most researchers.

missing [setting the] altimeter setting [to] 29.92.[5] The rest of the climb was done in steps, i.e., as we approach FL240 we were given FL260, etc. After level-off at FL350, ATC asked us to check our altimeter for 29.92. Ours were set at 29.61, thus making us 250–300 ft high."

(ASRS report # 394580)

The perturbation in this incident resembles the one discussed in the last chapter under "visitor" in which the flight attendant entered the cockpit just as the crew received a new instruction from the air traffic controller. In the "visitor" incident the crew we observed from the jumpseat chose to motion the attendant to wait for them to respond to the controller first. However in the incident described above the flight attendant called from the interphone, so it was not possible to signal the attendant to wait. Although this crew could have ignored the interphone temporarily they chose to respond immediately, but the ensuing conversation diverted attention at a time when the crew had been about to initiate the Climb checklist. The habitual flow of activities was disrupted and the crew forgot to execute the checklist and consequently failed to reset the altimeters to 29.92 inHg, as required at 18,000 feet of altitude. This example illustrates that when pilots are interrupted, their attention is diverted at least momentarily. They must then decide whether to suspend the ongoing task to address the interruption and then return to the suspended task, or to defer addressing the interruption until a more opportune time. In either case, pilots must remember to perform a deferred intention, which is an example of a prospective memory task. Later in this chapter we discuss the cognitive processes involved in prospective memory and analyze why these processes are sometimes vulnerable to errors of omission.

"We were tired due to a long day with delays, we had a change and were told to fly [the aircraft] instead of ride [as passengers, back to the home base] and we now had to rush over to the other side of the airport and hurry and takeoff. The preflight checks were rushed, we had to be deiced and there was packed ice and snow on the taxiways. With these icy conditions, our company procedure is to taxi out with the flaps up to prevent ice accumulation on the flaps, then set the flaps to takeoff position right before takeoff. This is a major change from our normal flap procedure. The Before Takeoff checklist was recently changed... The flap position check is now the first item on the Before Takeoff checklist (which is done while taxiing out) and is never checked again. As we taxied out for takeoff, I ran the checklist and left the flaps up as per the cold weather procedures. I informed the captain of this. As we approached the runway for takeoff, Tower asked us if we were ready, we said 'yes,' and they cleared us for immediate takeoff. The checklist then leads you to check the 'final items' as

---

5   See section *Takeoff, Climb, and Cruise* in the Ideal chapter for a brief explanation of the altimeter setting procedure.

you take the runway. These final items do not include another check of the flap position. I said 'checklist complete,' the captain advanced the throttles to takeoff power setting, and we got the takeoff warning horn. It was at this point that we realized that we had attempted to takeoff with no flaps—a potentially fatal error. We aborted the takeoff, reset the flaps, and took off."

(ASRS report # 263325)

(As discussed in the Taxi phase description in the Ideal chapter, the checklist to be executed prior to takeoff is often separated into two parts—the first is conducted soon after the beginning of taxi, while the second, "final items," is conducted right before takeoff, as soon as takeoff clearance is granted.)

This incident closely resembles the situation described under "call back later" in the last chapter, in which the first officer was busy with other tasks when the captain was ready to ask for the checklist. In that case, the captain was forced to defer the checklist but successfully remembered it later once the first officer became available. In the current incident, the crew was forced to defer setting flaps to takeoff position, and then forgot to complete that essential task. Crews normally perform cockpit tasks in the sequence prescribed by the FOM, and the many repetitions of the sequence of actions in these tasks causes performance to become automatic and normally quite reliable. But on occasion, situational factors or the unavailability of another person or of needed information require the crew to defer performing a task out of the normal sequence. For reasons that will be explained, this task deferral greatly increases vulnerability to forgetting to perform the task—yet again, a prospective memory task that may lead to errors of omission.

"I picked up a clearance from LGA [La Guardia airport controller] which was to 'taxi to runway 4 via taxiways A, F, B, hold short of [not cross] taxiway E.' After reading the clearance back, we were told to contact Clearance delivery for a change to the routing [a change to the en-route instructions to follow after takeoff]. I then stated to the captain our taxi clearance and said 'I am off on com #2, you have com #1.' I left the Ground frequency and proceeded to pick up our new clearance while the aircraft was taxiing. When I returned to com #1, I heard Ground state that we were told to hold short of taxiway E. Our position was just short of taxiway D which is south of taxiway E. At this point, the captain stopped the aircraft and asked Ground 'are we clear now to taxi to runway 4?' The answer was 'affirmative' and we continued taxi to runway 4. At no time were we in conflict with another aircraft. The biggest contributing factor to crossing over taxiway E when told to hold short was I was copying the second full route clearance while we were taxiing."

(ASRS report # 438470)

(Pilots can use either of the two VHF radios on board by using a switch to select between the two, as necessary. Standard procedure is to set those frequencies they know they will need during each phase of flight on one radio. If the need arises, as it did in this instance, to use a frequency not on the primary radio, the pilot responsible for communications will often temporarily switch to use the second radio. Here, when the first officer announces "going off" one radio, he is essentially informing the captain that he will be switching to the required frequency to pick up the new clearance on the other radio. When one pilot "goes off" one radio or one frequency, the other pilot becomes responsible for monitoring it. Here, when the first officer "goes off" the Ground frequency, the captain becomes responsible for monitoring it.)

The crew in "eavesdropping" in the last chapter was unexpectedly forced to integrate monitoring the situation on the ramp with their preflight duties, which they did, successfully. The crew in the present incident was not so fortunate. The pilots inadvertently violated the controller's instruction to hold short of (not cross) taxiway E on their way to the runway. Although the captain taxiing the airplane committed the primary error (for reasons that cannot be determined from the report narrative), the first officer also made an error by failing to monitor taxi progress so as to catch the captain's mistake before he had crossed taxiway E. The requirement to contact Clearance delivery for a change in flight routing was unexpected, and the first officer had to integrate switching frequencies and copying the revised clearance with his pre-existing, normal responsibility to monitor taxi progress. Unfortunately his attention was absorbed by this unexpected task, compromising his performance in monitoring the taxi. Switching attention between tasks, especially when one of them is a monitoring task and less structured than other tasks, is more vulnerable to error than is commonly recognized. As is discussed later in this chapter, humans in this situation often become absorbed in one attention-demanding task and forget to switch attention periodically to the monitoring task—yet another manifestation of a prospective memory task vulnerable to omissions.

"We were between 12,000 ft and 11,000 ft MSL on descent, preparing to accomplish the final items on the Approach checklist—1) cycling [momentarily turning off, then immediately back on] of the no smoking sign, our company's method of informing the flight attendants to have passengers stop using personal electronic devices and landing imminent, and 2) recheck altimeters, while being vectored for a visual approach to runway 26R. We had slowed the aircraft to 250 KIAS because we had previously been cleared to descend to 7,000 ft. We were then instructed to proceed to the FAF [final approach fix], descend to 2,500 ft, look for our traffic (a heavy jet), look for traffic turning in for the south runway, and also advised that we had a high overtake speed on our traffic. We accomplished all of those instructions and began to slow and configure the aircraft for landing. We proceeded to accomplish a normal landing. Throughout our entire descent and approach we had been instructed to maintain best forward airspeed. While deplaning the passengers, we were informed... that we had not cycled the no smoking sign. Apparently amidst the confusion and distractions from the checklist while being given the short approach we had not cycled the sign."

(ASRS report # 437750)

Like the crew facing the "everything changes" situation in the previous chapter, the crew in this incident was busy with multiple duties while flying the final stages of the approach. Unlike the crew of "everything changes" that successfully accomplished their duties, this crew forgot to signal the flight attendants that landing was imminent. A careful task analysis would show that the flight crew had to constantly switch attention among several concurrent tasks during this busy period. In these situations, it is easy for attention to become absorbed in one or more tasks, allowing another task to drop from awareness. The previous example illustrated how monitoring, perhaps because it is less structured, is particularly vulnerable to being dropped—this example shows that even habitual, well-practiced, structured tasks such as checklist items are not impervious to being forgotten when attention must be shifted back and forth among multiple tasks.

In the four ASRS incidents used here to illustrate the potentially hazardous effects of operational perturbations, no serious harm resulted. The error was either revealed by an external source (e.g., a controller, a warning device), or fortuitously did not combine with other factors to cause harm. However, the potential for harm was present in every one of the illustrated instances. The aircraft could have leveled off at the wrong altitude to find itself in the path of another aircraft, had it continued with an error in its altimeter setting display. The takeoff configuration warning horn could have malfunctioned and not warned the crew it was attempting to takeoff with the aircraft not configured properly. The aircraft could have found itself on a collision course with another aircraft traveling on taxiway E, after having violated the controller's instructions to hold short. The flight attendants might have not finished cabin service and might have still been standing when the aircraft landed. Thus the margin of safety built into the airlines' procedures was substantially reduced by an inadvertent crew error in each case.

Four Prototypical Situations

To develop measures to protect against these sorts of inadvertent errors of omission, we must first understand the cognitive processes underlying performance of tasks involving these diverse perturbations. Skilled performance and the errors made by experts, such as airline pilots, are the two sides of the same coin; because of this intimate relationship, by studying one we gain insight into the other.

Although the perturbations described in this chapter, the previous chapter, and in Appendix D are extremely diverse in their surface manifestations, we identified

four distinct patterns running through these examples. We now describe these
patterns as four prototypical situations:

1. Interruptions and distractions,
2. Tasks that cannot be executed in the normal, practiced sequence of
   procedures,
3. Unanticipated new tasks that arise, and
4. Multiple tasks that must be interleaved.

These are not four mutually exclusive categories; rather, they are prototypical
situations with both overlapping and distinct features. We organize the discussion
in terms of these prototypes both to identify commonalities among these highly
diverse situations, and to identify critical features that must be examined to
understand why experienced pilots are vulnerable to error in these situations.

Interruptions and distractions

Interruptions occur whenever some event diverts attention from an ongoing task,
causing it to be suspended, at least momentarily. Interruptions are so common they
may seem unremarkable. Before the cockpit door is closed for departure, crews are
interrupted by gate agents, mechanics, flight attendants, jumpseat riders and other
individuals who must interact with the crew to perform their own duties. After
the door is closed, pilots are interrupted by radio calls, intercom calls from flight
attendants, utterances by other crewmembers, and even by their own thoughts that
intrude upon attention.

The terms "interruption" and "distraction" are not used consistently in
aviation; for our purposes we use interruption to refer to discrete events that must
be addressed (e.g., the flight attendant's inquiry about possible thunderstorms,
turbulence, and the need to turn the seat belt sign on, as in the first ASRS report
above), and use distraction to refer to ongoing conditions that also tend to divert
attention but which do not have to be dealt with to accomplish the crew's immediate
responsibilities. The content and duration of distractions vary considerably, ranging
from a few minutes of non-essential conversation to worrying whether the airline's
financial problems will lead to layoffs. Pilots may attempt to ignore unwelcome
distractions, such as worrying about being furloughed, that can interfere with
performing their tasks, but they may welcome, even invite, other distractions that
seem benign, such as casual conversation during periods of low workload. These
welcome distractions may help pilots stay alert, especially when fatigued, but all
distractions effectively become concurrent tasks that must be interleaved with
cockpit duties and which are subject to the problems of interleaving discussed
later.

Interrupting events vary greatly in their urgency and in the demands they
impose. Being handed a fuel slip by the gate agent may intrude on the first officer's
attention for only a few seconds and may not immediately require full attention

An order for intravenous Diflucan was put though to the pharmacy, to be administered to a man at the emergency department. A mis-labeled bottle indicating "Diflucan" but actually containing Diprivan, a commonly-used sedative-hypnotic, was sent by the pharmacy to the emergency department. The nurse by the patient's bedside waiting for the pharmacy to deliver the Diflucan suspected something awry when she noticed the liquid she received was opaque. She happened to know that intravenous Diflucan is a clear solution.

The nurse decided to question the pharmacy for clarification. Her intention to place a telephone call to the pharmacist was unexpectedly interrupted by a physician's request for immediate assistance with another patient. A few minutes elapsed before she was able to return to the room of the first patient. By that time, she had forgotten her intention to call the pharmacist and proceeded with infusing the IV bag containing the sedative instead of the Diflucan. Less than a minute later the nurse had to attend to the IV because of a problem with the IV pump. It was then that she noticed again the color of the liquid and remembered her forgotten intention to check with the pharmacist. Her prompt intervention to stop the infusion saved the patient from experiencing any adverse effects.

(Agency for Healthcare Research and Quality, 2004)

(i.e., if the first officer has not yet started programming the FMC, which will require him to look at the slip, she can temporarily set the fuel slip aside), whereas being instructed to change radio frequencies during the approach may require the monitoring pilot to immediately interrupt other duties (i.e., monitoring the approach) to devote full attention to entering the new frequency and establishing contact with the next controller. Ongoing tasks also vary greatly in the degree to which they can be interrupted without disruption. Taxiing the aircraft in full visibility at a familiar airport along an uncomplicated route makes few demands on cognitive resources and generally allows the crew to accommodate the interruption of a radio call without difficulty. But programming a complicated route into the FMC, a task that makes substantial demands on cognitive resources, may be seriously disrupted by an interruption.

Interrupting events also vary greatly in their nature and timing, as well as in how predictable they are. Some interruptions, such as the issuance of a revised departure clearance as the crew is approaching the runway for departure and in the process of receiving takeoff clearance, are unexpected, both in content and in timing. Other interruptions, like the transmission of a landing clearance during the execution of an approach, are expected by the crew because they are required for proper execution of the flight. The exact timing and nature of even the expected interruptions, however, is generally unknown and unpredictable. The crew cannot be certain when the landing clearance will be delivered or if it will be delivered at all for that matter—another aircraft on the runway may lead the controller to have to issue a go-around instruction instead of a landing clearance. Nor can the crew predict what tasks they will be performing at the moment the controller's message arrives over the radio. Not knowing exactly when each interruption will occur, or what its nature will be, prevents planning other tasks to accommodate even anticipated interruptions.

Various factors, including the timing and nature of the interrupting events and the nature of the interrupted tasks affect the manner in which interruptions are addressed. For example, powerful, deeply ingrained social rules incline individuals to respond immediately to interruptions presented by another person, either physically present or communicating by radio. Individuals also tend to suspend ongoing tasks immediately to deal with interruptions that can be handled quickly to "get them out of the way."

What is common among diverse forms of interruption is that they divert attention from the task at hand and require the individual to decide whether to suspend the ongoing task in order to address the interruption or continue with the ongoing task to reach a natural stopping point before handling the interrupting event. In either case the individual must remember to perform a deferred task. In the former case the deferred task is the interrupted task; in the latter case the deferred task is responding to the interrupting event. In the section on Cognitive Aspects, we return to the challenges posed by deferring tasks and their link to inadvertent omissions.

Tasks cannot be executed in their normal, practiced sequence

Often, the operational situation may not permit a task to be performed in its normal sequence. For example, the crew in the second ASRS example above was forced to defer setting flaps to the take-off position, normally done before taxiing to the takeoff runway, because company policy required that taxiing in these conditions be done with the flaps retracted to prevent slush from the taxiways being thrown up on the flaps.[6]

In other situations, a task cannot be executed because information or a person expected to supply this information or with whom a task must be coordinated is not available when needed. For example, a first officer may be forced to suspend entering data into the FMC during preflight because the final passenger count has not yet been delivered to the cockpit by the lead flight attendant—the passenger count is a required data point—or a captain may be forced to defer executing a checklist because the first officer is busy with another task at that moment. (Most checklists can only be performed when both pilots are available.)

Deferring one task sometimes forces related tasks to also be deferred. For example, deferring setting the flaps for takeoff necessitates deferring running the Taxi checklist, which includes the flaps as an item to check. This compounds the

---

6   This was indeed the case with older aircraft, such as the one being flown by the crew in this example from 1994. This requirement does not hold for newer aircraft, as is explained in Chapter Six (The Research Applied).

risk of forgetting to set the flaps because crews may forget to run the checklist for the same reasons they are vulnerable to forgetting to set the deferred flaps before attempting to take off. (The cues that normally prompt execution of the checklist have been removed, and preparations for starting the takeoff occupy the pilots' attention).

When tasks must be deferred, for whatever reason, it is rarely practical to simply wait without performing other tasks until the opportunity arrives to perform the deferred task. For example, when setting the flaps is deferred, the crew must taxi to the runway, accomplishing various other tasks associated with this taxi, before the opportunity to set the flaps occurs. Further, time pressure in flight operations, especially during preparations for departure, is considerable. A crew that delays unduly while waiting for missing information risks losing their departure-time slot and upsetting their passengers. Consequently, pilots typically turn their attention to other pending tasks while waiting for an opportunity to resume the deferred task. Some phases of flight, especially the Taxi phase and the Approach phases, often present a continuous flow of task demands that occupy the crew's attention without pauses that would give the crew a moment to review whether all tasks have been completed. In competition with this continuous flow of ongoing task demands, the crew must attempt to remember at the appropriate time that a previous task was not performed in its normal sequence.

It was a busy night at the airport. The two maintenance technicians working the overnight shift had two different but time-consuming tasks to accomplish on a B737 parked at a mobile, remote workshop. The aircraft was going to be requiring replacement of its nose wheel spin pads and its toilet dump valve. To complete everything within the allotted time, the two technicians split the tasks. It was 3:30 in the morning when one of the technicians started working on the pad replacement task. He was under time pressure to complete the task so he could assist his colleague and also help another engineer working on a different aircraft. To ensure adequate illumination of the nose wheel area, he used a flashlight which he balanced on the nose wheel strut. While working on the spin pads, he knocked over some tools but rather than interrupt what he was doing, he decided to pick them up after completing the replacement. Later, while picking up the tools he was momentarily distracted by the workshop headlights and forgot his (implicit) intention to retrieve the flashlight from the nosewheel area before departing.

The aircraft was subsequently dispatched for flight, following a pre-service inspection. While taxiing to the departure runway, the flight crew found the nose wheel uncontrollable through the rudder pedals or the steering tiller. The flashlight remained stuck in the nose wheel area, unnoticed by the maintenance inspector and by the flight crew, who had conducted two exterior inspections prior to the flight.

(U.K. Confidential Human Factors Incident Reporting
Programme, Maintenance Error Management System)

Pilots also face challenges when they must remember to substitute an atypical action for one step of a habitual task. For example, on one aircraft type the most frequent flaps setting for takeoff is "five," but under special conditions the crew may have to remember to use a different flap setting. It can also be difficult to remember to *not* perform a normal step of a habitual task. For example, while flying a single engine approach in a particular twin-engine jet (i.e., when one of the engines has malfunctioned or has been shut down for precautionary reasons), the crew may forget to *not* extend the flaps all the way to the normal final landing configuration, rather than only part of the way, as required by the single-engine non-normal procedure. In the section on Cognitive Aspects, we discuss why it is much harder to remember to perform habitual tasks correctly when they must be executed out of their normal sequence or when a step of a habitual task must be replaced or omitted.

Unanticipated new task demands arise

Additional task demands often arise while the crew is executing procedures in the FOM-prescribed manner and sequence. In some situations, the additional task is to be performed at a later time. For example, while the aircraft is descending from 15,000 feet, the air traffic controller may instruct a crew to report passing through 8,000 feet (i.e., to transmit a verbal message to the controller when the aircraft is at that altitude). In this situation the unanticipated task must be added to the existing task requirements, and the crew must integrate it into the normal sequence of activities. The crew must hold the controller's instruction in memory for several minutes while busy with landing preparations, and must remember to retrieve the instruction from memory when the aircraft passes through 8,000 feet. Like an interruption, this situation poses the challenge of deferring a task—in this case a newly added, unanticipated task—and remembering to perform it later.

In other situations the new task must be performed immediately. In the third ASRS example above, the first officer was unexpectedly given instructions for a change to the original routing. At that moment, he was about to begin monitoring the captain who would be starting to taxi the aircraft to the departure runway. Responding to an instruction of this nature must be immediate—the information conveyed redirects what the crew will do next—so the first officer had no choice but to respond to the communication and attempt to integrate the new task it generates with his existing activities. Interleaving unpracticed tasks involving novel aspects with habitual activities is, as we shall see, another challenge that may lead to errors of omission.

Multiple tasks must be interleaved

In many situations pilots cannot defer one task long enough to complete another task and must attempt to interleave the two (or more) tasks. In the fourth ASRS report above, the crew faced a situation in which a routine approach became increasingly complex with multiple tasks requiring attention concurrently: fly the

---

9 June, 2005, evening, Logan Airport, Boston

Operations at Boston Logan's airport 6 intersecting runways were being monitored by the local east controller (LCE) and the local west controller (LCW) in the Air Traffic Control Tower. That summer evening an Airbus was preparing to make its way to runway 15R for takeoff, under the direction of the LCW. Another aircraft, a Boeing, was intending to take off from runway 9 under the direct control of the LCE. The two controllers were using different frequencies to communicate with the respective aircraft.

Runway 15R intersects runway 9 about 8,000 ft down its 10,000 ft length, so the LCW was required to obtain a release from the LCE in order to give clearance for an aircraft to depart from runway 15R. Accordingly, the LCW instructed the Airbus to taxi into position and hold on runway 15R and when, ten minutes later, the LCE "released" the Boeing for takeoff, the LCW gave the Airbus clearance for takeoff from runway 15R.

Things were proceeding per procedure to this point. Everything was to change five seconds later, when the LCE cleared the Boeing for takeoff from runway 9. That crew applied power and started traveling down runway 9, unaware of the Airbus that was also already headed towards the point of intersection of the two runways. The calm reaction of the Boeing flight crew averted the collision of the two aircraft over the runway intersection.

During the ensuing investigation, the LCE stated that at the time he "released" the Airbus he was very busy coordinating with airplanes and other controllers. Though he did notice the Airbus on its takeoff roll down runway 15R about 1 minute later, he was at that time being distracted by a third aircraft wanting to take off, so he was concerned to keep the traffic moving which, in this case, meant first moving the Boeing out of the way. The concurrent task demands led to his giving clearance to the Boeing for takeoff—but forgetting that the Airbus was still on its takeoff roll on the intersecting runway.

(U.S. National Transportation Safety Board, 2007)

---

approach with all the component tasks involved, which was made more challenging by the instruction to maintain best forward airspeed (the higher airspeed reduced time available and increased workload), look out for conflicting air traffic reported in the vicinity, and watch out for the aircraft in front, which they were closing on. Each of these tasks made substantial cognitive demands, so it was not possible to perform them simultaneously. In this sort of situation, pilots must switch attention back and forth among concurrent tasks, trying to avoid becoming preoccupied with one task to the neglect of the others. When attention is switched away from one task, that task is momentarily suspended while another task is addressed. However, in contrast to interruptions and deferred tasks, interleaving requires repeatedly suspending one or more tasks momentarily, engaging another task to perform a few steps, then suspending the new task, and re-engaging the previous tasks (or engage a third task) to perform a few more steps of it until all tasks are completed. This type of a situation poses a serious challenge that also sometimes leads to errors of omission.

Cognitive Aspects

From the preceding discussion it is clear that pilots typically respond to the concurrent task demands arising from the various operational perturbations we have described in one of two fundamental ways, either by *deferring* one or more tasks, or by *interleaving* multiple tasks. In some situations pilots may be able to perform multiple tasks more or less simultaneously, but these situations only occur when the tasks are highly practiced together in a consistent fashion, which means that these situations are not really perturbations. Pilots may also employ a strategy discussed in the first chapter and reduce task demands by changing how tasks are performed, either by lowering criteria for quality, accuracy, or completeness of performance, or by deliberately omitting one or more tasks altogether. This strategy may reduce workload in many situations, but in most cases it does not eliminate the need to defer or interleave tasks.

We next examine cognitive mechanisms involved when individuals attempt to respond either by deferring or interleaving tasks. This examination helps us understand why pilots are vulnerable to error in the four prototypical situations of interruptions, unexpected new task demands, tasks that cannot be performed in the normal sequence, or tasks that must be interleaved with other tasks. This discussion of cognitive issues also lays a foundation for ways to reduce vulnerability to error suggested in the final chapter of this book. The three cognitive mechanisms most relevant to the types of perturbation of operations we have been discussing are *prospective memory*, *automatic processing of habitual tasks*, and *attention switching*.

Our analysis is based on what is known about the cognitive processes of individuals, but it is noteworthy that, in the reports discussed above, the second pilot in the cockpit did not catch the first pilot's error. Thus, it is appropriate to consider these errors as crew vulnerabilities, and even more appropriate to think of them as system vulnerabilities, because it is the overall socio-technical system that creates the situations in which individuals and crews are vulnerable to error.

Prospective memory

Suspending or deferring a task with the intention to return to it later, or forming an intention to add a new task at a later time, requires the use of what is called prospective memory. (For simplicity we refer to suspended tasks, deferred tasks, and tasks planned for later execution all as "deferred tasks.") Research on prospective memory is a fairly new field, and much as yet remains unknown;

however, we can outline its general cognitive features (see reviews in McDaniel and Einstein, 2007 and Kliegel, Martin, and McDaniel, 2004).

The individual who wishes to remember to perform a deferred task must form an intention to execute that task when circumstances become appropriate and must retain that intention while attention is directed to performing other tasks. For instance, in the "flaps to go" example of the previous chapter, the completion of the landing checklist had to be deferred until the aircraft was slow enough to allow the flaps to be set to the landing position. The monitoring pilot announced his intention to set the flaps later and to complete the checklist by stating "flaps to go!" He then had to focus attention on various other tasks during the approach while maintaining in memory the intention to set the flaps and to complete the checklist once the aircraft reached the appropriate speed.

Generally, the tasks that are performed while waiting to execute a deferred task make sufficient demand on humans' limited attentional capacity that the deferred task cannot be maintained continuously in focal awareness and working memory; thus, the intention to return to the deferred task must be retrieved from long-term memory at the appropriate moment. The cognitive mechanisms of retrieval of deferred intentions are the subject of ongoing research, but they are clearly rather fragile, because individuals not infrequently fail to remember to perform deferred actions when the appropriate moment arrives (Guynn, McDaniel, and Einstein, 2001). Research to date suggests that retrieval of intentions from memory requires that the individual notice one or more cues associated with the intention and that the association in memory between the cue and the intention be strong enough to provide sufficient activation for the stored intention to be retrieved back into awareness (McDaniel, Guynn, Einstein, and Breneiser, 2004). In prevalent cognitive theory, "activation" represents the spread of neural activity from one neural circuit to other neural circuits. When a cue is processed in attention, activation spreads from attention to all the memories associated with that cue. In less technical language, these cues act as reminders that help prompt retrieval of intentions from memory.

Several factors greatly influence the probability of an individual remembering at the appropriate moment an intention to perform a deferred task. Ideally, when it is necessary to defer a task, the individual would *encode* that deferral—in other words, make an explicit mental note that the task is to be deferred. Research shows that encoding is most effective when the individual forms an "implementation plan" that specifies when and where the deferred task is to be performed and identifies what the individual is likely to be doing at that time, as well as the environmental cues likely to be present (Gollwitzer, 1999). For example, when it is necessary to defer setting the flaps and completing the Taxi checklist, pilots could explicitly state that they intend to complete these tasks when they reach the runway hold-short line, and encode an explicit intention in memory, so that when they observe the hold-short line it will act as a cue that will help trigger retrieval of the intention from memory.

Not all cues are equally effective. The hold-short line, for example, is a mediocre cue in this case because it is always present at the runway and is associated in memory with all previous flights, and is especially associated with the tasks that are normally performed as the aircraft turns onto the runway. Noticing the hold-short line is likely to trigger retrieval from memory of goals such as those associated with tasks normally performed when taking the runway, rather than with the goal (i.e., the deferred intention) of setting the flaps and completing the Taxi checklist

Reminder cues are much more effective if they are conspicuous, strongly associated with the deferred task, and positioned in a way that an individual is likely to notice them at the appropriate time (Brandimonte, and Passolunghi, 1994). Also, cues that are distinctive or unusual are more effective than cues that are commonplace or resemble other cues in the environment. If the cue is associated with many memories, then the amount of activation reaching any one of the memories is greatly diluted, something called the "fan effect" (Anderson, 1974). Distinctive or unusual cues have fewer associations in memory and thus spread more activation to relatively few related intentions stored in memory. Conspicuous cues are effective because they are more likely to be noticed and processed with adequate attention. Thus, leaving the checklist card sticking part way out of its holder, as did the pilot in the "flaps to go" example, was a relatively effective cue because it was conspicuous, strongly associated with the deferred task, and somewhat unusual.

However, even normally effective cues may fail, if an individual's attention is heavily occupied by demanding ongoing tasks. Leaving the checklist card out is rendered less effective when the pilots become busy with normally-scheduled, last moment preparations to take the runway. These demanding tasks reduce the likelihood that pilots will notice or fully process the cue associated with the deferred intention to extend the flaps. Because retrieving deferred intentions must compete with the cognitive demands of ongoing tasks, the probability of remembering to perform deferred tasks decreases with workload (Stone, Dismukes, and Remington, 2001). Further complications can arise because the goals of the ongoing tasks provide substantial activation to retrieve memories associated with those goals and do not support retrieval of the intention to perform a deferred intention. For example, on approaching the runway, the goal of taking off and associated tasks are in the foreground, rather than the goal to remember to set the flaps and complete the Taxi checklist.

Responding to interruptions is a special case of prospective memory. Interrupting a task implicitly creates a need to remember to resume the interrupted task later. However, interruptions are often so salient and abrupt that individuals may not have time to encode an intention to resume, or even think to do so, much less to create conspicuous cues to serve as reminders (Dismukes, 2007; Dodhia and Dismukes, 2008). With little or no encoding of the intention and without identifying or creating specific reminder cues, forgetting to resume interrupted tasks in a timely manner is common. However, individuals may still remember to return to the interrupted task if they happen to notice some cue in the environment previously linked with the interrupted task or if they pause to review the status of all tasks at the moment. This process is, unfortunately, haphazard, and cannot be counted on to be reliable. Checklists and monitoring are, of course, major safeguards against errors of omission; the effectiveness of these safeguards is discussed later in this chapter.

The vulnerability to error caused by interruptions is illustrated by the earlier ASRS example in which the crew was interrupted by a flight attendant's interphone call just as they were about to perform the Climb checklist and reset the altimeters. The pilots immediately turned attention to the call that raised issues important to the flight, but these issues further occupied their attention. The pilots probably did not think to encode an explicit intention to resume the interrupted tasks, nor did they create conspicuous reminder cues. (Quickly creating cues is often not practical in the cockpit.) Further, the pilots probably did not suspect they would be likely to forget to perform highly practiced tasks such as running the checklist and resetting the altimeters, and probably did not think that they would need reminding.

Habitual tasks and automatic processing

Broadly speaking, humans have two cognitive modes of processing information to perform tasks; one involves conscious control (called controlled processing in the scientific literature), the other involves automatic processes that operate largely outside of conscious control (Barshi and Healy, 1993; Norman and Shallice, 1986; Schneider, Dumais, and Shiffrin, 1984; Shiffrin and Schneider, 1977). The conscious mode is slow and effortful, and it basically requires performing one task at a time, in sequence. Learning a new task typically requires conscious processing, which is why learning to drive a car or fly an airplane at first seems overwhelming; the multiple demands of the task exceed cognitive capacity in this mode. Automated cognitive processes develop as one acquires skill; these processes are specific to each task, they operate rapidly and fluidly, and they require little effort and minimal attention, which is why, once we become proficient at driving or flying, we can perform those tasks while listening to the radio or talking to our copilot. Automatically performing a task reduces mental workload, allowing the individual to attend to other tasks.

Conscious control is required in four situations:

1. When the task is novel,
2. When the task is perceived to be critical, difficult, or dangerous,
3. When a habitual (automatic) response to a situation must be overridden to respond in an atypical way (e.g., not lowering the landing gear immediately after intercepting the ILS glideslope during approach), and
4. To choose among competing goals or activities (Norman and Shallice, 1986).

Human performance is usually a mixture of conscious and automatic processing. This is certainly true for cockpit tasks, though the mixture varies with the task. For example, to an experienced pilot, manual flying is largely automatic, but revising a flight plan in the FMC requires a considerable degree of conscious processing.

Habitual tasks that are consistently practiced in the same fashion and in the same sequence become largely automatic. Many habitual cockpit tasks involve a series of discrete steps, such as performing the items on a checklist. Furthermore, each task is itself a sequential step within a higher order task; for example, preflight procedural tasks are steps within the higher order task of preparing the aircraft for departure. As discussed in the Ideal chapter, practicing the large number of procedural steps required in each stage of flight in the consistent manner and sequence prescribed by the FOM helps pilots learn to execute procedures automatically, thus substantially decreasing their mental workload.

An essential aspect of automatic processing of a procedural task is that executing each step of the task automatically triggers retrieval of the next step from memory. For instance, the fuel quantity check in the flight preparation flow subconsciously serves as an internal trigger for the oil quantity check because these two actions are prescribed in this sequence by the written procedure and thus are consistently executed in this order. And because tasks are normally executed in a set sequence, performing one task automatically *triggers* the next task to come to mind, thus forming a chain of actions that requires little mental effort to recall and execute. External events also serve as triggers; appearance of the gate agent at the cockpit door just before pushback triggers the captain to remember to hand the gate agent the signed flight release form. Environmental *context* contributes to this triggering process; if the captain encountered the gate agent outside the cockpit he would be less likely to think of the release form.

Strictly speaking, individuals do not need to form explicit intentions for habitual tasks—the intention is implicit in the action schema for the task, and execution of each step of the habitual task normally occurs without deliberation. Habitual activities, because they become automatic, are largely under the subconscious control of trigger events and contextual cues, and this process is highly reliable when events occur in their normal sequence and in their normal context. But what happens when tasks are deferred or otherwise performed out of their normal sequence and context? Deferring a habitual task rearranges the normal sequence of tasks and removes critical triggers that have become subconsciously associated with specific actions and which normally serve to initiate those actions. The deferred task is detached from the preceding actions and events that normally trigger it, and, conversely, the deferred task can no longer trigger the task that normally follows it. In other words, the habitual chain breaks. Furthermore, performing tasks that normally follow the deferred task may create the misimpression that the deferred task has already been performed.

For example, normally the captain calls for the Taxi checklist, triggering the first officer to take out the checklist card and start running the checklist. The captain, for his part, relies on the transition from the ramp to the taxiway as the trigger to call for the Taxi checklist. But imagine that on some flight, the captain becomes busy negotiating a congested taxiway in foggy conditions with a long queue of traffic in front. He delays calling for the Taxi checklist until he feels comfortable that he can devote the attention necessary for its execution. The first officer may have subconsciously learned to rely on the external trigger of the captain's request to initiate the checklist. If the captain has taxied past his normal external trigger point before the congestion is resolved and so forgets to call for the deferred checklist, the normal trigger for the first officer is also removed, and she is at risk to also forget the deferred checklist.

Another consequence of rearranging the sequence of tasks is that the deferred task must be executed at a time when it competes with other tasks normally performed during this period. These other tasks are supported by their normal context and associated triggers, but the deferred task is not. Suppose that in the previous example, it was necessary to defer the Taxi checklist until the aircraft approached the runway threshold; the environmental context of the runway threshold is strongly associated with final preparations for departure, and reminds the crew to make those preparations. But the runway threshold is only weakly associated with the intention to perform the deferred Taxi checklist. What's more, because the Taxi checklist is normally completed prior to arrival at the runway threshold, the environmental context strongly supports the impression that the deferred Taxi checklist task has already been completed. When the Tower controller issues takeoff clearance, the crew is prompted to taxi onto the runway and complete the final items on the checklist (transponder and strobes on, scan panel for warning lights, etc). These final preparations are well supported through long association with the environmental context, external triggers, and internal triggers, but the deferred task is not supported unless the crew had the foresight to create a conspicuous cue, such as putting the deferred checklist in the throttle quadrant, or has established a habit of always asking themselves before taking the runway whether any items remain uncompleted.

This is exactly what happened to the crew in the ASRS example in which, after having to defer the flaps due to the icing conditions, the crew intended to set the flaps shortly before turning on to the departure runway (presumably when approaching the runway threshold). When the Tower controller gave permission for an immediate takeoff, the crew rushed to accept—crews typically try to assist air traffic controllers maintain the flow of aircraft; also, refusing the clearance would have delayed the flight. All activities associated with accepting the clearance and proceeding with the takeoff rose to the foreground, the environmental context and external cues supported proceeding with these activities, and the pilots did not review the status of the aircraft to determine if any deferred items were pending.

Problems can also arise in situations in which pilots must remember to substitute an atypical procedure in the place of a highly practiced procedure that has become habitual. In these situations, if the pilot does not monitor her actions carefully, she is vulnerable to reverting to the habitual action, a form of error called "habit capture" (Betsch, Haberstroh, Molter, and Glöckner, 2003; Reason,

1990, p. 68). For example, from long experience, a crew may come to expect a standard departure clearance at a particular airport that requires them to turn right to a heading of 300 degrees after reaching 1,000 feet of altitude. If on one occasion the departure clearance is modified to 330 degrees and the crew is busy during climb-out, they may revert to habit and stop the turn at 300 degrees. In this type of situation, as each step of the habitual sequence of actions is performed, it triggers automatic execution of the next step, and the atypical action is not substituted as intended. Here, too, creating explicit reminder cues that will be noticed during the turn can reduce vulnerability to this form of error.

Still another type of problem occurs when execution of habitual tasks is suspended, even briefly. In this situation memory of the many previous executions of the task may become confused with the current episode in which the task has not yet been completed, a problem called "source memory confusion" in the research literature (Johnson, Hashtroudi, and Lindsay, 1993). Consequently the pilot may have a vague feeling of having executed the suspended task and may not be prompted to check its actual status. Another possible manifestation of source memory confusion arises when a pilot remembers to resume a suspended task but returns to the wrong place in the task (Mycielska and Reason, 1982). For example, while performing a checklist, a pilot might be interrupted by a radio call that requires suspending the checklist in order to respond. After the interruption is over, the pilot might remember to resume the checklist but inadvertently resume one item later than the item he was about to call out when the interruption occurred —thus skipping an item on the checklist. Little research has been published on this form of prospective memory error, but, for example, the act of beginning to reach for a switch but not completing the act, might become confused in memory with having actually positioned the switch, especially since the pilot may have consistently executed that procedural step in thousands of preceding flights (See further discussion in Dismukes et al., 2007).

Pilots and other individuals may drastically underestimate their vulnerability to forgetting to perform habitual tasks that are interrupted or performed out of sequence because in their experience execution of habitual tasks seems simple and reliable, and requiring little mental effort. Consequently, individuals may not think to take precautions, such as creating conspicuous reminder cues, because such precautions are not necessary when habitual tasks are performed in the practiced fashion, context, and sequence.

Switching attention

Pilots do not normally have the luxury of deferring one task until another is completed; they must often interleave two or more tasks, which they accomplish by performing a few steps of one task, switching attention to the other task to perform a few steps, and back and forth in this fashion. When two tasks can be practiced together consistently and frequently, the steps of the two tasks become interrelated, and the two tasks merge into a single integrated task. For example, pilots first learning to fly instrument approaches struggle to keep up with multiple tasks: scanning and interpreting each of several instruments and making adjustments to pitch, power, and roll. With practice, the steps of the several tasks become linked, and the pilot switches attention among the tasks automatically and with much less effort—the separate tasks have become integrated into the superordinate task of controlling the aircraft by reference to instruments. Performance in these types of situation is normally quite reliable, in large part because cues occur that remind the individual when the time comes to switch attention from one task element to another. In particular, completion of one task element automatically triggers recall of the next task element from procedural memory.[7]

In many situations, however, pilots must interleave tasks that have not been practiced together consistently, if ever. For example, consider the situation of a first officer who discovers a numerical error on the load sheet and must re-program the FMC during taxi. Programming the FMC makes substantial demands on conscious processing, and so is ideally accomplished during preflight, when the first officer can devote full attention to it—which is the way prescribed by FOMs. When the FMC must be re-programmed during taxi, the first officer must shift attention back and forth between that activity and the normal duties accomplished during taxi, such as monitoring the progress of the taxi to help the captain catch any threats or errors. This interleaving requires looking down at the computer display to perform a few programming steps, looking up briefly to scan out the window, and then looking back down to find where programming had been left off, continuing with a few more programming steps, and then again looking up to scan.

This situation requires the pilot to self-interrupt each task periodically, which we have argued elsewhere to be a special case of prospective memory (Dismukes, 2007); it is problematic because of the lack of good cues to alert the pilot that it is time to switch attention from one task to the other. Because both tasks have novel aspects that are not extensively practiced together in a set fashion, performing elements of one task does not trigger retrieval from memory of the intention to switch attention periodically to the other task.

Attention-switching has been studied in great depth in the basic research literature (see Pashler, Johnston, and Ruthruff, 2001 for a review). It appears that

---

7   The way in which information is organized and stored in memory distinguishes between *declarative* and *procedural* knowledge (Eysenck, 1994). Declarative knowledge is that to which individuals have conscious access and can state directly in some form. In contrast, individuals do not have direct conscious access to procedural knowledge, which is demonstrated through action. Declarative knowledge, by its nature, is flexible, allowing general principles to be applied to diverse situations. Procedural knowledge is much more specific to situations; individuals develop a characteristic response pattern to specific situations to which they respond repeatedly—this is the basis of habit. Retrieval and execution of procedural knowledge is largely automatic, not requiring much conscious effort—indeed, effort is required to inhibit a strongly established habitual pattern of responding.

switching attention between tasks involves two components that require the brain's executive control systems. The first component controls shifting from the goal of performing the first task to the goal of performing the second task. The second component controls replacing the rules for performing the first task with the rules for performing the second task. Experimental studies using a paradigm in which participants either have to repeat the same task or alternate between two tasks within trials in a block have shown that alternating tasks imposes a switch cost—additional time is required after a switch to perform the next task (Rubinstein, Meyer, and Evans, 2001). Depending on the nature of the tasks, this cost ranges from a small fraction of a second to over one second. Such studies, however, do not adequately capture elements of real-world situations in which the pattern of switching required is not simple and constant, as it is in the laboratory. Still, we speculate that the switch cost may be related in some fashion to vulnerability to forgetting to switch in real-world situations.

Another component of attention-switching not fully captured by studies in the laboratory has to do with the issue of forgetting to switch tasks in a timely fashion—participants in the laboratory know when to alternate tasks between trials, and the time is so short between trials that prospective memory failures are rare. Complicating matters in real-world situations is that there is no established, agreed-upon schedule for how long it is acceptable to attend to one task before attention must be switched to the other task—this is situation-dependent, highly variable, and up to each pilot to work out for himself. This variability from one situation to the next contributes to errors. In situations that require interleaving tasks with novel aspects, pilots are vulnerable to becoming absorbed in one task and forgetting to switch attention to check the status of the other task and perform steps of that task if needed (Dismukes et al., 1998). This is especially true with tasks that demand a great deal of attention, as do programming and communication tasks. "Everything changes" is an example of successful task switching between re-programming the FMC and monitoring the taxi progress, whereas the ASRS report of violating the "hold short of taxiway E" clearance at LaGuardia earlier in this chapter illustrates failure to switch between a communication task (copying a clearance) and the task of monitoring taxi progress.

Little research exists to explain the cognitive processes that enable individuals in the situation of the pilots in "everything changes" to remember—at least some of the time—to periodically interrupt the ongoing task and check the status of other tasks. In some respects this situation resembles what is called *time-based* prospective memory (Brandimonte, Einstein, and McDaniel, 1996; Cicogna, Nigro, Occhionero, and Esposito, 2005). Most of the prospective memory situations described earlier in this chapter involve *event-based* prospective memory, in which the conditions under which an individual wishes to perform a deferred task are defined in terms of events (e.g., "We will set the flaps when we reach the hold-short line"). In contrast, in time-based prospective memory the conditions for performing the deferred task are defined in terms of time (e.g., "I will check the status of fuel transfer every two minutes").

The cognitive processes underlying time-based prospective memory may differ in important respects from those of event-based prospective memory, but these differences have not yet been studied extensively. Researchers have established that performance in time-based situations is considerably less reliable (Einstein and McDaniel, 1996), probably because the deferred intention is not associated with specific external cues that will prompt individuals to remember the intention at the right time. It is not known what does enable individuals to sometimes remember to perform time-based prospective memory tasks. In some situations individuals may set up a monitoring pattern in which they attempt to perform a few steps of an ongoing task and use the completion or outcome of those few steps to trigger remembering to switch attention to the other task. But the links between two tasks that have not been practiced together to any great extent is fragile; consequently this strategy is not always successful. Humans do have internal neural clocks, and it may be that such clocks help them keep track of the passage of time, but it is not known whether these clocks have any kind of alarm function. Here, too, the more demanding or engaging the ongoing task, the less likely it is that the individual will notice either internal or external cues signifying it is time to switch attention to the other task.

Switching among tasks is itself a task (if you will, a "meta-task") that makes further demands on limited cognitive resources. Furthermore, switching among tasks implies more than just the act of switching. Once the task switch has been accomplished, additional attention is required to acquire information and update situational awareness, a process that necessitates cognitive effort. This may explain why individuals report that having to switch among tasks increases the subjective experience of workload beyond that which would be expected from the simple sum of the demands of the two tasks (Kirmeyer, 1988a).

Having to concurrently accomplish several tasks that are not normally practiced together may also cause another kind of a problem, in that it often increases the total amount of work that must be accomplished in a set period of time. Crews have the authority to request additional time from a Ground controller who has issued a revised departure clearance, and sometimes they do, but the air traffic system provides considerable incentive to maintain the pace of operations and to avoid delays. Crews may be overly concerned with delays caused by losing a departure time slot or having to go around after falling behind in configuring the aircraft during approach. Subtle social factors may overly concern a first officer with not holding up a captain who is ready to proceed. These insidious pressures, which may be unconscious, push pilots to sometimes rush, which further increases vulnerability to error (Dismukes, et al., 2007).

Two crucial safeguards against errors of omission are checklists and monitoring (each pilot monitors the actions of the other pilot, the status of aircraft systems, and the path of the aircraft). But pilots are vulnerable to omitting checklist steps or entire checklists for the reasons discussed in the prospective memory section above. Monitoring is a concurrent task that often must be interleaved with other tasks. Thus, it is a kind of task-switching, vulnerable to errors of omission in the same ways as other task-switching situations. In the final chapter we discuss ways to improve the reliability of checklists and monitoring.

Applying These Cognitive Concepts to Cockpit Operations

With this cognitive foundation, we now analyze in depth four more examples from ASRS reports. These examples provide vivid and concrete illustrations of how crews respond to perturbations and the associated vulnerability to error. It will be apparent to the reader that these examples involve multiple operational issues, however, in each example we focus mainly on the cognitive processes that make any pilot in the reported situation vulnerable to error. Our analysis is necessarily speculative. The narrative of the ASRS report provides limited detail about what happened and what the pilots were thinking as events occurred. We flesh out the account with general knowledge of how airline operations are conducted, and we speculate on the cognitive demands from general knowledge of cognitive processes. Obviously, it is not possible to know exactly how cognitive processing actually took place in each of these specific incidents, but we feel that this approach provides a plausible account of the cognitive factors that would typically be at play in these situations. Thus, we are using these examples to expose our ideas about why concurrent task demands in routine flights are challenging and increase pilots' vulnerability to error.

Example 1: An interrupted procedure

Both reports presented below refer to the same incident that occurred to a crew flying the -200 variant of the B737 aircraft. The first report is the captain's account of events; the second is the first officer's account of the same events.

Report Number: 593973 (captain reporting):

"... At the precise moment that I would normally call for the flaps to [be set to] their proper position for takeoff, the first officer, upon [pressing the annunciator panel, as required by the After Start checklist], reported [that] the low pressure light on the #1 electric hydraulic pump illuminated. We started looking for the hydraulic circuit breakers. The first officer pulled out the QRH [Quick Reference Handbook] and I called company to inform them of the problem and that we would be going back to the gate. The first officer eventually found a popped circuit breaker and it was successfully reset so I called company to inform them that the problem was corrected. This process took about 2–3 minutes... we pushed on time. We were not rushing and we were not fatigued nor were there any other mitigating factors [that caused our] failure to accomplish the proper checklist. Later, I asked why my first officer had stowed the checklist and he said he didn't normally do so but this time had difficulty with the circuit breakers and needed both of his hands to accomplish the task of resetting the circuit breakers."

Report Number: 593896 (first officer reporting the same incident):

"...We checked [the] circuit breakers and did not [initially] see any circuit breakers popped. While the captain talked to Maintenance, I checked the QRH to look for [the] circuit breaker locations. I had to unstrap [my seatbelt] to look behind my seat at the bottom panel. I found one circuit breaker popped and informed the captain. He told me to reset [it]. The captain told Maintenance and they agreed we were good to go. This whole business took approximately 3 minutes. Normally, I leave the checklist [card] out after completing the After Start checklist. Today, in order to look for the circuit breaker, I put it back in its slot (before putting flaps to 5 degrees, and [before] performing the Before Takeoff checklist). After we solved our problem. I called for taxi [clearance]. We were rested, nobody was rushing, we were not talking about other things, we just did not do the Before Takeoff checklist ['Above the Line' items] (which we realized later). Taxiing to the runway, the captain asked for [the] 'Below the Line' [items]. I read [the checklist items], and he pushed the throttle forward—no takeoff [configuration] warning horn. Tower cleared us for takeoff. After advancing the throttles, the takeoff warning horn came on. We aborted the takeoff, checked the configuration, and realized that the flaps were up."

These two narratives describe a crew in the process of accomplishing the routine sequence of activities following a successful start of both engines. Per company procedures, while still on the ramp and before beginning to taxi, the first officer is supposed to accomplish the After Start checklist, the last item of which calls for a check of the annunciator panel, which the first officer accomplishes by pressing on the panel. If the system has detected an anomaly in any of the major aircraft systems, the corresponding light (and inscription) will illuminate on this panel to alert the crew. At the completion of this check (and of the checklist), the captain is supposed to call for flaps to be set to their takeoff position[8] and request that the first officer acquire the taxi clearance so as to release the brakes and begin taxiing. When taxi clearance is received, the crew must perform part of the Before Takeoff checklist (Above the Line items[9]) before the captain releases the brakes and sets the aircraft in motion.

---

8   Flaps are set to their "takeoff position" when they are positioned appropriately for the particular takeoff. This is usually setting 1 or 5, but depends on the particular aircraft and performance issues (e.g., weight, runway conditions) so the crew calculates it on each flight prior to pushing back.
9   Standard Operating Procedures vary slightly among carriers (see "Ideal" chapter). Some airlines (like the one referred to here) specify two separate checklists (Before Taxi and Before Takeoff)—others specify one checklist (Before Takeoff) and distinguish between

Here we see that, upon pressing the annunciator panel, the first officer discovers it indicates a problem with the hydraulic system of the aircraft. This prompts him to look up above his head on the hydraulics panel to identify the source of the problem. This unforeseen interruption must be addressed immediately, so it requires the first officer's attention and disrupts the normal flow of activities (which is to confirm that no annunciations exist, call the checklist complete, and proceed). The first officer is forced to suspend the checklist, which can only be considered complete when all annunciations have been addressed. The first officer *implicitly* intends to resume the interrupted checklist after determining the source and possible solution for the hydraulic problem, but he may not encode an *explicit* intention to do so. He does not attempt to devise an explicit cue to help him remember to complete the checklist. The urgent nature of the interruption, as well as the sense of time pressure as the aircraft is about to start taxiing, does not encourage the first officer to identify or create a suitable cue. As is his usual practice, he continues to hold on to the checklist card from which he has just read the checklist items.

The first officer now turns his full attention to the task at hand—the interruption. He reports the problem to the captain and together they determine that one of the pumps appears to be indicating low pressure. Based on their experience with previous encounters with such an indication, the crew decides to first check the related circuit breaker.[10] An initial visual check of the circuit breakers does not reveal anything amiss. The captain contacts Maintenance over the radio and the first officer takes the opportunity to double-check the circuit breakers. This time he looks at the circuit breaker layout depicted in the Quick Reference Handbook (QRH) to identify the exact location of the relevant circuit breakers. Their location, behind his seat and near the floor, forces the first officer to unstrap his seatbelt. It may be at this point that, without thinking too much about potential repercussions, the first officer places the checklist card he has been holding back in its slot on the glareshield, directly below the front windows. This will allow him more freedom of movement and the chance to accomplish a more thorough visual check. Indeed, this time, the check reveals a popped circuit breaker. The first officer informs the captain who requests that the popped breaker be reset. Resetting the breaker involves pushing the tiny button back in and the first officer finds that he will need

---

two portions (Above the Line and Below the Line items) to be completed before taxi and before takeoff correspondingly.

10   Quite often, the source of a problem is a "popped" circuit breaker. Like household circuit breakers, such devices in the aircraft interrupt electrical power to a protected system when they detect a malfunction. Many times, however, the circuit breakers have been pulled by the maintenance crew needing to make some adjustment/repair and are then inadvertently never reset. It is not uncommon for crews to fail to notice the position of a circuit breaker—there are over 100 tiny breakers to be checked on one panel. Specific rules dictate whether the crew is allowed to simply reset a popped circuit breaker and what precautions they may have to consider.

both hands to reset this particular breaker (if he has not already done so, he now places the checklist card back in its slot on the glareshield to free up both hands).

At this point, the first officer has not finished executing the After Start checklist. He normally keeps this card out because, immediately following the completion of the After Start checklist, he expects the captain to call for him to set the flaps, obtain taxi clearance, and perform the next checklist (Before Takeoff checklist). Having the card handy helps speed things up. Today, because of the situation with the popped circuit breaker, it is necessary to place the card in a secure location so that it does not fall or get misplaced, and that location is the slot where it is normally placed when not in use.

With the problem satisfactorily resolved, and having confirmed with the company dispatcher and with the maintenance crew that they will be proceeding with the flight as planned, the crew attempts to pick up their activities where they had left off. At this point, the tasks immediately pending on the captain's side are to call for flaps and taxi clearance. The tasks pending on the first officer's side are to ensure the After Start checklist has been accomplished and announce it "complete" and to respond to the captain's request for flaps and clearance. The captain asks the first officer to request the taxi clearance from the Ground controller, but in doing so, he inadvertently omits the normal call for setting the flaps for takeoff. The time spent dealing with the circuit breaker problem, contacting the company dispatcher, and contacting Maintenance has broken the normal sequence of closely linked actions, each action automatically triggering retrieval from memory of the next highly practiced step in the procedure. The situation now facing the crew is that after the delay they are ready to go (as far as they recognize), but they cannot proceed until they obtain taxi clearance. Thus the context of the situation provides better cueing for requesting taxi clearance than for calling for flaps.

The first officer, having just completed troubleshooting and resolving the unanticipated complication with the hydraulics, is also ready to get the flight going. Setting the flaps is so strongly associated with the cue of the captain's call for flaps to be set, that the first officer probably subconsciously depends upon this cue to prompt him, not just to act, but also to think about the need to set the flaps at this point. The captain's instruction to call for taxi clearance starts the first officer on the beginning of a habitual sequence of actions that normally occurs after flaps have been set. Thus, little occurs to prompt the first officer to think about setting the flaps, and starting the series of habitual actions that occurs after flaps are normally set may conceivably generate some sort of subconscious feeling that the flaps have been set—an example of source memory confusion. A deliberate search of the environment and memory for actions not completed at this point would probably have called both pilots' attention to the flaps. In the final chapter we discuss countermeasures, such as reviewing the status of items completed and uncompleted after a major interruption. It is especially important to conduct a review before moving on to the next phase of flight—in this case, starting to taxi.

To defend against inadvertent omissions, airlines use checklists of critical procedural steps. In this stage of the operation, standard operating procedures require the captain to call for the Before Takeoff checklist and for the first officer to execute these items before the brakes are released to begin taxi. One of the items on this checklist calls for the crew to confirm that the flaps have been set. As highly experienced pilots, the crew would have performed this checklist in its normal sequence on many previous flights. However, the circuit breaker interruption disrupted the flow of actions that normally prompt the crew to remember to perform this checklist, just as the interruption disrupted the flow leading to setting the flaps. Also, the first officer reports normally keeping the checklist card out after accomplishing the After Start checklist and until the Before Takeoff checklist; and very probably, through long association, the card serves as a helpful reminder to perform the Before Takeoff checklist. However, on this occasion the first officer put the card back in its holder, out of sight, in order to reset the circuit breaker, and this atypical action removed the cue that normally triggers the checklist.

The crew taxis to the runway and continues preparations for takeoff, both pilots unaware that they have forgotten to set the flaps and to run the Before Takeoff checklist that would have caught the omission. Although checklists provide a crucial defense against errors of omission, this incident reveals a subtle weakness in this defense. Situations that engender errors of omission, such as not setting flaps, can at the same time make the crew vulnerable to forgetting to perform the entire checklist that would catch the omitted procedural step.

This example illustrates features of the prototypical situation of "interruptions and distractions" discussed above. In this case, the interruption is an unanticipated new task—resolving the malfunction of the hydraulics system—which requires the crew to temporarily suspend preparing the cockpit for taxi. Suspending these preparations implicitly creates a prospective memory situation in which the crew must remember to resume preparations at the point at which they were suspended.

Example 2: A task cannot be executed in its normal sequence

Report #263589 (first officer reporting)

(The crew has just had the aircraft deiced twice and has resolved some problems with the Auxiliary Power Unit (APU) while still at the gate. Both engines have finally been started and the aircraft is ready for taxi):

> "... The captain elected to keep flaps up because of snow on the taxiways. Flaps are normally [extended] at this point which is part of the first officer's flow. We did not complete the [Taxi] checklist at this point because we were holding the flaps up. As we sat in line for takeoff we discussed [reasons for the problem with the APU]. When we were next for takeoff, the captain instructed me to tell the Tower we needed 1 minute on the runway [to run engines up... per aircraft manual] and with parking brakes set for me to go back in the cabin to check the wings for [ice or snow] contamination. As we taxied into position on the runway, I completed the last items of the Takeoff checklist.. I had not

noticed… that we had not completed the Taxi checklist… [which is] always done long before reaching the hold short line [of the runway]. During the wing contamination inspection I still did not notice the flaps were up... As the throttles were advanced... the takeoff warning horn sounded."

This crew has already spent more time at the gate than anticipated, due to a mechanical problem and the consequent necessity to repeat the deicing procedure, and is now finally ready to taxi to the departure runway. Both engines have been started. Normally, the captain would next call for flaps. After assessing the ambient conditions, however, he decides to defer the habitual action of setting flaps for takeoff. Depending on their experience with cold weather operations, both pilots have probably had to defer extending the flaps from time to time on previous flights.

Deferring the flaps, however, also requires deferring the Taxi checklist, since this checklist contains a step requiring that the crew verify the flaps are actually in the takeoff position. Appropriately, he intends to perform the checklist after setting the flaps—in this case, sometime before taking the departure runway. Both pilots undoubtedly intend to set the flaps and perform the Taxi checklist later, right before takeoff.

Setting the flaps is a strongly habitual action of such critical importance for safe takeoff that the crew may not suspect they are vulnerable to forgetting to perform it. Performing the checklist is also a highly practiced activity that is probably not considered a candidate for inadvertent omission. Because experienced airline pilots have accomplished these actions thousands of times previously, and because remembering to perform them pops into mind automatically and effortlessly when procedures are performed in the normal sequence, the crew is not aware of any compelling reason to take special efforts to guard against a possible omission on this occasion.[11]

Following the decision to defer flaps, everything else proceeds normally, and the crew devotes attention to taxiing under the demanding conditions posed by snow on the taxiways. They also report engaging in a discussion about the APU. Although the problem they had encountered earlier was resolved before pushback, it is normal for pilots to continue discussing the reasons behind the malfunction and how it might later affect the flight. However, conversation makes considerable demands on attention, and this discussion may make the crew less likely to review the state of preparedness of the aircraft before takeoff.

When the Tower controller issues a clearance for takeoff, the captain recognizes that the aircraft has spent more time idle than he may have anticipated. With appropriate caution (and following standard procedure) he asks for a visual inspection of the wings for snow or ice. This check is performed by the first officer who physically goes back to the cabin and views the wing surfaces from the side windows. (The crew asks the Tower controller for a slight delay, which is not uncommon in this situation.) The first officer visually determines that the wings

11   The crew reporting this incident did not mention having created a cue to help remind them of the deferred task, so we assume that they did not.

are clean. Intent on checking for ice or snow, however, he does not notice that the flaps are not extended. Though failing to notice may seem surprising, it is in fact a common phenomenon in which the way people frame a task strongly influences what aspects of a situation they notice and what aspects they do not notice (framing: Tversky and Kahneman, 1981; Loft, Humphreys, and Neal, 2004).

When the crew receives clearance for takeoff, the captain advances the throttles. All external cues as well as the environmental context are consistent with the normally-encountered Pretakeoff phase during which the flaps have been set and Taxi checklist has been completed, and the only thing pending is the completion of the Takeoff procedure and checklist. In some sense, this situation closely resembles that of the previous example. The forced deferral of setting flaps has broken the normal chain of events and actions that trigger retrieval from memory of taxi related actions (i.e., extending the flaps and performing the Taxi checklist). Those triggers belong to the past—and were "ignored" after the conscious decision to defer both setting the flaps and conducting the checklist. Now, with the aircraft close to the runway threshold, in the place of these triggers are other cues normally associated with initiating the takeoff; the crew's mental frame of reference is therefore oriented to taking the runway, and it's attention is occupied with the last minute tasks necessary for takeoff. Unaware that the flaps are still up, the captain advances the throttles. Fortunately, the takeoff warning horn prevents the impending disaster.

This example illustrates features of the prototypical situation of "tasks that cannot be executed in their normal, practiced sequence." Allowing for certain activities to be executed automatically, based on practice, habit, and the development of subconscious triggering events and cues, is an important feature of aviation operations. Were it not for the largely automatic execution of highly practiced procedures it would not be possible for pilots to accomplish all the tasks that must be performed to fly an airliner. But this incident illustrates that the cognitive processes underlying expert execution of practiced skills—highly reliable when procedures are executed in their normal sequence—are vulnerable when the normal sequence is disrupted. In this case, the task normally and automatically executed prior to taxiing (setting the flaps) cannot be executed and is deferred for later—the normally associated triggers are thus lost. Not specifying exactly when it will later be accomplished, or what the new trigger will be, the automatic action of setting the flaps and executing a checklist is later never triggered. In the final chapter we discuss ways pilots can use more deliberate, conscious cognitive processing to keep track of automatic execution of procedures, and other countermeasures to reduce vulnerability to error.

Example 3: A new task must be deferred

Report #443000 (flying pilot reporting):

> "... We were about to begin our descent... when a flight attendant knocked on the
> cockpit door... Upon entering the cockpit the flight attendant asked the captain
> and me about [non-essential conversation]... During the conversation, which

we all 3 [captain, first officer, and flight attendant] participated in, the Center controller told us to cross 35 miles E[ast] of KNOX at FL250 [25,000 ft]. This was read back to him and a quick calculation showed that we had about 25 miles to go before needing to start down. The conversation with the flight attendant continued and then concluded... I then proceeded to brief the approach... and totally forgot about the assigned crossing restriction."

In this example, the crew is interrupted by the flight attendant while in the cruise portion of the flight, when their workload is quite low—their main duties are monitoring the autopilot follow the pre-programmed flight plan and monitoring the radio for potential instructions from the controller. Both pilots become involved in the ensuing conversation, which is not uncommon during a phase of flight that places low demands on pilots' direct attention. The pilots probably assume the conversation will not prevent them from concurrently keeping an eye on the autopilot and monitoring the radio.

In these sorts of situations, casual conversation is a double-edged sword. Because humans are inherently quite poor at maintaining vigilance and alertness for long periods with minimal mental stimulation, conversation helps crews maintain alertness. But even a casual conversation makes substantial demands on attention, and it is easy to become engrossed in conversation and inadvertently let monitoring drop away (Dismukes et al., 1998). In this instance, the casual conversation does not, however, seem to distract the crew too much, and the two pilots monitor well enough to notice and acknowledge the controller's radio message assigning a crossing restriction.[12]

This example illustrates features of the third prototypical situation of an "additional, unanticipated task demand" discussed above. The controller's instruction is the new task demand added to the normal sequence of requirements and activities of this phase of flight. A quick calculation reveals they are about 25 miles from the point at which they must start their descent in order to comply with the crossing restriction; it will take three or four minutes at typical speeds to reach this point, and the crew returns to the conversation with the flight attendant. The additional task demand therefore also carries a prospective memory element to it, as the crew needs to create a deferred intention to start on a descent at a specific point that will allow them to reach the assigned point (35 miles east of KNOX—a navigational fix point depicted on their charts) at the instructed altitude.

The pilots were very probably unaware of the cognitive vulnerabilities to which they were exposed in this situation. Because crossing restrictions are commonly a part of descent clearances, and because the content of the restriction is simple and familiar in form, the pilots probably did not suspect they were vulnerable to

---

12   The sparse narrative of the ASRS report does not provide detail, but we infer that the crossing restriction required them to descend before they would have normally had to in order to get down to the airport.

forgetting to execute the intention and did not make any special attempt to encode the intention and create a specific cue for it. The conversation may have further limited the extent to which the pilots encoded the crossing restriction in memory, and it probably prevented them from rehearsing the intention to help keep it active in working memory. Thus, the intention to descend early to make the crossing restriction had to be retrieved from long-term memory when the aircraft reached the descent point.[13] The pilots had to observe the Navigation Display[14] to monitor their position. We do not know how frequently the pilots monitored the Display while continuing the conversation, but they did pay enough attention to their situation to recognize when they were at the point they would normally begin their preparations for descent, and at this time the flying pilot began his descent briefing.

Why did both pilots fail to retrieve from memory their intention to descend early at a specified point to meet the crossing restriction? Their cue to descend was provided by the Navigation Display, however this cue by itself was an imperfect trigger for retrieval from memory, even if they looked at it at the moment the aircraft reached the descent point. The display has many associations in memory (the "fan" effect) and has at best a fair chance of triggering retrieval of the intention to descend early unless the pilots establish a procedure of periodically monitoring the display and determining each time they check it if they are yet at the descent point. In principle, the pilots could interleave monitoring the display this way with their conversation, yet, as discussed in the next example of a prototypical situation, interleaving has its own vulnerabilities.

Example 4: Interleaving new tasks with ongoing tasks

Report #259087 (first officer reporting):

> "As the aircraft approached the airport we received [navigation instructions from the controller] for runway 17R. The reported weather changed several times [during final approach]. Air Traffic Control asked if we wished to land on runway 18L. [Based on reported visibility conditions] we elected to accept runway 18L. The aircraft was configured on schedule to flaps 30 degrees as briefed. I began to re-program the computer for runway 18L [in order to obtain improved situational awareness]. This task was complicated by an inoperative 'execute' button [on the FMC]. The captain requested flaps 40 degrees and briefed a new

---

13   This is typical of situations in which pilots form intentions to perform an action at a later time. Although in this incident the pilots could have put aside non-essential conversation and rehearsed the intention, it is not common for people to maintain intentions in working memory by continuous rehearsal except for very short periods of time such as between looking up a phone number in a phone book and actually dialing the number.

14   In older aircraft that lack Navigation Displays the pilots must monitor position with a Horizontal Situation Indicator and Distance Measuring Equipment. We do not know what type of equipment this aircraft had.

approach speed. I selected flaps 40 degrees and continued re-programming the computer. The runway approach lights could be seen illuminating a thin layer of fog. We were still [flying in] VMC [visual meteorological conditions]. I heard the ground proximity warning [horn] sound. I scanned the instruments and saw the captain begin raising the nose and advancing the thrust levers [to abandon this attempted approach and landing]… I reported the Missed Approach [to the Tower controller]."

Weather conditions precipitate a change in the arrival/landing plans for this aircraft during approach. This is not uncommon, and the crew prepares to handle the additional tasks incurred by accepting a runway change. The first officer decides to re-program the FMC, which will provide additional flight path information to support situation awareness. Re-programming the FMC must be interleaved with the normal duties of the monitoring pilot (the first officer): monitoring the status of the aircraft, executing commands given by the flying pilot, and performing checklists. To accomplish all these tasks, the first officer has to restrict performing each task to a few seconds at a time, and must attempt to remember to switch attention back and forth among the several tasks.

We have already discussed the reasons pilots are vulnerable to becoming absorbed in one task and forgetting to switch attention to other tasks with sufficient frequency when interleaving. This is especially a problem when the ongoing task demands full attention, as does re-programming the FMC. In this incident, an additional complication arose because the Execute button on the FMC was inoperative, and this complication undoubtedly increased attention demands (and time pressure) still further. Perhaps the first officer anticipated being able to re-program the FMC so quickly that he would not be head-down very long, not recognizing that any unexpected complication may cause him to lose track of other interleaved tasks.

This example illustrates how unanticipated new task demands may force pilots to attempt to interleave several tasks concurrently (the third and fourth prototypical situations). In this sort of situation, with the first officer head-down and mentally absorbed in the FMC task, little existed to prompt the first officer to remember to frequently suspend the FMC task and look up to monitor the aircraft situation. The captain's call for flaps 40 briefly pulled the first officer's attention away from the FMC task, but the first officer then returned to that task which now preoccupied him because it took longer than anticipated due to the Execute button problem. The first officer was slow to look up again until the ground proximity warning aural alert interrupted his preoccupation. Apparently the captain had let the aircraft descend too low or had allowed an excessive rate of descent, triggering the warning. Incidents such as this have occurred with such frequency that some airlines now advise pilots to consider not re-programming the FMC when runway changes are given close to the airport. Instead, the monitoring pilot can back up the flying pilot with data from the cockpit instruments more quickly and with less prolonged diversion of attention.

Conclusion

In this chapter, we have provided what we think is a plausible account of the reasons the demands of managing concurrent tasks in real world flight operations increase pilots' vulnerability to errors of omission. This account is of necessity somewhat speculative because much more empirical research is needed, but it is consistent with existing scientific knowledge. The ideal of how flight operations should be conducted, as manifested in FOMs and associated training is frequently perturbed in diverse ways, but most perturbations resemble one or more of four prototypical situations:

1. Interruptions and distractions;
2. Tasks that cannot be executed in their normal, practiced sequence;
3. Unanticipated new task demands arise; and
4. Multiple tasks that must be performed concurrently.

Each of these situations creates task demands that must be managed, if not performed, concurrently. Of necessity, pilots respond to these prototypical situations either by deferring tasks or attempting to interleave tasks. With both types of response, pilots—and any other individuals dealing with concurrent task demands—may forget to perform intended tasks in a timely manner. In the final chapter we explore the implications of our analysis and suggest countermeasures that might reduce vulnerability to errors of omission.

Chapter 6
The Research Applied

In the Ideal Chapter we showed that operating procedures for normal flight situations are designed as if flight operations are linear, predictable, and under the complete control of the crew. Moreover, we argued that the training that is based on such procedures, and which to a large extent is designed to teach and practice these procedures, further conveys this implicit perspective about the nature of flight operations. However, as we showed in the Real Chapter, this perspective is inconsistent with the reality of day-to-day airline operations. The Analysis Chapter explained some of the risks resulting from the interaction between the nature of human cognition and these discrepancies between the ideal and the real. In the present chapter, we discuss specific implications and applications of our work for the design of procedures and training. We also describe how one major carrier applied our analysis, and we conclude with a more general discussion of ways in which individuals and organizations can reduce risks and improve human operators' ability to manage the complex demands of real-world operations in all types of dynamic work environments.

Airline pilots undergoing training are required to learn by rote the exact steps and actions within procedures, as well as whole sequences of procedures, and then practice them repeatedly, always in the same manner, until whole procedures are committed to memory and can be performed in an almost automatic fashion. (This is also true of the training of operators in many other complex systems involving formal procedures.) Steady improvement in accuracy and fluid execution of procedures is often used to indicate progress during training. Performance is regularly assessed in tests that require pilots to operate a flight simulator and perform many normal and non-normal procedures to demonstrate their mastery of these procedures. Because of regulatory requirements, as well as time and cost constraints, these tests are focused primarily on the pilot's control of aircraft and operation of its systems, including procedures to configure those systems for flight and for rectifying problems that may arise with those systems. Training and testing do not fully capture how these procedures are used in actual line operations; in particular, the complexity of actual operations and the necessity of managing multiple tasks concurrently are drastically under-represented. In other words, these tests and the training that prepares a pilot to pass them are often conducted as if the pilot is the only pilot in the sky, and the aircraft the only aircraft in the sky.[1]

---

1   It is interesting to note that this same attitude often underlies aircraft design as well. Thus, FMC logic is designed to optimize performance of the particular individual aircraft as if no other aircraft share the same airspace. As a result, optimal flight paths dictated by

Thus, the training and the testing reinforce the ideal perspective and exacerbate the discrepancy between the ideal and the real.

As the many examples from our observations, from ASRS reports, and our analyses of these events show, anytime the assumptions of linearity, predictability, and controllability of operations are violated, the risk of erring increases. What's more, procedures and training that are based on these ideal assumptions unintentionally set traps into which pilots sometimes fall. The risk of erring further increases with increasing demands of concurrent task management, as when crews are in any of the prototypical situations we examined earlier. In the next section, we describe how the analyses we have presented in the preceding chapters led one major airline to review and revise its operating procedures to remove these traps and reduce these risks.

Reviewing and Revising Procedures

At the completion of our observational study, we delivered our findings to the airlines that had granted us access to their cockpits. One of these airlines decided to revise its procedures, in part because it became particularly concerned that its operations could be vulnerable to the operational perturbations we reported having observed during its daily flights. The airline decided to revise its normal procedures by questioning everything in its then-current normal procedures, and enlisted our assistance with the review and revision process. A team was assembled, and tasked with reviewing the airline FOM and with proposing changes to improve safety and efficiency. We provide here some details about the team's composition and the process they followed (for further details, as well as in-depth discussion of reviewing and revising operating procedures, see Barshi, Mauro, and Loukopoulos, in preparation). We then use one example to illustrate the outcome of the team's effort, focusing on the types of issues treated in this book. We believe that the work of this team could serve as a model for any organization (i.e., not just an air carrier) wishing to reduce the kinds of risks our analyses expose.

As should be clear from the discussions throughout this book, designing good procedures is neither trivial, nor obvious. Simply understanding the relevant equipment and how it is to be used is not enough. Operating equipment safely and efficiently also requires a thorough understanding of the operator, of the environment in which the operations take place, and of the operations themselves. It is crucial, therefore, that all these different perspectives be taken into account in the design process for the resulting procedures to be optimal.

---

the FMC often have to be interrupted in response to ATC instructions which attempt to accommodate other traffic. These path interruptions often have adverse effects on safety in addition to their impact on efficiency.

Following this principle, the airline staffed its review team with active line pilots of varying levels of experience and seniority, including check pilots,[2] senior and junior captains as well as experienced and junior first officers. The team also included representatives of the Training Center, the Safety Department, and the Pilots' Union. When needed, the team also called on the expertise of regulatory bodies, the Engineering Department (both at the airline and at the airframe manufacturer), Scheduling and Dispatch departments, and even Customer Service for issues that had implications for their passengers. In arranging this broad representation, the airline assured adequate input throughout the review process from all stakeholders, as well as commitment to the process and buy-in for the final product.

The team started its work with a thorough analysis of the existing procedures and developed an extensive catalogue of hidden *traps*, that is, instances that resemble the prototypical situations described in the previous chapter and that hold the potential for errors. In particular, using their own expertise as pilots and additional jumpseat observations of their own, team members looked for conflicts, such as those that arise from the opposing demands sometimes placed by procedural requirements and those placed by the nature of the operation (i.e., by operational perturbations), or those between procedural demands and cognitive capabilities.[3] An example of the first (conflicts between procedural and operational demands) would be a Taxi checklist that has to be executed during taxi, or a procedure to be performed at a time when the crew is likely to receive a radio call from ATC. Performing a checklist during taxi creates a conflict because the crew must focus on a number of operational tasks, such as the control and movement of the aircraft, the continuous awareness of the layout of the airport's taxiways, the proper execution of the taxi clearance received from ATC, the location and movement of other aircraft and vehicles, and the communication exchanges on the radio to maintain situation awareness€. Requiring the crew to divert their attention from all these tasks in order to focus on executing a checklist at the same time is one of the reasons for the large number of surface incidents and runway incursions that occur annually (FAA, 2007). Similarly, there are known altitudes and locations where there is a high likelihood of receiving radio calls from ATC. These are the altitudes and locations where "hand-offs" take place, such as when the departure controller hands a flight off to the low-altitude center controller, or where one enroute center

---

2 Check pilots (or check airmen) are experienced line captains especially trained and designated by the FAA to conduct advanced training and all testing and certification of pilots at their airline. They also act as quality assurance officers, maintaining the standards according to the airline's FAA-approved certificate of operations.

3 The review team searched for and identified other types of conflicts such as between procedural demands and current equipment or between procedural demands and current company philosophy. Here we focus on those elements of the team's work most closely related to the theme of this book. For a more comprehensive discussion of this team's work and of such a process in general, see Barshi et al., (in preparation).

controller hands off a flight to another center controller. These hand-offs require two separate communication exchanges, one with each controller, and a radio frequency change in between. Requiring the crew to perform a procedure during such a time sets a trap that increases risk, because completing the procedure will have to be deferred until the communication exchange with ATC is finished.[4]

The review team first combed through their existing procedures, examining them through the lens of the reality of everyday operations to identify conditions that could lead to any of the prototypical situations we described earlier. Next, the team explored alternative means of completing the same tasks as a way to alleviate the potentially risk-inducing conditions. Proposed changes were extensively tested and evaluated in flight simulators, leading to an iterative process of refinement. The final product was implemented and shown to result in substantial reduction in error rates and in improved efficiency of flight operations. Many of the traps were successfully removed, thereby minimizing the opportunity for any of the prototypical situations to occur. The revised procedures were also shown to be easier to learn than the old procedures, thus enhancing the airline's training program. To illustrate some of that process, we turn to one detailed example. We look at the analysis conducted on that particular problem area by the review team, at the procedures before and after the revision process, and at the way in which these procedural changes alleviate the risk-inducing conditions and increase the safety of operations.

Setting flaps for takeoff

To complement its analysis of procedures and operational perturbations, the review team used pilot reports collected through the airline's own safety reporting system to identify challenging areas in the airline's operations that threatened to give rise to serious incidents or even accidents. One significant problem area identified was the situation in which crews inadvertently omit setting the flaps prior to takeoff, a situation already referred to in other ASRS examples in this book. The attempted no-flaps takeoff error is serious because it can have fatal consequences. Large transport category aircraft are not designed to take off with flaps[5] retracted. To prevent this serious omission, the takeoff configuration warning horn provides an aural warning when the throttles are advanced on the ground and flaps are not set for takeoff. When pilots fail to execute the prescribed procedure and omit

---

4   Responding to ATC instructions must be accomplished as soon as possible, so it typically takes precedence over any other ongoing tasks.

5   All references to "flaps" in this discussion include both leading edge and trailing edge devices. In most aircraft, and certainly in the Boeing 737 which is used throughout this book, leading edge lift devices (such as slats) and trailing edge devices (flaps) are activated together by a single control.

setting the flaps, their lives hang by the single thread of the warning system[6]; they are only one fault away from catastrophe. Cases in which the crew inadvertently omitted the flaps and the warning horn malfunctioned have ended in fatal crashes (e.g., NTSB 1969, 1988, 1989). More importantly, the team also noted that when crews report having omitted setting the flaps, this omission was often only the most noticeable error because flap position is wired to the warning horn and is thus linked to a visible/audible outcome. In many cases, forgetting to set the flaps for takeoff, in fact, also involves the omission of the whole procedure and corresponding checklist in which setting the flaps is to be performed.

The original pretakeoff procedure

The original FOM described the After Start procedure, which was followed by a short After Start checklist, "silently" performed from memory by the first officer who also announced it "complete." The FOM then went on to discuss taxi considerations, following which it described the Pretakeoff procedure. The first item was "Wing flaps" for which the FOM stated:

> "The Captain will call for the flaps to be set. The First Officer repeats the command and places the flap handle to the takeoff flap setting and verifies that the handle position and flap gauge agree."

The procedure then continued with two additional items (controls check and performance computations) and a portion of the Pretakeoff checklist (Above the Line), followed by 8 more items and a second portion of the Pretakeoff checklist (Below the Line).

The original Pretakeoff checklist contained 24 items. The eighteen items listed as Above the Line were to be performed during taxi, whereas the 6 items listed as Below the Line were to be performed once the flight was cleared to cross the hold-short line (that is, either cleared for takeoff, or cleared into position on the departure runway). In the Above the Line subset of the Pretakeoff checklist, "Wing flaps" was the 10th item, just about in the middle of the list.

A section discussing "Weather Procedures" under Supplemental Procedures of the original FOM provided the following guidance: "If taxiing through slush or standing water in low temperatures, leave the flaps up. Taxiing with the flaps extended subjects them to snow and slush blowup from the main landing gear wheels. Leading edge devices are also susceptible to these slush accumulations."

Evaluating the operational context and cognitive demands   Taking our findings into account, and discussing with us how these findings may apply to their

---

6   Such situations of a potential single-point failure were also a specific focus of attention for the review team. The intention was to provide multiple layers of defense and minimize the number of cases where a critical item is protected by just a single layer.

operations, the review team came to understand that failing to set flaps and similar errors of omission are linked to basic human cognitive vulnerabilities. Recall that the operational demands for concurrent task management often give rise to one or more of the four prototypical situations and expose the fragility of prospective memory, the downside of automatic processing, and the difficulty with switching attention between tasks. To understand how each of the prototypical situations (or their combination) may give rise to the omissions involved in the attempted no-flaps takeoffs, the review team considered the broader operational context within which flaps are supposed to be set. Their analysis revealed that the original procedures unintentionally created several traps that increased vulnerability to error.

Flaps must be set prior to takeoff. They can only be activated once sufficient hydraulic pressure is available, after the engines have been started. But besides these two boundaries at the extremes (engine start and takeoff), there are no particular requirements or specific conditions for the timing of setting the flaps for takeoff. Also, setting the flaps does not interact with other required actions or procedural steps in the Pretakeoff phase of flight (their activation does not depend on the execution of other items except for starting the engines and engaging the hydraulic pressure pumps; likewise, the execution of other typical pretakeoff items does not depend on the setting of the flaps). As a result, the captain's call for the first officer to set flaps for takeoff in many airlines' procedures has been what we have come to call a "floating item." *Floating items* are actions that are not specifically pinned down in time according to a specific procedure, though they may have to be accomplished within a given time frame (e.g., calling for the flaps must take place at some point after engine start and prior to takeoff, but can happen anywhere within this time frame).[7] By definition, because they are not pinned down in time, performing floating procedural items is inherently a prospective memory task, and as such is vulnerable to forgetting. In analyzing the interaction between the operational context and the operator from this perspective, the review team recognized that allowing a critical action such as the call for the flaps to float sets a trap for the crew.

The ground phase of operation prior to takeoff can sometimes be a very busy time of the flight, as the many examples given in the preceding chapters clearly show, and as LOSA data confirm. One LOSA study, for example, claims that 75 percent of safety-threatening factors occur during the Pretakeoff phase (Helmreich, Klinect, and Merritt, 2004), although the consequences of these factors may not occur until after takeoff. Risks associated with surface incidents and runway incursions have received much attention in recent years (Lacagnina, 2007; US GAO, 2007). Navigating the airport's taxiways can be very challenging

---

7   Note that this call is different than the "flaps" item on the taxi checklist which directs the crew to verify that flaps have been set earlier. The checklist is often performed during taxi and definitely before takeoff, implying that the crew has called for flaps to be set sometime before calling for the checklist.

even under the most benign conditions. Pilots must pay close attention to a large number of variables in a highly dynamic situation. Aircraft are large and taxiways may be narrow; taxi clearances can be complex and signage may be confusing; many airplanes and vehicles operate in close proximity and the distances are hard to judge. There are organizational pressures of schedule and fuel efficiency. The crew may even be distracted by personal matters, preoccupied with issues they bring with them to the cockpit from conversations in the pilot lounge or at home, or stressed from the drive to the airport or from the layover at the hotel. In the midst of it all, the crew must remain alert and prepared to respond to any number of variables that can change from one moment to the next (instructions to stop/move, change in taxi routing, departure information, or aircraft sequencing, etc). The challenges are substantially greater in conditions of reduced visibility, stormy weather, or heavy traffic—conditions that often mean delays and place further pressures on flight crews. In short, operating aircraft on the ground is often extremely demanding.

In this highly dynamic environment with its many demands, the captain must remember to call for the flaps to be set, while also being responsible for and directly engaged in controlling the moving aircraft. Because the call for flaps is a floating item, the captain must rely on fragile prospective memory processes to remember to make that call. Without being able to explicitly articulate the risky nature of this complex situation, many captains are intuitively aware of the floating nature of this call and of the fragility of their own memory, and so define for themselves a particular external cue to rely on. Some captains call for the flaps as soon as they receive their taxi clearance. Some when they begin their taxi. And some use the straight taxiway parallel to the departure runway as the reminder, because it represents a period of reduced workload.

The review team collected and documented personal stories throughout the airline and evaluated the kinds of cues pilots were routinely using to make sure they don't forget to make the flaps call. The team found that such cues usually worked well, but not always. Because of the intensely dynamic nature of ground operations, cues can be easily obscured or rendered inapplicable. A captain relying on the beginning of taxi as the cue to call for the flaps can be interrupted by a radio call, or distracted by a provisioning truck maneuvering in close proximity to the airplane. Procedures that call for taxiing with flaps retracted in icy or slushy conditions render that same cue irrelevant since the flaps cannot be set at the beginning of taxi. A revised taxi or departure clearance introduces an unanticipated new task that may divert a captain's attention from his normal cue, and executing checklists while taxiing requires concurrent task management by definition, another situation that may hide a well-intended cue. In analyzing the operating environment faced by their pilots on a routine basis, the review team realized that pilots were at risk of forgetting to make the call to set the flaps for takeoff because the conditions under which the flaps are supposed to be set provide many opportunities for one or more of the four prototypical situations to occur.

The review team also focused on the effective strength of the cues pilots were using for flaps. The more strongly the cue is associated with the intended action, the greater the chance of the task being recalled. External cues (in the environment) are usually more effective than internal ones (in the person's head), because they are more predictable than the stream of consciousness. Consider the difference between setting the flaps for takeoff and setting the flaps for landing. Flaps are crucial for both maneuvers, and in both cases the task of setting the flaps is a floating item and hence a prospective memory task. Namely, the pilot must remember to call for the flaps to be set for the intended maneuver. But it is extremely rare that pilots omit setting the flaps for landing, whereas setting the flaps for takeoff is highly vulnerable, as the various ASRS reports and the airline's own experience clearly show. The difference between the two maneuvers is in the number, strength, and reliable presence of external cues available to the pilot. Prior to landing, the pilot must descend and must slow the aircraft down from descent speed to approach speed. Even at idle thrust, the aircraft will pick up speed during descent unless additional drag is used. Speedbrakes and idle thrust are used to reduce speed, but flaps must be used to properly manage the descent path, pitch attitude, and speed. Not only are there clear external cues to remind the pilot to extend the flaps prior to landing, there is also clear feedback from the aircraft behavior once it is done. Control pressures, pitch attitude, speed, and descent path, all respond to the flaps extension. If the pilot were to forget to extend the flaps, it would be impossible to maintain aircraft control under the correct descent conditions of pitch attitude, speed, engine power, and descent path. In contrast, on the ground, there are no obvious external cues to remind the pilot to extend the flaps, and no change in aircraft behavior reflecting flaps extension. The aircraft feels the same way and taxis the same way regardless of the flaps' position. On the ground, prior to takeoff, the cues must be devised by the pilot, or better yet, designed into the procedures.

We must note here that some may argue that the real problem is one of workload. The demands described above might be simply treated by pilots as increased workload, and errors could be considered to be the result of this workload exceeding a given threshold of the number of tasks a person can perform at once. Such a view is based on the assumption that people can multitask reliably, that is, they can perform several tasks at the same time with no impairments to their performance of any one of the tasks. As we have already seen, however, simultaneous performance pertains only to tasks that have become automated and do not require appreciable attentional resources, and even then performance is not perfect. Non-automated tasks require controlled processing that can only be focused on one task at any given moment. Thus, even when it is possible to accomplish all tasks within the time available, performing more than one non-automated tasks at the same time means concurrent task management, in other words switching of attention back and forth among the tasks at hand with all the implications we have seen that has for performance. Thus, although high workload may exacerbate concurrent task demands, there is much more to the prototypical situations than the mere increase in the number of tasks that must be handled.

Interruptions and distractions were the common theme of the first prototypical situation described in Chapter 5 (Analysis). The time on the ground prior to takeoff is often busy and replete with interruptions and distractions. Taxi is a time when ATC may interrupt the crew with complex taxi instructions or amendments to the departure or enroute clearance, necessitating changing the FMC programming, or reviewing charts. We can safely assume that the longer a checklist, the longer it takes to execute it, and thus the more likely it is that some external event might interrupt its execution. The review team readily recognized that presenting a very long checklist (18 items Above the Line) at an interruption-prone phase of flight creates a conflict between procedural and operational demands, and substantially increases the crew's vulnerability to inadvertent omissions of checklist items.

Tasks that cannot be executed in the normal, practiced sequence of procedures were the common theme defining the second prototypical situation. Not only does the procedure calling for deferring the extension of flaps until the end of taxi when taxiing through slush or ice force the pilots to deviate from the normal practiced sequence, it also requires them to interleave an unanticipated task later in the sequence, the third prototypical situation. This procedure creates a prospective memory task, but does nothing to support encoding into memory the intention to extend flaps later or retrieval of that intention when the right time comes, at the end of taxi. The crew is, therefore, on its own with no procedural support, at a time when the flight is likely to be under many pressures. The weather conditions necessitating this procedure often create delays and congestion (both on taxiways and on radio frequencies), which lead to higher workload and time pressures. The review team recognized that there are no strong external cues to extend flaps and complete the Above The Line checklist at the end of the taxi, but in contrast there are plenty of cues (e.g., the sight of the runway, clearance to hold short of the runway or to takeoff) to prompt the crew to perform the Below the Line items. The crew is also vulnerable to implicitly assuming, based on habit built on the way things are normally done, that the Above the Line items must have already been performed if the aircraft is about to take the runway. These factors, plus the intrinsic pressure on the crew to depart without delay and not risk losing their place in the departure queue, create a high risk of omitting the flaps and probably the whole Above the Line checklist under these conditions.

Multiple tasks that must be performed concurrently were the defining characteristic of the last prototypical situation. A checklist that is performed during taxi is clearly such a case. Because airplanes can only maneuver on two axes rather than the three available in flight, because they are restricted to the relatively narrow taxiways and runways, and because so many airplanes, ground vehicles, and ground personnel operate in close proximity to each other, the risk of collision is much greater on the ground than in flight. The review team recognized that a Taxi checklist creates another conflict between procedural demands and operational demands. The pilots are expected to pay full attention to the taxi and at the same time pay full attention to the checklist. And since neither of these tasks can be performed adequately in an automatic fashion, they can not be safely accomplished simultaneously. Rapid switches between the two tasks may not be good enough under these conditions and pilots are at risk of overestimating their abilities to multitask. The review team understood that, given cognitive constraints, this concurrent task management situation in reality means that at least one, if not both, of the tasks suffer; either not enough attention is paid to the taxi, or checklist items are not checked as carefully as they should be.

Contemplating these findings from their review of the original procedures, the team proceeded to design new operating procedures to support the pilots by eliminating, as much as possible, the potential traps it had identified in the original procedures.

The new pretakeoff procedure

In designing the new procedures, the review team employed a number of different strategies:

Re-distribution of tasks   We saw earlier that the original description in the FOM went from the After Start procedure, to the Pretakeoff procedure and corresponding checklists (Above and Below the Line), and that the call for flaps was the first item of the Pretakeoff procedure, but the verification check of the flaps was the 10th item in the Above the Line subset of the Pretakeoff checklist. In the revised procedures, the team re-distributed the procedural items across the various phases of operation. The call for setting the flaps is now part of a series of memorized steps that are performed after the engines have been started. Specifically, following the confirmation of engine and related systems indications, the first officer is to perform from memory an After Start flow which ends when he places his hand on the flaps lever and announces "standing by flaps!" This announcement serves as an unmistakable trigger for the captain to call for the particular flap setting for the forthcoming takeoff. The FOM specifically states:

- (First Officer) Position your hand on the flap lever and announce, "Standing By Flaps."
- (Captain) Command the planned flap setting. (Example: "Flaps 5.")
- (First Officer) Restate the flap position (Example: "Flaps 5") and set the flaps.
- (Captain) Verify that the flap lever is moved into the proper detent and the flaps are in transit.

Following this After Start flow, the revised FOM goes into a new, Before Taxi checklist with the clear statement that, as the name implies, it is to be executed before initiating the taxi: "the parking brake remains set until the Before Taxi checklist is completed." This checklist now contains several of the items previously contained in the "silent" After Start checklist as well as the Pretakeoff (Above the Line) checklist. The FOM also provides the following guidance: "There is no need to rush this checklist. Reading the checklist at a normal pace will allow the flaps to reach the desired position[8] as the final checklist step 'Flaps' is read." And indeed, the short Before Taxi checklist only lists 7 items and ends with the call to confirm the flaps' position. The FOM then instructs the pilots that once the Before Taxi checklist has been completed, their attention can be turned to taxi considerations, to requesting taxi clearance from ATC, and to the actual movement of the aircraft.

Having already completed the checklist, there are no longer any procedural demands for the crew to handle during taxi out to the departure runway. Furthermore, the revised FOM clearly instructs the pilots that any unanticipated tasks must be verbally coordinated, and that any demanding tasks require stopping the aircraft and setting the parking brake before addressing them. Under the heading of "Managing Intensive Tasks During Taxi," the revised FOM uses the following language: "(first officer) If unexpected changes require significant flightdeck tasks (for example, FMC programming for a runway change), inform the captain and receive verbal acknowledgement." And it directs the captain in clear terms stating: "(captain) If flightdeck-intensive tasks need to be performed, stop the aircraft and set the parking brake." The FOM goes further to say that "If the reported visibility is less than 4000 RVR,[9] or 3/4 mile, any flightdeck-intensive tasks, by either pilot, will be performed with the aircraft stopped and the parking brake set." As for flaps, the FOM is very specific and directs the captain that if revised performance calculations (as in the case of weather or runway change) require a new flaps setting, the captain must "stop the aircraft, set the parking brake, reset the flaps, and re-accomplish the Before Taxi checklist." In short, based on a thorough analysis of the nature of the operations and the nature of the procedures, the revised FOM *anchors* the timing of the critical action of setting the flaps for takeoff and provides the crew with a robust cue for doing so.

In revising the taxi portion of the FOM, the review team made a first effort to prevent, or at least alleviate, conflicts between procedural demands and operational demands by redesigning the basic procedure, and by providing explicit guidance on how to deal with specific situations that may threaten the integrity of that procedure. In the new FOM, executing the Pretakeoff checklist is no longer competing with taxiing the aircraft for the crew's attentional resources; the need for concurrent task management is reduced, and the opportunities for the prototypical error situations to arise are also significantly reduced. This change turned out to

---

8   It takes time for the flaps to transition from one position to the next, after the flaps handle has been moved by the pilot in the cockpit.

9   RVR stands for Runway Visual Range which is measured electronically at specific points along the runway. RVR is distinct from "visibility" which is measured (or estimated) from the control tower.

be consistent with official guidance that appeared a year later, urging operators to avoid all checklists while taxiing (FAA, 2003).

Trimming of the checklist   As mentioned earlier, the length of the Pretakeoff (Above the Line) checklist increased exposure to interruptions and distractions while conducting the checklist during the busy Taxi phase. The opportunity to be interrupted while performing the checklist was significantly reduced simply by shortening the checklist from 18 items in the original Pretakeoff (Above the Line) checklist, to the revised 7-item Before Taxi checklist.[10] This shortening of the checklist was made possible by reviewing each checklist item separately and re-evaluating its criticality and reason for being on the checklist. In doing so, the team discovered that some of the original items in the Above the Line portion were no longer relevant due to upgrades in equipment, and that some items could be moved to a new, Before Push checklist which is executed just prior to pushing the aircraft away from the gate, a static position with a low risk of interruptions. The opportunity to be interrupted was reduced even more by also performing the whole Before Taxi procedure and completing its related checklist prior to any aircraft movement. That particular time—after the cockpit door is closed, the cabin secured, the aircraft has been pushed back from the gate, the engines started and the pushback crew released, and prior to requesting a taxi clearance from ATC—is a very quiet time that is indeed under the complete control of the flight crew. With a much smaller chance of being interrupted, there is also a much smaller chance of having unanticipated new tasks arise under the revised procedures compared to the original procedures. Thus, two of the four prototypical situations are, to a large degree, avoided.

Re-consideration of operational factors   The revised FOM no longer mentions the traditional guidance to taxi with flaps retracted in icing conditions. A careful check with the aircraft manufacturer and with historical records revealed that this guidance was a relic from older aircraft designs that had been carried over through the years. The wing surfaces of older airplanes were indeed susceptible to contamination from ice, snow, or water on the taxiway surfaces, as described in the original FOM. The Boeing 737, however, have enjoyed various design improvements including some to the landing gear and to both leading edge and trailing edge lift devices. As a result, taxiing these new models in slush or standing water during periods of low temperatures no longer poses any risks to the flaps or the slats. Thus, in operating this type of aircraft, it is acceptable to set the flaps in the normal practiced sequence of events under all conditions, and to taxi with flaps set for takeoff even if operating in icing conditions. With their commitment to truly start from scratch and to question received traditions, the review team was able to avoid another prototypical error-inducing situation, that of being forced to defer critical actions and having to remember them later.

---

10   The original Below the line items have remained largely unchanged under the revised header of the Before Takeoff Checklist.

Anchoring floating items We showed above that a floating item is a prospective memory task by its very nature, and as such is highly vulnerable to being forgotten. The team eliminated floating items and firmly anchored single actions and even entire procedures in the revised FOM. Attaching the call for flaps to the end of the After Start flow is an example of anchoring a single action. Having pilots execute the whole Before Taxi checklist with the parking brake set, prior to any aircraft movement, ascertains that the procedure is now firmly anchored with strong external cues that cannot be easily obscured. The very change of the name, from "Pretakeoff" to "Before Taxi" is an explicit reminder of that anchor. Similarly, throughout the revised procedures, checklist titles make it clear that the purpose of the procedure and associated checklist is to confirm that the aircraft is properly configured for the upcoming phase (e.g., Before Push, Before Taxi, Before Takeoff, Before Landing) and that the appropriate procedure and checklist are to be accomplished immediately prior to commencing that phase.

Facilitating crew coordination The review team also noted lack of crew coordination as the source of many operational errors, so it strived to achieve better crew coordination under the revised procedures than was likely under the original procedures. In our cockpit observations, using the old procedures, it was common to see the captain initiate the taxi and then call: "Flaps 5, Pretakeoff checklist when you are ready!" The call indicated that the captain was aware of the fact that the first officer was still busy with other tasks. Although the call might appear to show consideration on the part of the captain, it was, in fact, an added source of workload (and indirect pressure and stress) for the first officer at a time when the latter was often already very busy catching up for operational reasons beyond his or her control, and rushing to complete earlier, pending tasks. Under these circumstances, the call was not always heard, and the flaps were sometimes not set, or set to a default value rather than the one earlier calculated for the particular flight. In contrast, the revised procedures allow the first officer to set the pace. Although it may appear strange to have the first officer set the pace of the operation, rather than the captain, in this particular phase of the flight, immediately following the starting of the engines, the first officer is the crew member who is most task-saturated and as such, the "weak link" in the chain, hence the one who should be allowed to set the pace for the whole crew. When the first officer, using the new procedures, announces "Standing By Flaps," it is clear that the first officer is ready to hear the flap setting, and this announcement also serves as a powerful cue for the captain to call for the flaps.

Additional safeguards In the original 18-item Pretakeoff (Above the Line) checklist, the Wing Flaps item was number 10 in the sequence. As is well known from research on memory, the items in the middle of a list are those most likely to be forgotten (Crowder and Greene, 2000; Healy, Shea, Kole, and Cunningham, 2008), compared to items in the beginning or the end of the list. Thus, items in the middle of the checklist are those most likely to be omitted. And of course, the longer the overall list, the more "middle" items are likely to be omitted, given working memory capacity limitations (Barshi and Healy, 2002) (Some caution is required in extrapolating this research to the situation of executing highly-practiced checklists.) Also, the longer the list, the greater the risk of interruption.

The review team provided additional safeguards against accidental omission of the critical flaps action: in the much shorter 7-item Before Taxi checklist, setting the flaps is number 7. The final item is more likely to be performed than a middle item in any list. Recall, also, that movement of the lever to extend the flaps occurs when the captain calls for this action, right before the Before Taxi procedure and checklist. Consequently, placing this action last on the checklist allows sufficient time for the flaps to reach their intended position and for the various indicators to clearly show it. So not only is the basic execution of the task more likely, for the reasons we saw above, but confirmation of the execution through the use of the checklist is also better secured under the revised procedures than it was under the original procedures.

Beyond the Pretakeoff checklist, the revised procedures incorporated yet two more verification steps for the flaps. Under the "Approaching the Departure Runway" section, the revised FOM includes the following:

"(Captain) Approximately one minute before departure (about 2000 feet taxi distance remaining or # 2 in the departure sequence), …
Check the aircraft configuration.
Perform a visual scan of the planned flap setting and stabilizer trim. Ensure that the speedbrake lever is in the forward and down detent."[11]

The FOM then goes on to say:

"(Captain) With the parking brake released, momentarily advance one thrust lever from idle to midrange and back. Check that the takeoff configuration warning horn is not activated."[12]

These two additional layers of defense against errors of omission further reduce the possibility of the crew being surprised on the takeoff roll.

It is worth noting that advancing a thrust lever as a quick check prior to takeoff to make sure that the warning horn doesn't sound was a technique we observed pilots perform, prior to the work of the review team. As was mentioned earlier,

---

11   These three items of the takeoff configuration, flaps, trim, and speedbrake are wired to the Takeoff Configuration Warning Horn which would activate upon throttle advancement if not properly set for takeoff.

12   This so called "throttle burst" works on aircraft whose takeoff configuration warning horn is linked with thrust lever position. Some variants of the Boeing 737 aircraft do not have the same feature and for this reason there are air carriers that have added a takeoff warning test button that performs the same function prior to departure.

part of the team's effort was to collect such techniques from the pilot group, and to assess their usefulness. When appropriate, as in this case, these techniques were incorporated into the new procedures. By doing so, the team availed itself of the experience and expertise of the whole pilot group, as well as increased the likelihood of the changes being accepted by the pilots.

In summary, the revised taxi procedures significantly reduced the opportunity for the four prototypical situations that are conducive to error. By performing the procedure during a quiet time and by shortening the length of the checklist, the opportunity for interruptions and distractions is reduced. And by reducing the opportunity for interruptions, the chances of unanticipated new tasks are also reduced. By separating procedures and checklists from the operational task of taxiing, the crews no longer have to perform multiple tasks concurrently. And by eliminating the requirement to taxi with flaps retracted in icing conditions, there is no longer any need to perform a task outside of the normal, practiced sequence of the procedure. What's more, by anchoring the procedure to a specific time and place, it is no longer a floating item. By taking all these steps, the revised procedures eliminated, to a large degree, the need for concurrent task management and for prospective memory, thus greatly reducing the opportunity for error.

Crew performance during the Taxi phase was measured in several cycles of evaluation, first using the original procedures, and later the revised procedures, during both their design phase (to test different versions of the suggested revisions), and at various time intervals following their implementation. With the revised procedures, the number of attempted no-flaps takeoffs was reduced to zero,[13] and throughout flight, the overall number of errors was dramatically reduced.[14]

We used the discussion of setting the flaps for takeoff as an illustration of the approach taken by an airline team for the review, analysis, and revision of that organization's normal procedures. The review team applied the same process throughout all phases of flight to eventually produce an entirely new set of normal procedures, and the outcome was met with similar success (Barshi, et al., in preparation). Recognizing and avoiding the circumstances leading to any of the four error-inducing prototypical situations was one of the main principles that guided this revision process. And this recognition was rooted in the careful analysis of the daily operations and the procedures designed to guide those operations. The

---

13   Since those measurements were taken, a few cases of attempted no-flaps takeoff occurred. All these cases were found to be instances of pilots intentionally violating the requirement to perform the Before Taxi checklist with the parking brake set and prior to any aircraft movement. The overall number of these cases is still significantly lower than it was under the original procedures, and further efforts are being made to educate pilots on the consequences of such choices to violate the procedure.

14   It is important to remember that the revised procedures include other operational, engineering, and cognitive aspects beyond those relevant to concurrent task management and prospective memory. We only provided here the details that were most closely related to the theme of this book.

key to reducing errors of omission was to minimize the need for concurrent task management and for prospective memory tasks.

Aviation and Beyond

The work of this team can serve as a model for any organization wishing to support its operators in their job and to reduce the likelihood of inadvertent errors. The considerations used in assembling the team, the methods used for review of existing procedures and practices for identification of error-conducive situations, and the process followed for guarding against them can be applied to almost any type of operation. In the remainder of this chapter, we step away from the particular review process and discuss additional, general guidelines for reducing the likelihood of error in operations. Once again, although the details of the examples are taken from aviation, the underlying principles apply to all work domains involving complex human performance.

Improving the effectiveness of checklists and crew monitoring

Checklists have long been used as a defense against errors of both omission (prospective memory errors) and commission (e.g., mis-setting control trim before takeoff). But the use of checklists is itself subject to error. As pointed out previously, entire checklists or sections of checklists may be inadvertently omitted, especially if conducted when other tasks are competing for pilots' attention. Another insidious vulnerability occurs because pilots execute checklists so often that their performance becomes automatic rather than fully attentive. The verbal response to a checklist item (read aloud by the other pilot) is so habitual that it is often uttered before the pilot's eyes can turn to the item checked to assess its status. Expectation bias (Austen, and Enns, 2003) also operates here—because the item checked is almost always in the expected position or condition, the pilot sees it that way even on the rare occasion when it is not. The combined effects of insufficient attention due to automaticity and distraction by concurrent task demands can lead to inattention blindness or to "looking without seeing" (Simons and Rensink, 2003). It is not unusual for a pilot to direct her gaze to a gauge, for example, and read the expected or normal value rather than the indicated value when it differs from the expected one. Furthermore, having flown a particular model of aircraft thousands of times, perhaps even several times previously that same day, pilots may confuse the present occasion with previous instances in which the item was checked. In general, because fast, fluid execution of procedures is an overall hallmark of expertise and is emphasized in training, pilots do not necessarily recognize that relying on automaticity rather than on full attentive processing reduces the reliability of checklists.

Checklists are used by human operators in many work domains. Improving and maintaining checklist reliability can be achieved if operators force themselves to check each item in a slow, deliberate manner that allows attentive processing. Pointing to or touching each item checked and withholding the verbal response momentarily aids this process. It does take some effort to make this pattern one's habitual manner of performing checklists, because it runs counter to automatic processing that dominates unless kept in check. It also takes self-discipline because operators are often under time pressure, and rushing is a normal human response to time pressure. However, rushing a checklist saves at best a trivial amount of time but enormously increases vulnerability to error. Organizations can help their operators in this matter by carefully deciding when checklists are to be run and by providing formal guidance and training on how checklists are to be executed (see Dismukes et al., 2007 for more detailed discussion of checklist effectiveness in aviation).

Another defense against errors makes use of the fact that work is most often accomplished by teams, not single operators. Transport aircraft cockpit, for example, are occupied by more than one pilot. The concept of crew monitoring in aviation holds that each pilot has a formal responsibility, in addition to all other duties, to cross-check crucial actions of the other pilot and to periodically assess the flight path of the aircraft and the status of its systems (Sumwalt, et al., 2002, 2003). For example, when the captain is taxiing the aircraft the first officer should monitor to ensure that the aircraft is correctly following the assigned route, that conflicts with other aircraft do not occur, and that the aircraft does not enter or cross a runway without a clearance to do so. As with checklists, however, monitoring is also vulnerable to lapses. Organizations can mitigate these lapses by formally describing in their operating manuals what is to be monitored and how, and by treating monitoring as an essential task rather than as secondary. It is worth noting that many airlines now designate the pilot who is not flying a particular leg the *monitoring pilot* (as opposed to the older designation of "pilot not flying"). Training is also required to make operators aware of the importance of monitoring and how to conduct it effectively (Ibid).

Strategic management of concurrent task demands

In Crew Resource Management (CRM) classes, pilots are taught techniques for managing workload that to some degree can help with concurrent task management. Pilots are cautioned to be alert to signs of overload: feeling rushed or confused or getting "behind the airplane." When they experience these symptoms, pilots are shown how to ameliorate the situation by distributing tasks among crew members so that no one person is disproportionately loaded, or by negotiating with ATC for extra time (e.g., delaying taxi on the ground or requesting a holding pattern in the air). Also, when it is simply not possible to accomplish everything they are expected to do, pilots should strategically assess which tasks are most crucial and then defer or omit lower priority tasks in order to focus attention on those that are essential.

The concepts of CRM have been adapted to various other domains, such as medicine, and operators in these domains can adopt similar strategies to deal with overload. But, as we have explained, concurrent task demands create vulnerability to error even when operators have enough time to perform all tasks. Thus, we recommend that CRM training be expanded to include the issue of concurrent task management and to provide specific techniques operators, as individuals and as a team, can use to reduce associated vulnerability to error, especially errors of omission, when confronted with any of the four prototypical situations. Some such techniques are described in the next section.

Training and personal techniques

Good procedures can go a long way towards reducing the opportunity for error. But the operational environment is ever dynamic and will always have a certain level of unpredictability associated with it. Crew members will never be able to rely exclusively on procedures, however well-designed, and must therefore be properly trained and adequately prepared to handle unexpected circumstances with the same level of safety as they handle routine operations. What's more, there will always be some situations in routine operations that require concurrent task management and that present prospective memory tasks, regardless of the careful design of procedures. Thus, besides the thorough design of procedures, explicit training is another key to reducing error in operations.

To assist in avoiding errors of omission, such explicit training must include learning to recognize the circumstances conducive to making these errors, especially those that arise from the prototypical situations discussed in this book.[15] This training should also include strategies for forming clear explicit intentions and strong retrieval cues for any prospective memory tasks, as well as for developing the habit of performing a deliberate search for any incomplete procedure or deferred intention at regular intervals during the operation. Further, this training should include both the principles we have discussed and concrete examples relevant to the specifics of the given operation, so operators can understand how the principles apply to their daily work.

Training and procedures go hand in hand in supporting all operators. For example, the last item in the Before Takeoff procedure mentioned above, the "throttle burst" prior to taking the runway to make sure that there are no conditions, such as flaps not extended, that would activate the takeoff configuration warning horn, is akin to stopping at the door prior to leaving the house to ask "do I have everything I need?" Some people check to make sure they have the keys before shutting any door that locks behind them. Similarly, a periodic deliberate check for

---

15   Learning to recognize factors ("threats") that could jeopardize the safety of a flight is at the heart of Threat and Error Management (TEM) training programs (Gunther, 2004; Veillette, 2005), though this training does not focus specifically on situations that make demands for concurrent task management and/or prospective memory.

deferred intentions or other forgotten items is critical in searching for anything that might have slipped through the multiple layers of defense built into the design of systems and procedures. "Are we forgetting anything?" "Have we been interrupted in the middle of anything that we should have resumed?" "Have we been focusing our attention for too long on a single aspect of our workload or the environment?" "Are the circumstances we are in similar in any way to any of the prototypical situations conducive to error?" These are the kinds of questions operators must learn to ask on a regular basis throughout routine operations to avoid the traps that we (and they) know are out there. An especially crucial time for pausing to check for uncompleted actions is at transitions from one phase of operation to the next, for example, before taking the runway for takeoff, when leveling off from climb or descent, before starting a landing approach, and when exiting the runway after landing.

Asking these kinds of questions forces the brain to search memory for deferred intentions relevant to the current situation. But that search is likely to be ineffectual if the individual has not explicitly encoded an intention to perform the deferred action at a later time. Pilots, like all individuals, often fail to encode intentions adequately in memory because of time pressure or the abruptness with which interruptions seize attention. Individuals may also fail to recognize that remembering habitual tasks is no longer reliable when performed outside the normal sequence of procedures, and thus requires encoding an explicit intention both for the fact that there is a deferred task, as well as for *when* the deferred task is to be performed.

Under routine circumstances, operators don't usually encode intentions for deferred tasks so explicitly, rather they implicitly rely on environmental cues, their expertise, and the nature of the operation to remind them. This approach works often, but not always. Unfortunately, the many times when individuals successfully remember to perform deferred tasks may lead them to underestimate their vulnerability to forgetting, and hence to not develop a habit of explicitly encoding intentions to complete the tasks later. Most people's personal experience[16] clearly shows that this approach can fail. ASRS and NTSB reports reveal that the danger and consequences of forgetting are substantial; thus explicit strategies to boost prospective memory performance are essential.

One such strategy is to create the operationally relevant equivalent of a "sticky note" (e.g., a Post-it® note). This type of note provides two key ingredients for reliable recall: it explicitly registers the intention in memory and it serves as a clear cue for its retrieval. However, the cockpit and most operational environments do not always support the use of the paper sticky notes; the operators must be creative in finding the best approximation to a sticky note to meet both goals: clear

---

16 We have all been in situations where we found ourselves saying "I can't believe I forgot to do it!" This expression shows that we intended to perform a task at some point later than the time at which we thought of it, and assumed that we would remember it at the right time, but didn't.

encoding and strong cueing. In our observations and in informal conversations with pilots, we came across many personal strategies aimed at doing just that. When pilots encounter a situation in which they know they are at risk of forgetting to do something later (namely, an obvious case of a prospective memory task), they often employ their own equivalent of the sticky note. They may, for example, place the checklist card between the throttles to serve as a reminder that the checklist was interrupted, or place an empty coffee cup on the landing gear handle to remind themselves of their decision to lower the gear at a later point than usual, or hold their fingers crossed as long as they were cross-feeding fuel to remember to return the fuel pumps to their normal configuration. These creative cues are conspicuous and distinctive and have the added advantage of physically preventing the pilot from taking downstream actions before performing the deferred task.

Creating cues, however, only works for operators who are acutely aware of the deferred task, of their vulnerability to forgetting to perform this particular deferred task, and of the fact that no reliable cues other than this strategy were available. The failures we have been presenting throughout this book are cases in which pilots were probably not as aware of their vulnerability to forgetting. Again, explicit training which is focused on these situations and which provides guidance and opportunities to experiment with such strategies could help increase operators' awareness of these potential traps, and in providing them with strategies to avoid them. Research is needed to develop the most effective training strategies.

Managing fuel in flight is a good example of a prospective memory task that could be used in pilot training (if relevant to the particular airplane model). Slight differences in performance between an aircraft's two engines sometimes lead to a fuel imbalance, which requires cross-feeding. Normally, each engine draws fuel from its respective wing tank; that is, the right engine draws fuel from the right wing tank and the left engine from the left wing tank. If, for example, on a given flight the left engine uses slightly more fuel than the right engine, then over time the right wing will become heavier with the greater amount of fuel remaining in the right wing tank compared to the left wing, and induce a right roll moment (i.e., the aircraft will roll to the right). If left unattended, this situation could compromise aircraft control. Thus, it is critical to correct this fuel imbalance, and this correction is done by rerouting the fuel flow such that the left engine also draws fuel from the right wing tank. This cross-feeding of fuel is maintained until the two wing tanks are equal again, and then it must be stopped lest the imbalance again occurs but in the opposite direction.[17]

---

17 Some times, the pilot may choose to cross-feed for a bit longer than just the equal point and intentionally create a small imbalance in the opposite direction with the expectation that the difference in fuel consumption between the two engines will bring the tanks back to the equal point and reduce the number of time cross feeding would be necessary.

Once cross feeding has been initiated, remembering to return the fuel pumps to their normal configuration when the fuel imbalance is corrected becomes a prospective memory task. The deferred intention requires a periodic scan of the fuel system panel to maintain awareness of the progress of the fuel balancing process. However, due to its location on the overhead panel above and behind the pilot's head means that it is not always part of their frequent scanning of the flight and engine instruments. The fuel gauges are on the center instrument panel, but even they are in the area between the two pilots such that they are not right in front of either pilot's eyes. In other words, monitoring the fuel balancing process requires an intentional shift of attention that is not part of the pilot's habitual scan of cockpit displays. If the aircraft is on descent to its destination and the engines are idling, it may take a long while before balance is restored. It is very difficult to maintain the intention to stop the cross feeding over such a long period of time, particularly because many other things are happening during that time that distract the pilot from maintaining the intention in her focus of attention. In short, stopping the cross feeding becomes a deferred task that cannot be eliminated by a well-designed procedure, and the pilot is back to a prototypical error-prone situation, that of having to interleave the task of monitoring the status of the fuel gauges periodically with other tasks ongoing in the cockpit at the same time.

Unfortunately, it is difficult to maintain this sort of periodic monitoring— individuals are vulnerable to getting caught up in the other tasks and forgetting to monitor. Scientific research has not yet provided specific techniques to maintain monitoring in these situations, however, the general techniques applicable in all prospective memory situations can provide a fair degree of protection. If the pilot was well trained to recognize prospective memory situations, then he would know the importance of clearly encoding the intention in memory, and of creating a strong cue for the retrieval of the intention. The pilot might, for example, involve the other crewmember in the task. Something as simple as "don't let me forget the cross feed!" increases the chances of recalling the intention.

Summary of Recommendations

For organizations

Organizations can easily adopt and adapt the approach taken by our collaborating airline in reviewing and revising procedures. Starting from scratch and questioning everything is an excellent way to uncover implicit assumptions and unrecognized vulnerabilities to error. It is crucial to thoroughly analyze reported and observed problems in routine operations, and to go beyond their surface manifestations to identify, and understand the true nature of the problems encountered with existing procedures prior to designing and implementing new procedures. Likewise, it is critical to perform a careful analysis of the procedures, the training, and of the actual operations to identify underlying assumptions, and to characterize the discrepancies between the ideal and the real operating environment. This analysis should identify situations in which procedural demands conflict with operational demands. It should also identify the ways in which the four prototypical situations manifest in the particular type of operation. Moreover, the analysis must identify the ways in which the given procedures might lead to such situations, especially those in which:

- operators are likely to be interrupted or distracted, as well as other situations that lead to prospective memory tasks,
- tasks may not be executed in their normal practiced sequence,
- unanticipated tasks are likely to arise, and
- tasks must be performed concurrently.

Once the analysis has been completed, the organization can turn to redesigning the procedures to avoid these situations, and to creating multiple layers of defense; the more critical the item, the more layers are needed. Specifically, the procedures should minimize the need for concurrent task management and for prospective memory tasks. The redesign should consider anchoring all floating items, shortening and grouping procedures, identifying or creating quiet points in the timeline of an operation to execute procedures to completion, and removing as many conflicts between procedural and operational demands as possible.

In addition to aligning the procedures with the reality of the operation and the characteristics (strengths and vulnerabilities) of human operators, the training should also reflect the real, rather than the ideal situation. It should provide guidance for successfully handling prospective memory and concurrent task management situations. Operators should be explicitly trained to recognize the circumstances that are conducive to error (e.g., the prototypical situations and how they manifest themselves in the particular operation) and how to avoid and/or manage them. The training must emphasize that when operators have to defer a task, it is almost always necessary to attend to other tasks during the period before the deferred task can be performed, and that because attention is focused on these other tasks, the intention to perform the deferred task at the appropriate time cannot readily be maintained in working memory and is likely to slip from awareness. Operators must be led to realize that the great challenge of prospective memory tasks is recalling the deferred intention at the appropriate time, because typically there are no prompts to alert them that the appropriate time has arrived—they must somehow "remember to remember." Training can help operators increase their chances of accurate and timely recall by providing strategies for explicitly encoding deferred intentions and for creating strong retrieval cues.

Procedures are seen as representing the safest, most efficient way of performing work under relatively benign conditions. However, complex operations by their very nature cannot be scripted with perfect reliability. As the Real Chapter clearly shows, routine operations are highly dynamic and unpredictable, even if within predictable bounds. Thus, it is not possible to have a procedure for a given task that would work under all conditions, in all situations, and for all operators. It is not even desirable to attempt to cover all of the known exceptions, because it would require unmanageably large FOMs. Given that some situations may fall outside the scope or language of the available procedures, operators must be trained to recognize that these situations will increase the likelihood of error. They must learn to appreciate that, even when equipped with procedures that have been well designed, there will be times when they will be called to devise ways to flexibly but safely accommodate operational demands. Training should help operators to recognize, accept, and appreciate their own vulnerabilities, and to develop effective and safe personal strategies. Organizations may choose to require operators to route such strategies through appropriate channels for evaluation and possible formal implementation.

Beyond helping operators best deal with the reality of the operational environment, organizations should also take the time to examine whether the organization's own priorities and the ways those priorities are implicitly or explicitly promoted exacerbate the complexity of that environment. Organizations must recognize and address the ways in which operators are implicitly pushed to compromise safety by the inherent tension between safe operations and production pressures. Production pressures in aviation (e.g., on-time performance, cost savings) show up in forms such as short turn-around time at the gate, publications comparing on-time arrivals with those of other airlines, and emphasis on the increasing costs of fuel. Air traffic control conveys its own production pressures in last minute runway changes and in "slam-dunk" approaches (which are situations in which arriving flights are kept high until very close to the airport to facilitate traffic flow, and then instructed to make steep descent to a landing). These pressures, combined with others created by social and legal concerns create situations in which workload and concurrent task demands are high. Crews often respond by rushing, which further increases the vulnerability to error associated with concurrent task management. Organizations should examine both their formal guidance and their implicit reward structures to encourage operators to strike an appropriate balance between production throughput and careful, deliberate management of tasks. In many cases, explicit guidance about how the organization expects the operators to safely handle conflicting demands is sufficient, provided the organization's structure for rewarding and reinforcing operator performance is consistent with that guidance.

Checklists and monitoring are crucial defenses against errors and equipment failures, but in practice these defenses are often not fully effective because operators unwittingly slip into automatic rather than attentive execution. Companies can bolster these defenses by providing training on the nature of this vulnerability and by providing formal guidance on how checklists and monitoring in deliberate and fully attentive ways should be performed.

Finally, for any organization contemplating revising operational procedures to help operators avoid errors, we emphasize the importance of collecting data on its operators' performance, both before and after any changes. Continuously evaluating the effectiveness of procedures and training, and continuously monitoring for the occurrence of errors and deviations are central to the health of any organization.[18] Evaluating the success of any procedural or training redesign is important for the identification of any unintended consequences arising from the implementation of changes.

For individuals

Individual operators can, in addition to encouraging their organization to adopt the recommendations listed above, develop their own personal techniques to reduce the risks associated with prospective memory tasks and with concurrent task management. You can learn to recognize the prototypical situations in your work, and realize that you are especially vulnerable to forgetting anytime you are interrupted, have to manage concurrent tasks, or when anything forces you to deviate from the ideal or habitual flow.

Recognizing the ways in which the prototypical situations manifest themselves in your own work environment can help you develop techniques to prevent them. For instance, recognizing the risks associated with interruptions can lead you to be very careful when you have to interrupt somebody else, and to adopt a strategic approach to letting yourself be interrupted. Such an approach will help you decide when to attend to an interruption after explicitly encoding your place in the interrupted task, or when to hold off the interruption until the current task gets to a good stopping point. Similarly, recognizing the need to respond to several different demands at once, you can call on a co-worker for help, or offer your help when you see somebody else in that situation.

Regardless of formal training, you can practice associating intentions for deferred tasks with strong external retrieval cues. When forming these explicit intentions, it is important to identify the time or circumstances when the deferred intention should be performed and to identify or create specific cues that will be present at the appropriate time. In other words, determine and set your work environment equivalents of the sticky notes, making use, when appropriate, of any alerting devices (alarm clocks, timers) that are available to you. You can also practice periodic, deliberate searches for incomplete tasks and for deferred intentions, something which can prove useful in your home environment too, not just at work. Deliberate searches are particularly useful in the transition points between distinct phases of an operation, and following interruptions. Practice can help make this deliberate search a habitual action that can better persist even in time-pressured and otherwise stressful situations. Last, but not least, you can also develop the habit of enlisting your co-workers to help with prospective memory tasks, for example by letting them know when you are deferring a task and/or by

---

18 Examples of guidelines for evaluating whether "best practices" have been successful in reducing errors in other domains can be found in the literature, e.g., Rogers, Cook, Bower, Molloy, and Render, 2004 (wrong-site surgery).

asking them to help recall it later, and by inviting them to also perform a regular "sweep" for incomplete or deferred tasks.

It is important for you to realize the ways in which organizational pressures affect your workload, and may create error-inducing situations. Your vulnerability increases with increases in workload and time or production pressure, or in off-nominal operational conditions, as well as under conditions of fatigue or stress. So it is best to develop a strategic approach to the management of workload, one that doesn't devolve into a reactive mode when workload increases. Traditional CRM measures are relevant here: prioritize, delegate tasks, reduce task demands, shed tasks, and buy time when possible. It is tempting to try to comply with production pressures, but you must remember the dangers of rushing and the vulnerability to error under these conditions. To mitigate these dangers, avoid deferring critical tasks to the extent possible, and discuss your plans with your team members. For instance, when you must defer a task, identify exactly when to perform the task, the cues that will be available, and how the deferred task will fit in with tasks ongoing at that time. In short, build your own defense layers against the prototypical situations conducive to error, whether they are brought about by organizational pressures or by the reality of the operation.

Concluding Thoughts

We have drawn upon recent research in cognitive psychology, especially in prospective memory, to suggest ways in which the challenges of concurrent task demands can be better managed and vulnerability to omitting intended actions can be reduced. Although in this book we emphasize safety, these measures are equally relevant to efficiency and cost. For example, although we know from ASRS reports that failure to set flaps before attempting to take off occurs on a monthly basis in the airline industry, in almost all instances the takeoff configuration warning horn alerts the crew to abort the takeoff safely. But rejected takeoffs impose significant fuel and time costs—in some of these instances, the crew must taxi off the runway and allow the brakes to cool, thereby delaying the flight even further. Other industries could improve the efficiency as well as the safety of their operations by adopting measures comparable to those we have described for aviation.

We are confident that the measures we suggest will be effective if applied thoughtfully and diligently, but these are by no means complete solutions. Considerably more research is required in many areas to develop powerful countermeasures. For example, as far as we know, no research is being conducted to devise ways to help operators who must interleave multiple tasks with novel content that requires attentive processing. This can be attributed not to lack of interest on the part of scientists, but to the paucity of research funding for this sort of inquiry.

It is also crucial to recognize that operator error cannot be fully understood in isolation. The organizational environment and the operational environment play critical roles in creating the circumstances that lead to error. We must recognize that procedures and training that are based on the assumptions of the ideal operating environment are not helpful, since operators out in the field have to face the complex reality of the operation and the discrepancies between the ideal and the real examined in the early part of this book. Not only must the procedures be designed with a thorough understanding of the complexity of real world operation and the strengths and vulnerabilities of the real operator, but also the training must reflect that understanding. Part of this understanding is recognizing the ways in which the prototypical error-conducive situations manifest themselves in the particulars of the given operation. Another part is recognizing how the performance of individuals and teams is affected by the inherent characteristics of human cognition, organizational factors, and the interaction of these factors with cognitive characteristics.

Aviation operations are very carefully scripted in explicit procedures and manuals. These written records facilitated our analysis and enabled us to demonstrate the discrepancies between the ideal setting and the real operational environment. But medical operations, and operations performed by nuclear power plant workers and by train engineers, and by countless other professionals in their work environments are all susceptible to the same discrepancies and to the same errors. The examples taken from everyday life in the Preface and Chapter 2 (Multitasking) clearly show that even simple aspects of personal life show the same vulnerabilities to forgetting deferred intentions and to the challenges of concurrent task management. The operation of a cell phone while driving, or the intention to return to the food that is cooking on the stove after chopping some additional ingredients may not be as exciting or as critical as remembering to extend the flaps before pushing the throttles of a large jet aircraft for takeoff, but they tell the same story. What's more important, the strategies for reducing error in flight operations can be just as useful in everyday life as in all systems requiring high reliability.

All operators are vulnerable in similar ways. Unfortunately the myth that one can multitask without degrading performance and risking accidents is all too prevalent in modern life. Inadvertent errors of omission are generally not careless oversights, nor are they evidence of lack of competence or of conscientiousness. The reality is that cognitive constraints on attentional resources, on the ability to manage concurrent tasks, and on prospective memory are shared by all people everywhere, in all endeavors.

Appendix A
Methods

No single research method can adequately capture the multi-faceted reality of actual flight operations, thus a multi-disciplinary approach was taken. We drew on several research disciplines, especially ethnography for its field observation techniques and of cognitive psychology and human factors for their approaches to analyzing tasks and expert performance.

To understand and truly appreciate the many complexities of actual flight operations we conducted field observations of actual revenue flight operations while occupying the cockpit jumpseat. Observation, of course, requires significant expertise in the tasks being observed, not only to understand what is being observed, but also to infer the implications of events and how they covertly affect operators' decisions and actions. Jumpseat observations were therefore informed by qualitative and detailed analysis of manufacturer and carrier operating manuals and pilot training courses and amplified through informal interviews with pilots and instructors (see "Ideal" chapter). Further understanding of relevant issues came from analysis of ASRS incident reports and NTSB accident reports. Analyzing the cognitive mechanisms underlying the skilled performance and occasional errors of pilots managing cockpit task demands required reviewing diverse research literatures in cognitive psychology and human factors based on laboratory research (see "Analysis" chapter). Combining methods and diverse sources affords a powerful and realistic perspective of the challenges faced by pilots in the course of routine flight operations. This approach, in turn, makes the findings applicable to both the operational and the applied research communities.

Our study was mainly conducted at two major U.S. passenger airlines. Previous studies and informal observations from the jumpseats of many other airlines convince us that our findings are generally representative of airline operations, although details vary among operators and the specifics of aircraft types differ.

Analysis of Manuals

Piloting a jet airplane requires considerable expertise in the form of "stick-and-rudder skills." Piloting an airplane for a commercial air-carrier also requires in-depth knowledge of facts about the aircraft and the carrier operations, as well as procedures necessary to operate the aircraft in the air and on the ground in compliance with both national and carrier-specific regulations. Most of this information exists in the form of operating manuals. Pilots are required to have excellent working knowledge of their carrier's manuals and are expected to faithfully follow the contained guidelines. Operations manuals are so important that they are essentially used as textbooks during training and, as a result, are largely memorized by pilots.

For our study, a thorough examination of aircraft-specific Flight Operations Manuals (FOMs), which describe cockpit operating procedures for the particular airline, and Flight Reference Manuals (FRMs), which describe the aircraft systems, was carried out. This analysis had two purposes. First, it informed us about the formal procedures used by the airline and how those procedures were supposed to be executed (albeit in an ideal world), which in turn allowed us to understand the objectives of the crews we observed and to some extent see the challenges of managing cockpit tasks from their perspective. This understanding was critical for conducting and interpreting our jumpseat observations. Second, it allowed us to make a detailed analysis of the character and flow of task demands as they would occur in the ideal world portrayed in the manuals and in the training based on those manuals.

Participation in Training Courses

We observed two types of airline training: training for newly-hired first officers and training for first officers and captains who were transitioning from one type of aircraft to another. New- hire courses typically last around six weeks and transition courses around four weeks. The content of both types of courses is similar, except that the new-hire course also includes material orienting pilots to the specific ways business is conducted at the airline (e.g., how to place bids for certain schedules). (In major U.S. airlines, new hires already have substantial flight experience in complex aircraft, either through military service or smaller airlines). Training focuses on the specifics of the type of aircraft to be flown and the procedures used at the airline. Aircraft systems (power-plant, controls, electrical, fuel, automation, etc) are studied extensively, using the FRM as a guide. Traditionally, classroom lectures have been used for this phase of training, but many airlines are now using computer-based self-study, allowing classroom time to be used for questions and answers. Pilots memorize operating procedures described in the FOM and practice executing the procedural flows used to prepare the aircraft for flight, using cockpit mockups. In the final stages of the course they practice flight maneuvers and normal and emergency procedures in highly realistic flight simulators. Assessment of progress involves oral and practical examinations requiring demonstration of both technical knowledge and performance skills.

Experiencing the training first hand was achieved by participating as trainee pilots in a new-hire and an upgrade/transition courses for the Boeing 737 at the two airlines collaborating in this study. The authors' involvement as students in these courses allowed full immersion in the natural environment of all aspects of training: facilitated sessions in the classroom, computer-based training (CBT), cockpit procedure trainers (CPTs), as well as fixed-based trainers and full-mission flight simulators (FBTs, FFSs, respectively). The first author, who was attending civilian flight training for the first time, observed the first 4 weeks of a transition course for pilots transferring from other types of aircraft to the B737 while maintaining their positions as first officers or captains within the airline. This author observed numerous training flights from the simulator jumpseat and discussed her observations with the flight instructors. The second and third authors, who already had substantial aviation experience and various ratings, spent 3 weeks at one location obtaining their B737 type-rating before attending a 6-week new-hire training course at another airline. These authors also participated as trainee pilots in the flight simulation portion of the training.

Observation of Routine Flights

Although modern flight simulators are so similar to actual aircraft cockpits in layout of instruments and controls and use such realistic visual displays and motion platforms that they are used for both training and certification of pilots, simulation scenarios typically do not capture the full range of operational demands occurring in line operations. This is especially true of the unscripted aspects of operations that are the focus of our study. Thus, it was necessary to observe actual flight operations as they typically play out in a wide range of weather conditions at diverse airports and along various routes. Further, it was important to observe a substantial number of crews to avoid mistaking possible idiosyncrasies for norms.

Our approach to observation of cockpit task demands and crew management of those demands was ethnographic (Emerson, 2001). The observer occupied the cockpit jumpseat and took notes on events and crew actions during actual passenger-carrying revenue flights. The Boeing 737 is well suited for this type of observation because the jumpseat is located between and behind the two pilot seats. The observer can easily see most instruments and gauges on the cockpit panels and can watch the pilots' actions, including their typing inputs to the Flight Management Computer (FMC) via the Control Display Unit (CDU) and their manipulation of the Autoflight System (AFS) via the Mode Control Panel (MCP). Communication exchanges between the two pilots and among pilots and other agents on the radios can be monitored directly by means of headphones connected to the aircraft communication system.

The advantage of the ethnographic approach is that the observer is directly immersed in cockpit operations and can experience the flow of events first-hand rather than rely on second-hand accounts. Although the crew is well aware that the observer is present, their attention is focused on task demands during critical phases of flight, and the observer is not intrusive.

The jumpseat observer was introduced to the crews by means of a letter signed by an upper management official for the particular carrier asking for the voluntary cooperation of the flight crew. The letter and the observer emphasized that the data collected would be de-identified and that the study would in no way expose the crew to professional jeopardy. (The performance of airline pilots and their adherence to company procedures and federal regulations is frequently evaluated, and deficiencies can harm careers). Also emphasized was that entry to the cockpit was to be allowed only with the concurrence of both pilots. During the study, all crews readily granted their permission for access to the cockpit. The observer was familiar with the Federal Aviation Administration (FAA) regulations on jumpseat occupancy and fully complied with the sterile cockpit rule barring all non-pertinent communication in the cockpit while the aircraft is below 10,000 ft of altitude. Once the flights were at cruise, crew workload diminished greatly, and during this period the observer was able to ask the pilots both specific questions about events that occurred earlier in the flight and general questions about their perspectives on managing task demands.

Rather than attempting to identify what types of events and crew responses might occur and creating a data sheet to record the anticipated events, we decided that it would be more fruitful to use an open-ended approach to explore any events that might make cockpit tasks more complicated than portrayed by FOMs. Desiring to provide a comprehensive account of situations that perturb the ideal execution of procedures and crew responses to those perturbations, we set out to capture all relevant events, the source and timing of the perturbation, and crew response (e.g., distraction or modification of a procedure). As we quickly came to realize during these observations, perturbing events sometimes occur at such a rapid rate that attempting to screen and selectively record them on a data sheet would have been impractical. Thus all perturbations during a given phase of flight were recorded as they occurred, using free-style handwritten notes. When conditions permitted during cruise or after the flight, the observer discussed these notes with the pilots to confirm and expand her understanding.

Formal data collection began in August 2000 and ended in July 2001 and included more than 100 flight hours of jumpseating by the first author. (Informal observations by the other two authors before and after this period served to cross-check the data). Sixty flights were observed, each between 1 and 3 hours long. This sample allowed a wide range of locations and weather conditions to be sampled. The first 22 flights were on board aircraft of carrier A. Their duration averaged about one hour, with the exception of the 4-hour "commuting" flights from the observer's home airport to carrier A's hub. A typical data collection day involved flying out of the hub in the morning and proceeding through 3 or 4 different southwestern U.S. destinations within the day so as to return to the same location in the evening. The time spent in the airport terminals between flights, typically between 1 and 1.5 hours, was devoted to augmenting notes taken during the just-observed flight. In November, flights with the same carrier were flown in the Northeast region of the country, in and out of another major hub airport. Flights were again about one hour long. Carrier A pilots are typically paired together for 3- to 5-day trips and often stay with the same aircraft for the duration of the trip. Crews observed within a given day, therefore, were different from flight to flight as the observer moved from one arrival gate to the next departure gate in order to maintain a set itinerary.

Between the months of May and July, 2001, 38 flights on board carrier B aircraft were observed along the Northwest and Southwestern U.S. regions. A typical data collection day involved flying out of the observer's home airport in the morning and consisted of 3–4 flights with a return to the same location in the afternoon. Carrier B pilots are also typically paired together for a 3- to 4-day trip. Because of the scheduling format of this carrier, the flights observed within a day were in many cases flown by the same pair of pilots as part of their designated trip. In one instance, a particular crew was "shadowed," i.e., the jumpseat rider remained with them for the duration of their scheduled 3-day trip, which allowed more extensive interviewing and discussion.

Analysis of ASRS incident reports

To extend our observations of perturbing events during flight operations and to see what errors might be associated with those perturbations, we conducted a search of the Aviation Safety Reporting System (ASRS) database. This database contains voluntarily submitted aviation safety incident reports by pilots, air traffic controllers, mechanics, ground personnel, and others involved in aviation operations (ASRS, 2008). More than 2500 reports are received each month, and the database currently contains more than 600,000 entries. All reports are de-identified before being filed, providing anonymity to the reporters. Each report includes a narrative in which the reporter describes the incident, surrounding circumstances, and his or her perspective on the causes of the event. Reporters often acknowledge that their own errors contributed to the incident, and their narratives range from a few sentences to several pages.

Although the ASRS database is invaluable to both the operational community and researchers, some limitations should be kept in mind (Chappell, 1996). Because the reports are voluntarily submitted, the number of reports about a given situation probably does not mirror the incidence rate of that situation in operations. Pilots are motivated to submit reports for multiple reasons, including concern for safety and the partial immunity from disciplinary action when deviations from FAA regulations are reported to the ASRS. Also, the validity of pilots' analysis of the causes of incidents is a function of their memory and understanding of the situation. Thus, the database is most useful for getting a sense of what kinds of situations arise and what kinds of errors occur in those situations, rather than for quantitative analysis of incidence rates.

Because our analysis of incidents was designed specifically to complement our jumpseat observations, we tailored a directed search in which the perturbing situations observed from the jumpseat were used to generate words and terms with which to search the database. We restricted our search to reports about air carrier operations conducted within the last 10 years. Some search terms were generic in nature and referred to potential sources of a perturbation, e.g., we looked for words such as "interrupt" or "interruption" and "distract" or "distraction." Other terms referred to potential effects of a perturbation and included words such as "forget," "omit," "neglect," and "failed." Naturally, we did not expect pilots to always describe situations using the words we would choose to use to describe analogous situations. Some events, e.g., the requirement to postpone setting the flaps to the takeoff position before taxi, may simply not be characterized as "interruptions" by pilots. Our directed search was therefore extended to also include key words that would be part of a generic description of situations we identified from the jumpseat to vary from the expected, ideal sequence of events. Thus we created composite search terms such as "forget and flaps," "fail and trim," "interrupt and warning," and "distract and checklist". A last set of search terms involves specific situations which we were curious to see if were being reported. For example we used "takeoff configuration horn" to obtain reports in which the crew attempted a takeoff with flaps or trim set incorrectly.

Reports that were selected as a result of the directed search were screened for relevance and those containing enough detail are listed in Appendix D.

Analysis of Cognitive Aspects

To go beyond a phenomenological description of perturbing events and crew responses, we attempted to analyze the cognitive demands posed by these events and to develop an account for the associated vulnerability to error, especially errors of omission.

We started this part of the study with a cognitive analysis of cockpit tasks to evaluate the cognitive demands imposed by attempting to respond to the various perturbations observed. Although the details and surface manifestations of these perturbations are quite heterogeneous, we found that almost all of the essential features fit into four prototypical situations and that crew responses fell into three basic types, described in the Analysis chapter. Once the dimensions of the problem were reduced in this manner, it was possible to explore the cognitive processes likely to underlie responding to these situations.

Reviewing diverse areas of experimental literature in cognition and human factors, it was clear that memory and attentive processes must be central to this account. However, most experimental studies use greatly simplified task demands, and great caution is required in extrapolating the results of these studies to real-world performance of experts, such as pilots, involving complex interplay of many cognitive processes, modulated by subtle social and organizational influences. Further, experts are highly adaptive in responding efficiently to real-world situations, and may respond differently as a function of subtle features of situations and task demands. We identified three cognitive themes that seem central to both successful and unsuccessful crew performance attempting to respond to perturbations: prospective memory, habitual actions and automatic processing, and attention switching. Using these three themes we developed a high-level conceptual framework for understanding pilots' performance. Because this framework is an extrapolation from basic research literatures that are far from complete accounts of complex real-world performance, the framework is inherently speculative, though we think it is plausible and well grounded in the existing literature. If it serves to stimulate the thinking and research of other scientists, it will have served its purpose.

Appendix B
Human Agents

Human Agents who routinely interact with the flight crew (in alphabetical order):

- **Air Traffic Control (ATC)** is responsible for the orderly flow of air traffic and for adequate separation (in terms of physical distance) between aircraft. ATC is organized according to geographical and functional areas of jurisdiction which roughly correspond to phases of flight. ATC interacts with the flight crew via radio communication (voice and/or text), and flights are "handed over" from one controller to the next as the flight progresses. Because controllers do not know the cockpit workload, their calls may interrupt the flight crew at very busy times; for instance, taxi instructions to clear the runway after landing might be delivered during the landing rollout when the pilots are fully focused on deceleration and directional control. Pilots usually treat ATC calls as high priority and often suspend on-going activities to listen and respond to ATC calls, and to follow ATC instructions.

  ATC functions are listed below in the chronological order in which the flight crew is likely to experience on a routine flight. The descriptors in parentheses denote the address used in radio communication. (For more information about ATC and its interactions with the flight crew, see the FAA Aeronautical Information Manual (FAA, 2008)

- **Clearance Delivery** (Clearance) provides the crew with the specific route for the flight, in response to the flight plan submitted by Dispatch. Normally, the first officer contacts Clearance during preflight. Subsequent changes to the flight routing are delivered to the crew by the ATC facility in radio contact with the flight at the time of the change.

- **Ramp tower** (Ramp) (at some, large and high capacity airports) has control over movement (pushback and initial maneuvering in the gate area) of all aircraft around the gates it supervises. Ramp is often operated by an airline when it has large gate areas, or a private company. Because all incoming and exiting aircraft must be coordinated, Ramp determines the exact time at which each aircraft must be pushed back from their particular gate. This time is estimated and relayed to the first officer upon his or her request over the radio, and confirmed again when the aircraft is ready to push back. The exact time of pushback from the gate very much depends on traffic at the ramp areas. At airports with no Ramp control, Ground is instead responsible for issuing pushback times and clearances.

- **Ground control** (Ground) (physically located on the airport grounds, usually in the tower) maintains responsibility over the movement of all aircraft on the airport taxiways (i.e., excludes runways, ramp, and parking areas). In order to monitor and sequence the traffic, Ground controllers may also be responsible for determining when an aircraft can push back from the gate, and hence get ready to taxi. The first officer typically contacts Ground before commencing the pretakeoff flow to receive information about expected pushback time, anticipated delays, or special considerations (e.g., de-icing, ramp or taxiway construction or equipment). Depending on aircraft traffic volume at the particular airport and the particular time of day, the Ground Control radio frequency can be very busy. The first officer must make sure not to "step on" communications between Ground and other aircraft before placing any calls. Monitoring the frequency prior to taxi is advantageous as it keeps the first officer aware of any evolving situations on the taxiways. An exact taxi route each aircraft must follow from the gate to its departure runway is determined by Ground and transmitted to each aircraft via radio communication to the first officer when he or she requests it. Ground instructions must be followed without delays and exactly as called for so as to ensure the safe and efficient movement of all aircraft on the airport grounds. As during preflight, depending on the traffic volume, the Ground Control radio frequency can be very busy. Some very large airports (e.g., LAX) have two or more frequencies assigned to Ground control (e.g., North and South) and specific procedures outline which frequency must be contacted depending on the exact location of the taxiing aircraft on the airport surface and/or the departure runway.
- **Tower** (sometimes called the Local Controller) is responsible for the airport runways and the airspace in the immediate vicinity of the airport; maintains responsibility over all aircraft taking off, landing, or crossing the airport runways, as well as those flying through its designated airspace. The first officer must contact the Tower frequency once the aircraft approaches the takeoff runway and in anticipation of takeoff instructions. The first officer must remember when to switch radio frequencies from Ground (which was being monitored while taxiing) to Tower. Tower is also to be contacted anytime the aircraft is to cross an active runway during taxi. Typically, Ground control will include an instruction to do so after issuing a command to hold short before an active runway that the aircraft must cross as part of its taxi clearance. When close to the airport and while preparing for landing, the monitoring pilot contacts the Tower according to instructions from Approach Control in order to receive a landing clearance.
- **Terminal Radar Area Control (TRACON, Departure/Approach)** is responsible for the airspace around large airports, and controls departing and arriving traffic for all airports within its geographical area, as well as traffic flying through its designated airspace. After takeoff, the monitoring pilot contacts Departure following the instruction to do so from the Tower; on

arrival, the monitoring pilot contacts Approach following the instruction to do so from Center. TRACON has responsibility for a flight during its climb and descent between the underlying Tower airspace and the overlying Center airspace.

- **Air Route Traffic Control Center** (Center) Twenty-one centers throughout the US provide en route services. ARTCCs are further sub-divided into high (above 24,000 ft MSL) and low (below 23,000 ft) sectors. The monitoring pilot contacts Center during climb following the instruction to do so from Departure. Center has responsibility for a flight during its final climb segment, all of its cruise, and through its initial descent. Flights in low altitudes and in heavily populated areas can sometimes be controlled solely by TRACONs.

- **Ancillary services** (e.g., galley suppliers, cleaning crews, baggage handlers) make their services available to the aircraft either by default or after being contacted by a member of the cabin crew. Their arrival and exit from the aircraft is typically coordinated and supervised by the cabin crew.

- **Cabin crew** (flight attendants) is responsible for ensuring the cabin and its safety equipment are all prepared for flight and that passengers board and disembark the aircraft in a safe and efficient manner. The total number of cabin crew members depends on the number of passenger seats on the aircraft—there are usually three in a Boeing 737. The captain and the lead cabin crew member must interact sometime during preflight so as to determine the status of cabin preparations and to establish that boarding has been completed before the flight crew initiates the pushback. The lead cabin crew member must also present the captain with an accurate and final passenger count once everyone has been seated and the aircraft doors have been closed. In some cases, part or the entire contingent of cabin crew may change over at the beginning of the flight. The captain is responsible for conducting a short pretakeoff brief with each new cabin crew. During routine flights, the cabin crew could be a source of interruptions for the flight crew as when cabin crew members inquire about the pilots' needs, or when they relate passenger needs to the crew (e.g., the number of wheel chairs needed at the arrival gate). As in the case of ATC, cabin crew members can not always know and/or appreciate the cockpit workload situation and may attempt to contact the flight crew at a busy time. Unlike their interactions with ATC, however, the pilots are likely to defer responding to a cabin crew member call than to suspend an on-going activity.

- **Company agents** (Company) (i.e., air carrier agents, physically also located somewhere on the airport grounds) are responsible for coordinating all in- and out-bound flights at the particular airport by providing assistance with gate assignments, aircraft and crew exchanges, and other matters. They communicate with the pilots via radio and/or ACARS. These interactions are usually initiated by the flight crew when the aircraft is in motion, but are often initiated by the company agent when the aircraft is parked at the gate. Thus, such interactions can be a source of interruptions to the flight crew during preflight preparations.

- **Dispatch** shares legal responsibility for the flight with the captain; the flight release must be signed by both the captain and the responsible dispatcher. Dispatch conducts the planning and route preparation for the flight and provides the crew with its flight plan as well as weather and other operational information for the flight. Dispatch also determines the amount of fuel required for the flight given FAA regulations, company policies, route and weather conditions. In many cases, Dispatch is the main point of contact for the flight crew's interaction with the company, including Maintenance. During flight, the flight crew often consults with Dispatch in cases of rerouting around weather, delays, or any deviations from the flight plan. In flight, the flight crew often monitors the company radio frequency for calls from Dispatch, and also to remain aware of the larger context of operations gleaned from conversations between Dispatch and other crews.
- **Fuelers** arrive to each incoming aircraft and coordinate pumping the necessary amount of fuel after coordinating with the captain. Refueling is often still underway when the pilots begin their Pretakeoff procedure. Prior to pushback, the captain must ensure having a fueling slip indicating the amount of fuel that was pumped into the aircraft tanks so as to confirm that the fuel required according to the flight release has been supplied.
- **Gate/Operations Agents** are responsible for ensuring that the flight is boarded with passengers as per company and airport procedures and have final authority over certain issues related to the loading of the aircraft. They are also in charge of delivering or accepting various pieces of paperwork relevant and necessary to the particular flight. They may be in charge of filling out a final Load sheet listing aircraft weight and balance information important for calculation of performance data by the pilots. They present this sheet to the captain sometime during preflight. The flight crew's preflight preparations depend on information provided by the gate agent; thus, the agent's actions affect the pacing of the flight crew activities during preflight, and can cause significant deviations from expected progressions.
- **Maintenance** is responsible for responding to the cockpit or cabin crew calls about malfunctioning items anywhere on or in the aircraft. They must troubleshoot and either repair them on the spot or declare them unserviceable. In the latter case, they must label the corresponding system "inoperative," with repercussions determinable by the pilots who consult their Minimum Equipment List (MEL) and in coordination with Dispatch. In some cases, the inoperative item is inconsequential for the flight; other times, a certain performance penalty must be imposed (for example, only certain types of approaches may be flown) and the crew must remember to impose it at the appropriate time during preflight and/or flight. Yet in other instances, the aircraft is grounded and the flight is discontinued until another aircraft can be used instead. The maintenance crew must contact the crew when boarding and

exiting the aircraft and must make entries regarding their findings and actions in the aircraft logbook before returning it to the cockpit. The crew, in turn, must ensure the placement of correct labels (placards) and the accuracy of logbook entries to ensure compliance with company policies and FAA regulations.

- **Ground (Pushback) crew** is responsible for physically pushing the aircraft back from the gate when instructed to do so by the captain. To prepare for this, the team must connect their tugcart to the aircraft nose gear after confirming that the parking brake is set. The lead team member communicates directly with the captain via the cockpit interphone and/or with hand signals. With the pushback tug connected to the nose gear, the driver on the interphone, and the wingmen in place, the team waits for the captain to ask for a pushback, once that clearance has been given and the crew has finished their Pretakeoff procedure and checklist. The team pushes back the aircraft from the gate being careful not to induce any collisions or block traffic in the ramp area. The captain and first officer are supposed to monitor the pushback from their respective cockpit windows. While pushing the aircraft back, the team is also responsible for providing the crew with clearance to start the engines (one at a time, or both) and must monitor their correct spin-up and spooling. Initiating the pushback is a complex coordination effort as the first officer receives the pushback clearance from Ramp or Ground, has to communicate it to the captain who has to communicate with the pushback crew.

- **Other aircraft** may intrude on the flight crew through conversations over the radio. The flight crew monitors radio frequencies which are shared by other aircraft. Listening to other conversations can be very helpful in updating the crew's understanding of the situation, as well as in creating proper expectations for future clearances and instructions. However, such conversations can also be distracting as when interesting but operationally irrelevant information is being exchanged. Crews are also vulnerable to errors when they interpret ATC clearances according to expectations based on, seemingly identical but actually different, clearances given to other crews.

Appendix C
Observed Perturbations

Note: CA = captain, FO = first officer, PF = pilot flying, PM = pilot monitoring, FA = flight attendant (cabin crew member, TCAS = Traffic Collision Avoidance System, and ACARS = Aircraft Communication Addressing and Reporting System).

Perturbation source	Consequence
Pretakeoff	
The FO had just started the pretakeoff flow when he spontaneously remembered his intention from well over 45 minutes ago. He had encountered some difficulties at a busy airport earlier that day, and knew he needed to confirm with his Company that the correct pushback time data had been received and recorded.	He interrupted the pretakeoff flow and proceeded to contact the Company agent. Upon verifying that the correct times had been received, he returned to the interrupted pretakeoff flow which he started from the beginning.
The arrival of a company pilot seeking permission to occupy the cockpit jumpseat interrupted the flight crew who was, at that time, conducting a departure brief.	The CA had to quickly assess the urgency of dealing with the jumpseat formalities and did so effectively while continuing to talk through the brief. He decided to deal with the jumpseater after the brief and motioned him to wait.
The CA was conducting the pretakeoff flow that called for testing the fuel quantity gauges. When he pressed the test button to verify the display's operation, he found one of the gauges to be unresponsive.	He interrupted the flow and contacted Maintenance with a request to have the gauge checked. When his request went through he resumed the flow at the item that normally follows the fuel flow check.
The FO monitored the Ground radio frequency throughout preflight to maintain overall situational awareness about operations at the ramp area and on the airport surface areas. A call with information relevant to their impending pushback interrupted her as she was setting the pressurization system, a step in the prescribed pretakeoff flow.	She finished the calculation and verification of numbers she was inputting in the pressurization panel and only then interrupted her flow. She dealt with the radio call while keeping her finger on the landing altitude knob so that she would have an immediate reminder of where to resume the flow at.

Perturbation source	Consequence
Pretakeoff	
The CA asked the FO for clarification on a segment of the airport he was not familiar with and was going to be traversing during the taxi. The FO was busy verifying the numbers on the Load sheet.	The FO had to search for the airport diagram under the paperwork he was reviewing.
The CA had just given clearance to the ground crew to start the pushback. The tug driver had started pushing back the aircraft when the FO received a message from the Ground controller to push back to the left to allow enough space for an incoming aircraft to park safely at the neighboring gate.	The FO acknowledged the call and turned to the CA to repeat the instruction to him too. The CA, in turn, had to repeat the information to the pushback crew who assured him they had the incoming aircraft in sight and were acting as necessary.
The FO called Ground for taxi clearance but received no response for about 2 minutes. The CA monitored the Ground frequency as well, while watching the tug driver negotiate a safe passage between this and an incoming aircraft.	The CA asked the FO to try the frequency again while still watching the tug driver. After another minute she asked the FO to verify that he was contacting the correct frequency.
The CA asked for flaps and taxi clearance while the FO was involved in conducting the silent After Start checklist.	The FO nodded his head to acknowledge the CA's request but continued the checklist. When he finished it, he reached over to set the flaps and contacted Ground for taxi clearance.
While taxiing, the crew received an instruction from the Ground controller to "wait for company 737 joining you on taxiway D." *(i.e., a Boeing 737 type aircraft belonging to their company)*.	The crew discussed their current position and the point at which they anticipated the 737 aircraft to join them. When another 737 appeared to their right, the crew quickly determined it did not belong to their company and continued to taxi while monitoring to give priority to the aircraft in question.
The crew was forced to spend a long time on the taxiway with the parking brake set during their taxi in sequence behind six other aircraft on a busy day at a large airport. The FO took the opportunity to rearrange his headphone cord and clean his glasses.	When the controller issued a new instruction for the aircraft to resume taxiing, the FO acknowledged the call and the CA released the parking brake and set the aircraft in motion. The FO found himself having to rush to put things away in order to resume monitoring the taxi progress.

Perturbation source	Consequence
Pretakeoff	
A new load sheet was delivered to the cockpit via the ACARS printer as the crew was taxiing. Its arrival over the printer was accompanied by a chime which caused the FO to notice it and take it in her hands.	The FO compared the new load sheet to the one she had used to program the FMC at preflight and found no changes. While verifying the numbers she continued to monitor the taxi progress by alternating her gaze between an out-the-window view and the paper.
The Ground controller instructed all aircraft on the ground to expect delays because of reduced visibility conditions at the airport at that time. The CA decided to turn one engine off to save fuel.	When the aircraft finally arrived closer to the runway, the CA determined it was time to prepare the aircraft for takeoff. The crew performed the Before Start checklist, started the engine, and completed the After Start checklist, just as ATC issued a takeoff clearance.
Unanticipated weather changes along the filed route were brought to the CA's attention by the Ground controller. The CA decided to discuss this with the company dispatcher.	The CA tried to contact the dispatcher but was unsuccessful. He asked the FO to request permission from Tower to pull of to a side taxiway where he parked and tried to contact the dispatcher via cell phone.
In the middle of taxi, and not anticipating any delays, the CA reached up and "off-loaded" the APU. He started the timer so as to ensure 2 minutes would go by before actually turning the APU off.	While primarily focused on the view out the window, he occasionally glanced at the timer so that he would know to reach up and turn the APU off.
While monitoring the traffic situation during taxi to runway 15 the CA wondered whether he would be instructed to change the filed flight plan and to take off from runway 34 instead. He asked the FO whether the aircraft takeoff weight was within limits for runway 15.	The FO complied with the CA's request, and went head-down to consult the appropriate performance charts. In doing so, he was distracted from monitoring the taxi progress.
The FO discovered math errors on the load sheet while verifying the performance calculations during taxi.	After informing the CA, the FO went head-down to re-calculate and re-enter the data in the FMC. In doing so, he was unavailable to monitor the taxi progress.
The FO was accomplishing the final items on the Takeoff checklist when the CA took a left turn to bring the aircraft onto the runway.	The FO was required to check down-wind for other aircraft while still running the checklist.

The CA turned the controls over to the FO when turning on to the departure runway, as this was to be the FO's leg to fly the aircraft. The FO was performing the final items on the Takeoff checklist.	The FO had to rush through the last item of the checklist while putting his hands on the controls and verbally confirming he had control of the aircraft.
The crew was performing the Taxi checklist. The item calling for verification of the data already entered in the FMC reminded the FO that he had never received a final passenger count from the cabin crew.	He suspended the checklist and called the FA over the intercom. The FA reported a final count. The FO proceeded to enter the data in the FMC before resuming the checklist.

Perturbation source	**Consequence**
Other Phases of Flight	
After takeoff, the PF called for "flaps up" at the same time that ATC instructed the crew to contact the Departure controller.	The PM reached and moved the flaps lever. While keeping an eye on the gauge to verify their full retraction he pressed the toggle switch on the radio and contacted Departure. While receiving the controller's response, he pointed to the flaps gauge to indicate to the CA that the flaps were now fully retracted.
During climbout, the PF turned the anti-ice on as the aircraft entered a cloud layer. He announced it out loud.	The PM was contacting Company when he pointed to the anti-ice switch a few moments later, reminding the PF that it should now be turned off.
The PM announced he was "going off" to contact Company as the aircraft approached the target altitude of 12,000 feet.	While waiting for Company to respond, the PM continued to monitor the climb and announced "1000 to go[1]."
The FA entered the cockpit with beverages for the crew. At that time, ATC issued an instruction for the crew to "climb and maintain 27,000 feet."	The crew momentarily ignored the FA's salutation. The PF instructed the PM to set the new altitude in the MCP as his hand was on the throttles (monitoring thrust).

1   When an aircraft is on climb or descent to a controller-assigned altitude, and that altitude has been programmed in, the altitude alerter emits an aural warning tone about 1,000 ft before the aircraft reaches that altitude. Many airlines' standard procedures require pilots to monitor and make the verbal call "1,000 to go" or "1 to go" before the alerter goes off.

Perturbation source	Consequence
Other Phases of Flight	
The PM picked up the logbook to start completing the necessary data. The aircraft passed FL180 and the PF announced it, reset the altimeter on his side and turned the aircraft lights off.	The PM finished the logbook data entry, put it away, and then reset the altimeter on his side.
The PM went "off" to contact Company and announced it to the PF. The PF was at that time head-down consulting the arrival charts.	The PF decided to defer looking at the charts while the PM was unavailable to monitor the instruments and the radio
The PM was busy swapping charts from those he used for the departure to the ones he would need for the approach. A call from ATC came through.	The PF noticed that the PM was preoccupied and had missed the call. He brought it to his attention.
ATC asked the crew to contact other company aircraft - the altimeter was showing 18,000 feet.	The PM announced FL180 and changed the altimeter on his side before making the radio call, per the controller's request.
The PF noticed the center fuel pump lights come on while on the radio with the Company agent.	He reached up and turned the center pumps off while still talking.
The FA notified the crew of a passenger request for a wheelchair. The crew was busy monitoring the descent.	The PM went "off" to communicate the request to Company, allowing himself to briefly become distracted from monitoring the descent.
An ATC request interrupted the crew who was performing the approach brief. At the same moment, the aircraft approached the altitude at which it would level-off and the altitude alerter sounded.	The PF interrupted the brief to let the PM respond to the controller's request. At the same time, he pointed to the altitude window on the Mode Control Panel to indicate acknowledgment of the impending aircraft level-off. As soon as the PM became available, he started the approach briefing from the beginning all over again.
The PF asked the PM to find out the destination gate. The PM was not familiar with how to use the ACARS system to request the gate number.	The PF went head-down to assist the PM in figuring out how to get that information. Both pilots became briefly preoccupied with the ACARS system.

Perturbation source	Consequence
Other Phases of Flight	
The latest ATIS report mentioned landings on a runway that was not acceptable to the crew given the aircraft's landing weight.	The PF announced that they would have to remember to request a different runway once they established contact with the Approach controller.
ATC requested that the crew "report aircraft in sight" *(i.e., when they had visual contact with a specific aircraft in the area).*	Both pilots became preoccupied looking out the window for the other aircraft which they knew was in the proximity. While doing so, they were not monitoring the autopilot perform the descent.
ATC directed the crew to "descend and maintain 8,000" while the PM was "off" on another radio frequency, coordinating the need to have an agent bring two wheelchairs at the gate upon arrival for two of his passengers.	The PF dialed the new altitude in the MCP. When the PM returned his attention back to monitoring the flight, the PF pointed at the MCP and verbalized the selected altitude.
The PM was performing the checklist and was about to make the announcement for the FAs to be seated. He told the PF he wanted to allow the cabin crew some extra time to finish up their service, as there had been some turbulence earlier that had likely delayed them.	He put the checklist card part-way in its slot so as to indicate the deferred announcement. Later, after he had made the FA notification, he announced the "checklist complete" and pushed the card all the way in.
The PM could not establish contact with the appropriate navigational aids when the Approach checklist called for identifying navigational aids and radios.	The PM continued with the remainder of the checklist. He kept the checklist card in front of him and announced "radios to go" indicating his intention to accomplish this item later, at which time he would also announce the checklist complete.
The FA entered the cockpit at the same time as a TCAS alert was issued. The PM was "off."	The PF motioned "one moment" with his finger while he looked out the window for the aircraft displayed on the radar display.
ATC issued an instruction to contact a specific frequency. The PM was already "off" and communicating with the Company agent.	The PF dialed in the instructed frequency but waited for the PM to finish his call to Company. When he was done, he informed him of the instructed change. The PM acknowledged the call and contacted the next controller.

Perturbation source	Consequence
Other Phases of Flight	
The TCAS issued a traffic alert at 5,000 ft causing both pilots to look out the window for the aircraft showing on the radar screen.	The crew was having difficulty identifying the other aircraft. The PF decided to suspend their descent until they succeeded.
The PF requested "Flaps 15, landing checklist" at the same time that ATC issued a call.	The PM decided to first set the flaps, and then respond to ATC. He reached for the checklist card and held it in his hands as a reminder to run the checklist after communicating with ATC.
The PM was performing the Landing checklist. She reached the item calling for final flaps verification but realized that final flaps had not yet been called for by the PF.	She placed the checklist card by the flaps lever and announced "flaps to go." When the PF called for flaps again, she announced the checklist "complete" and put the card away.
The PF had just asked the PM to set the flaps and initiate the Landing checklist when ATC instructed the crew to contact Tower for landing clearance.	The PM gave priority to the ATC call, switched radio frequencies, and established contact with the Tower controller, then turned to the PF and prompted him to resume his request for flaps and the checklist.
The PF asked for "flaps 10" while the PM was switching radio frequencies from Approach to Tower.	The PM first set the flaps per the PF's request, and then placed the call to Tower. He continued monitoring the flaps gauge while talking to the Tower controller.
The PM switched to Tower but found that frequency busy.	He continued responding to the PF's requests for flaps, while monitoring that frequency for the first available opportunity to let the controller know the aircraft was approaching the airport.
ATC instructed the crew to contact Tower as the PF asked for "gear down."	The PM contacted Tower and lowered the gear. At the same time, Tower responded with a landing clearance. While monitoring the gear descend into place, the PM acknowledged the Tower's clearance.

Perturbation source	**Consequence**
Other Phases of Flight	
The PF was still pulling back the thrust reversers after landing when Tower instructed the crew to exit at taxiway P.	The PM acknowledged the controller's instruction. The PF kept his hands on the thrust reversers, while quickly glancing over at the intersecting taxiway the aircraft was just crossing. He asked for the PM's confirmation that this was taxiway O and that they would be taking the next right.
ATC delivered complex taxi instructions to the crew just after landing. The PF was focused on stopping the aircraft using maximum thrust reversers while keeping it on the runway centerline.	The PF turned off the runway at the first available taxiway. The PM realized he had not fully encoded (nor acknowledged) the controller's taxi instructions and contacted ATC to request the taxi route again.
The FO used the time it takes for the CA to taxi the aircraft back to the gate after landing to configure the pressurization panel for the next flight. This action is normally performed during the pretakeoff preparations.	While at the gate preparing for the next flight, the flight plan changed. The FO had to remember to re-set the pressurization panel before the CA called for the Before Start checklist.

Appendix D
Errors Cited in ASRS Incident Reports

Note: CA = captain, FO = first officer, PF = pilot flying, PM = pilot monitoring, FA = flight attendant (cabin crew member), QRH = Quick Reference Handbook, TCAS = Traffic Collision Avoidance System, TA = TCAS Traffic Alert, RA = TCAS Resolution Advisory.

ASRS Report	Perturbation Source (Quoted directly from report)	Consequence
Pretakeoff		
424986	"Rushed through checklist in an effort to get the flight out on time and missed that the aircraft had not been refueled … Checklist was interrupted by cabin crew."	Omission—Aircraft not refueled. Realized the error after takeoff. Returned to airport.
425830	"When I first noticed the logbook was missing, I allowed myself to get sidetracked by FA concerns in the back. We allowed jumpseat rider to disrupt our normal flow of checklist procedures in the cockpit."	Omission—Departed airport without aircraft logbook.
152017	"Early in our taxi we were interrupted with a sudden change in our taxi instructions involving [the need] to identify several other aircraft [on the taxiways]. This distraction occurred at the point we normally complete the Before Takeoff checklist."	Omission of checklist. Takeoff configuration warning horn at takeoff. Aborted takeoff.
194641	"Minimum taxi time from gate to runway. #2 engine started during taxi … Before Takeoff checklist interrupted by conversation with Ground and Tower."	Checklist interrupted and resumed after interruption. Omission—Flaps skipped over when checklist resumed. Takeoff configuration warning horn at takeoff. Aborted takeoff.

ASRS Report	Perturbation Source (quoted directly from report)	Consequence
Pretakeoff		
238083	"Interruptions from the pushback crew while checklist was being read."	Checklist interrupted. Omission—Fuel pumps skipped over when checklist resumed. Engine flame-out during flight due to fuel starvation.
263325	"Ran Taxi checklist but left flaps up per cold weather procedures [packed ice and snow on taxiways]. Cleared for immediate takeoff as we approached the runway, we checked the final items [Before Takeoff checklist]."	Procedure item (flaps) and associated Taxi checklist deferred. Omission of deferred checklist prior to takeoff. Takeoff configuration warning horn at takeoff. Aborted takeoff.
263405	"Due to ATC, jumpseat rider, and clearance changes we were distracted during the [Pretakeoff] checklist."	Omission—Fuel quantity not checked. Discovered insufficient fuel on board while taxiing. Returned to gate.
264622	"Preoccupied with both a change in the departure clearance and a discussion about a 'packs off' operation."	Call for flaps 5 not confirmed. Omission—Flaps not set for takeoff. Flaps set to 1 instead of 5. Takeoff configuration warning horn at takeoff. Aborted takeoff.
317660	"I was busy starting the #2 engine, performing After Start flow and Taxi flow in time to run the checklist prior to reaching the runway"	FO failed to adequately monitor CA. Aircraft taxied past hold short line.
323839	"We became distracted… rushing to get airborne before our holdover time expired [after deicing]."	Omission—Stabilizer trim skipped over. Takeoff configuration warning horn at takeoff. Aborted takeoff.
357401	"Second engine had just stabilized when Load sheet came over ACARS. I immediately began to load the FMC to free myself for short, congested taxi to runway"	FO failed to adequately monitor CA. CA began taxiing without verbally and visually releasing pushback crew. Crew rushed to disconnect headphone and rang cockpit bell, alerting the crew just in time to avoid injury or damage.

ASRS Report	Perturbation Source (quoted directly from report)	Consequence
Pretakeoff		
372046	"As we approached the runway. We were moved up [positions in the aircraft queue waiting for takeoff]… We jumped from taxi mode to flight mode… Tower cleared us to line up on runway. I called for the checklist."	Crew rushed to perform checklist. Aircraft took off without clearance.
372293	"Tower suggested different runway to expedite getting airborne. I asked FO if we could use that runway at our takeoff weight and he said yes."	Crew rushing to takeoff before airport closure. FO rushed to perform aircraft performance calculations. Miscalculation of performance data. Aircraft took off heavy.
379824	"I had verbally released pushback crew. Completed checklists, got clearance"	Omission—Crew did not receive 'all clear' signal from pushback crew. Pushback crew had trouble disconnecting the towbar. Emergency stop signal from pushback crew.
397388	"Initial change in standard taxi route with numerous aircraft movements ahead. Advised of aircraft on our right. Very busy Ground frequency. Tower interrupted Pretakeoff checklist…"	Omission—No call for flaps before taxi. Omission—Flaps were not verified. Takeoff configuration warning horn at takeoff. Aborted takeoff.
398017	"I was interrupted during my preflight check."	Omission—Pressurization system not set for flight. Insufficient cabin pressurization after takeoff. Cabin altitude warning light in flight.
400553	"We were continually interrupted during our checklist (agents, fueler, FAs, etc)."	Omission—New departure not programmed in FMC. Aircraft flew past designated turn during climb. Crew disconnected autopilot and flew departure manually.
414095	"I was distracted momentarily in cockpit after pushback. I looked out to see tug pulling away."	Omission—Departure of pushback crew not verified before taxiing. CA confused other pushback tug in proximity as own. Aircraft ran over tow bar.

ASRS Report	Perturbation Source (quoted directly from report)	Consequence
Pretakeoff		
438470	"Ground issued change to taxi routing [during taxi]... I was copying the new clearance."	FO head-down during taxi, copying new clearance. FO failed to adequately monitor CA. Aircraft taxied past hold—short point at taxiway per taxi clearance.
445237	"Distracted during taxi discussing special procedures for destination"	Omission of deferred action (start second engine on taxiway). Aircraft aligned with runway. Crew realized omission. Cleared runway and stopped at taxiway to start second engine and perform checklist.
445810	"5 minutes before scheduled departure time, maintenance [crew]... needed logbook and promised to return it right back... I engaged in discussion of departure and weather system we would encounter after takeoff... distracted in our attempt to depart on time"	Omission—no check if logbook on board prior to pushback. Aircraft departed without logbook.
472309	"I was in the process of updating the FMC with the correct weights."	FO head-down during taxi, copying new clearance. FO failed to adequately monitor CA. Aircraft taxied past hold—short point at runway.
480583	"During the Pretakeoff flow I was interrupted by a question form the CA. Tower cleared us for immediate takeoff"	Omission—APU left running on takeoff. Fire warning horn on climb. Crew extinguished fire following QRH procedure.
489805	"Congestion on taxi-out, shutting down and restarting engine, problems with passengers getting out of seats."	Omission—flaps not set for takeoff. Takeoff configuration warning horn at takeoff. Aborted takeoff.
491660	"10 minutes prior to departure received revised clearance... we were busy getting ready to push back."	Omission—Navigational aids not set. Omission—Repeat of briefing for new departure not accomplished. Aircraft deviated from intended track on departure.

ASRS Report	Perturbation Source (quoted directly from report)	Consequence
Pretakeoff		
498489	"While running Before Takeoff checklist, Tower offered takeoff clearance ahead of two other aircraft."	Omission—FA notification skipped over. FAs not warned to take their seats for takeoff. Aircraft took off—FAs had to rush to their seats.
521812	"Running late. Crossing active runway on way to departure runway… advised to cross expedite, traffic on short final… Takeoff checklist interrupted by Tower delivering takeoff clearance."	Omission—resume interrupted checklist. Flaps not set for takeoff. Takeoff configuration warning horn at takeoff. Crew extended flaps during takeoff roll.
542468	"Running late. Fuel problem. Had to brief 3 runway changes due to weather… loaded FMC 5 times."	Flaps not set correctly for takeoff. Omission—verify flaps set for takeoff. Takeoff configuration warning horn at takeoff. Crew extended flaps during takeoff roll.
573040	"During the After Start checklist, I interpreted the probe heat lights for the engine anti-ice lights which were on for the icing conditions… reduced visibility… required increased vigilance outside the aircraft during taxi."	Omission—probe heat not set on during preflight. Omission—verify probe heat on. Crew confused illuminated indications. Master caution on takeoff. Aborted takeoff.
Other Phases of Flight		
259087	"Elected to accept runway change [weather changes as aircraft approaching airport]. I began to re-program the computer… the task was complicated by an inoperative button on the FMC… I heard the ground proximity warning…"	PM head-down during approach to land—programming new runway in FMC. PM failed to adequately monitor PF. Ground proximity warning horn. Crew aborted landing (go-around).
394580	"Climbing through 16,000 ft FA called and inquired as to seat belt, rough ride, etc."	Omission—climb checklist not performed. Altimeters not reset at FL180 (18,000 ft) to 29.92. Aircraft leveled-off at wrong altitude. Crew alerted by controller.

Other Phases of Flight		
422185	"As we started to do an After Landing checklist we were interrupted by Ground to wait for another aircraft."	Omission—flaps not retracted after landing. Checklist item skipped over after interruption. FAA inspectors alerted to check crew upon arrival at ramp.
425528	"Controller cleared us for the approach but forgot to switch us to Tower frequency"	Omission—failure to contact Tower. Aircraft landed without clearance
426080	"I started the large heading change to 110 degrees [using the MCP] but must have stopped heading bug at 140 to set new altitude in order to get out of turbulence"	Omission – failure to execute deferred intention to set heading bug to 140. Aircraft traffic in area—Controller alerted crew. Aircraft given new altitude clearance to avoid potential collision.
426510	"We were busy detouring around weather and making altitude changes… began pointing out some weather on the radar to rest of crew"	Crew failure to monitor aircraft altitude. Aircraft climbed past assigned altitude.
426580	"During descent I was high and fast and became concerned about making crossing restriction."	Crew failure to monitor aircraft altitude. TCAS TA at same time as altitude alerter. Crew preoccupied looking for traffic. Aircraft descended past assigned altitude.
426760	"I was distracted [calling Ops concerning arrival] as we approached a fix that required a turn."	PM failed to adequately monitor PF. Aircraft flew past assigned turn point.
426830	"Copying ATC instructions as aircraft climbed through FL180)	Crew failed to monitor aircraft altitude. Omission—altimeters not reset at FL180 (18,000 ft) to 29.92. Aircraft climbed past assigned altitude.
429237	"Right after we started down a FA came into the cockpit and engaged us in a conversation…"	Crew failed to monitor aircraft altitude. Omission—altimeters not reset at FL180 (18,000 ft) to 29.92 Crew received TCAS alert.

Other Phases of Flight		
429647	"Thunderstorms on filed route… decided to detour a few miles R of course… I am used to international flying… where there are numerous tracks and much traffic… was lulled into complacency by the lack of traffic"	Omission—failed to send message to ATC that PF had deviated from course due to weather. Aircraft flew >20 miles off course.
430060	"On approach. Received a hold… We got so busy inserting last minute holding pattern [in FMC]… our expected clearance was such that fuel was a concern, Dispatch needed to be contacted, and making sure aircraft is programmed and flying correct pattern distracted me…"	Crew failed to monitor aircraft altitude. Omission—altimeters not reset at FL180 (18,000 ft) to 29.92. Aircraft descended past assigned altitude.
431560	"I had gotten my attention diverted by setting up and identifying approach frequencies and completing checklist."	PM failed to adequately monitor PF. PF failed to slow down, as instructed by ATC. Aircraft violated speed restriction.
437750	"… Preparing to accomplish final items on Approach checklist (passenger signs and recheck altimeters). Distracted while being vectored for short approach."	Omission—checklist not completed. FA had to rush to a seat when aircraft about to land.
438340	"Distracted with making heading changes and watching for traffic"	Crew failed to monitor autopilot. Aircraft failed to start timely descent.
439599	"I became quite busy maintaining visual with preceding aircraft as well as traffic on the ground. Sun low on the horizon reducing visibility."	Omission—did not switch to Tower frequency. Omission—failed to obtain landing clearance. Aircraft landed without clearance.
439651	"I was reading the Approach checklist and calling Tower"	PM failed to monitor PF. PF forgot to set autopilot to capture localizer. Aircraft overflew assigned runway.
441740	"I asked for the Approach checklist… then the Before Landing checklist… by the time we were configured to land we were inside the 2 mile fix and busy making standard profile callouts"	Omission—did not call 2 mile final fix, as required. Omission—failed to obtain landing clearance. Aircraft landed without clearance.

Other Phases of Flight		
444359	"Departure called for an early turn for traffic at approximately 800 AGL"	Omission—flaps to be retracted not called for. Omission—no verification that flaps retracted. Aircraft buffeting—flaps overspeed.
453870	"While on approach… could not get ILS to tune or display. During this period we arrived inside the outer marker and turned our attention to the landing, with no one ahead of us and runway clear."	Omission—failed to switch to Tower frequency. Omission—failed to obtain landing clearance. Aircraft landed without clearance.
460500	"On arrival. Given a hold. ATC continued to make radio calls to us. In the process of adhering to instructions we entered the holding fix into our FMC and executed it."	Failure to check that correct hold entered in FMC. Aircraft flew wrong direction in holding pattern.
460697	"Preoccupied with runway assignment change, difficulty programming FMC, frequency change, need to have VOR back up."	Aircraft failed to adhere to required crossing altitude.
462230	"… had to chase down the glideslope after being vectored too close to the intercept altitude."	Omission—did not switch to Tower frequency. Omission—failed to obtain landing clearance. Aircraft landed without clearance.
463950	"FA came in cockpit… we get clearance to 24,000 ft and direct SBV. FO was talking to FA so I told him to go direct SBV."	PM omitted part of instruction (altitude) when repeating it to PF. Aircraft failed to begin timely descent.
467190	"Received a TA after rolling out on assigned heading during climb. Looked outside for traffic."	PM head-down during climb. PM failed to adequately monitor PF. Aircraft deviated from assigned altitude.
468200	"Received a TA in cruise. As I looked outside to spot traffic, PF started to descend."	PM head-down during Cruise phase of flight. PM failed to adequately monitor PF. PF started descent early, at habitual point of descent.

Other Phases of Flight		
469100	"I turned on both center pumps to deplete fuel [in center tank]... started clock to estimate time to turn pumps off... discussed max altitude aircraft was capable of obtaining with moderate turbulence, referred to performance manual."	Omission of intended action— pumps not turned off on time. All fuel in center tank depleted.
472320	"Distractions of checklists, visual separation, configuration changes, concern for stabilized approach.	Omission—failed to switch to Tower frequency. Omission—failed to obtain landing clearance. Aircraft landed without clearance.
490420	"After joining the localizer, told to call airport in sight. Following another aircraft... starting to have a hard time seeing it due to background of ground lights. Both of us focused on watching other traffic"	Omission—failed to switch to Tower frequency. Omission—failed to obtain landing clearance. Aircraft landed without clearance.
495500	"Instruction to hold... PM attention given to notifying company and passenger about hold, finding a waypoint on chart, ensuring navigational aids were properly set up for hold."	PM failed to adequately monitor PF. Omission—altimeters not reset to 29.92 at FL180 (18,000 ft). Aircraft descended below assigned altitude—crew alerted by ATC.

Glossary

Advanced Qualification Program (AQP): a voluntary alternative to the traditional regulatory requirements for certain types of pilot training and checking. Under this program, the Federal Aviation Administration (FAA) may approve significant departures from traditional requirements, subject to justification of an equivalent or better level of safety. The program entails a systematic front-end analysis of training requirements from which explicit proficiency objectives for all facets of pilot training are derived. For further details, visit the FAA website at http://www.faa.gov/education_research/training/aqp/

Altitude Alerting System: designed to alert the crew when the aircraft approaches and departs a pre-selected altitude. The Altitude Alerting System typically references altitudes set in the MCP and consists of an aural warning (momentary "beep") accompanied by an illuminated annunciation when the aircraft approaches within 900 feet and/or deviates by more than 300 feet from the selected altitude.

Anti-Ice System: designed to prevent ice from forming on aircraft surfaces (vs. deicing system which removes already formed ice). Ice can form as a result of low temperatures combined with moisture in the air and is very dangerous because it affects the aircraft's performance. The anti-ice system typically uses hot, high-pressure bleed air from the engines to protect the leading edge surfaces and engine intake lips.

Annunciator panel: centrally located panel of labeled fault indications corresponding to different aircraft systems. Generally, the indications are amber and are accompanied by an amber "Master Caution" light to direct pilots' attention to the annunciator panel.

Approach: procedures and parameters that define the manner in which an aircraft will approach the destination airport and ultimately land. Pre-defined approached are published for each airport—one runway at a large airport may be reached using several different kinds of approaches, depending on the weather conditions and the technology in use. Common types of approaches include:

- Visual approach: conducted in visual reference to terrain.
- Instrument approach: conducted using instrument references.
- Precision/Non-precision approach: with/without an electronic glideslope.
- ILS approach (*see* Instrument Landing System).
- Coupled approach: flown by an autopilot that is coupled to the flight controls.

- Missed approach: transition from descending on the approach to climbing to a pre-established missed approach altitude.
- Final approach: the final portion of the approach that terminates with the landing.
- Stabilized approach: a final approach descent that is stabilized with respect to specific criteria, typically including airspeed, aircraft configuration (gear down and flaps set), establishment within on-course and on-glidepath tolerances, and engine thrust.
- Unstabilized approach: violation of any of these criteria at a specific altitude above ground or distance from the runway.

Automatic Terminal Information Service (ATIS): recorded terminal (airport) area information (e.g., current surface weather conditions, landing and departing runways, runway and taxiway conditions, communication frequencies) of importance to arriving and departing aircraft. Broadcast continuously over a frequency specific to each airport and, in many locations, also data-linked to equipped aircraft, reports are updated every hour and identified by a sequential letter of the alphabet (referred to using the phonetic alphabet, e.g., "Alpha" for the letter A, "Bravo" for the letter B, etc.). Upon initial contact with the Air Traffic controller, a crew reports the most recent ATIS information it has received (e.g., "Carrier 123, we have information Delta."

Automated Flight System (AFS): controls both the navigation (Autopilot) and the thrust management (Autothrottles) of an aircraft together, or separately. At the heart of the AFS lies a Flight Management Computer (FMC in Boeing terminology) which accepts inputs from the pilots, manages it using information stored in regularly-updated databases (e.g., location and other facility information for airports, runways, and navigational aids; route structure; approach procedures) and with information it also receives from the aircraft instruments, and calculates performance parameters necessary for various modes of flight. The desired flight mode is selected and data input by the pilot using buttons on a Mode Control Panel (MCP) and a Control Display Unit (CDU). The selected mode at each moment in time is indicated on the Flight Mode Annunciator, displayed on the pilots' instrument panels.
Examples of automated flight modes are:

- Level Change mode: pitch and thrust are coordinated so that the aircraft climbs or descends to a selected altitude while maintaining a selected airspeed.
- Heading Select mode: roll is controlled so that the aircraft turns to and maintains a selected heading.
- Lateral Navigation mode (LNAV): roll is controlled so as to intercept and track a selected route stored in the FMC database.
- Speed mode: controls thrust so that the aircraft maintains a selected airspeed.

- Vertical speed mode: controls pitch and thrust to maintain a selected climb or descent rate.
- Altitude hold function: controls pitch to maintain a level altitude and thrust to maintain a selected airspeed.

Autopilot: provides automatic aircraft pitch and roll inputs. The AP physically moves the aircraft flight control surfaces (ailerons, elevator), which may of course also be manipulated by the pilot flying the aircraft. See Automated Flight System Auxiliary Power Unit (APU): small gas turbine engine that provides power to start the aircraft main engines. Electrical and pneumatic power generated by the APU is also used to run the heating, cooling, and ventilation systems of the aircraft on the ground prior to engine start or, as a backup, in flight in case of an engine failure or hydraulic pump failure.

Aviation Safety Action Programs (ASAP): program designed to enhance aviation safety through the prevention of accidents and incidents. Its focus is to encourage voluntary reporting of safety issues and events that come to the attention of employees of certain certificate holders. An ASAP is based on a safety partnership between the Federal Aviation Administration (FAA) and the air carrier, and may include a third party such as the employee's labor organization.

Aviation Safety Reporting System (ASRS): incident reporting system run by NASA. It collects voluntarily submitted aviation safety incident reports from pilots, air traffic controllers, flight attendants, mechanics, ground personnel, and others involved in aviation operations. Analysis of the de-identified data helps identify deficiencies in the National Aviation System, and supports efforts taken towards their resolution and prevention. More than 600,000 reports have been submitted to date.

Briefing: verbal conference conducted between the pilots before the beginning of certain phase of workload that will be requiring coordination and therefore an agreed-upon plan; i.e., before takeoff, before starting an approach to the destination airport. A briefing is also conducted between flight crew (pilots) and cabin crew (flight attendants) prior to a sequence of flights. In their standard operating procedures, many carriers specify the important points that must be covered in a particular briefing.

Callout: specific utterances made by the monitoring pilot that serve to aid and enhance the general situational awareness of the flying pilot. Callouts are specified by each air carrier's standard operating procedures, most often refer to instrument readings, and are specific to each flight phase (e.g., during the takeoff roll the monitoring pilot will call out the aircraft speed as indicated by the airspeed indicator—"100 knots"… "V1" … "Rotate"). In some cases, callouts are indicated only if certain parameters have been exceeded and the ongoing action must be discontinued (e.g., during the approach to landing, the monitoring pilot will call out the deviation from any of a number of parameters for a stabilized approach, as set forth in the Flight Operations Manual).

Challenge: A verbal utterance made by the monitoring pilot to alert the flying pilot that a specific flight parameter limit has been exceeded or an undesired aircraft state is occurring. These challenges are specified in airline standard operating procedures as a required function of the monitoring pilot; thus they do not connote interpersonal friction or insubordination. Besides being meant to inform the other pilot, they are also intended to prompt the other pilot to respond. Challenges must continue until any adverse situation is corrected. Also, see Checklist for another context in which this term is used.

Control Display Unit (CDU): keyboard and monitor of the Flight Management Computer (FMC). Also referred to as "the box." Two CDUs are typically installed on the lower portion of the instrument panels, one on the left and the other on the right side so that they are most immediately accessible to the pilot on the respective seat. Performance- and route-related information is entered on data-entry "pages." There are more than 10 separate pages (e.g., Route, Climb, Takeoff Reference, Descent, Hold). Each page displays specific fields for data entry (e.g., the Takeoff Reference page has fields for entering the runway wind heading and direction, the aircraft center of gravity, the trim setting, etc.) Procedures specify which pages must be completed at each point during any given flight and calls for the monitoring pilot in flight (the First Officer on the ground) to "program" them and for the other pilot to verify the data entered. The most programming-intense times of flight are during preflight and before the beginning of an approach. Programming is also required whenever there are changes to an anticipated plan, for example a change in the departure or approach, when a hold is required, etc. See Automated Flight System.

Crew Resource Management (CRM): a set of principles that pilots are taught to make effective use of all available resources: human, equipment, and information. Interaction and coordination among team members are emphasized. The concept of "team" includes but is not limited to flight deck crew members, cabin crew, air traffic controllers, dispatch, and maintenance. CRM principles are couched in various ways but in general address topics such as workload management, coordination and communication, leadership and support, situation awareness, and decision-making.

Deicing: the process of removing ice that has already accumulated on aircraft surfaces. This can be achieved either on the ground or in the air. Ground deicing is accomplished by spraying a glycol-based liquid over the airframe. There are different types (I, II, and IV) of liquid depending on their effectiveness in preventing further ice formation (anti-ice protection). Deicing in the air is accomplished using air from the pneumatic system (to inflate, then deflate the surface thus cracking the ice off) or engine-bleed air (to heat the surface and thus melt the ice).

Flaps: structures used to modify the surface of the wing of an aircraft. When extended, they increase the wing's lift by increasing its curvature and its surface area, thereby allowing the aircraft to fly at relatively slow speeds without losing lift. This is particularly important both at takeoff and the final stages of an approach (before landing). Flap position settings in the Boeing 737 are 0, 1, 2, 5, 10, 15, 25, 30, and 40 degrees. The desired setting is selected by positioning the flap lever on the control stand and monitored on the flap position indicator on the first officer's instrument panel. Flap settings are calculated based on the performance characteristics of the aircraft, its weight, the prevailing weather conditions, and possible speed restrictions prior to every takeoff and landing. Flap positions 0-15 provide increased lift and are normally used for takeoff. Flaps 15-40 provide both increased lift and drag to permit slower approach speeds and greater maneuvering capability, and are normally used for landing.

Flight Management System (FMS): *see* Automated Flight System.

Flying Pilot (FP): the pilot who controls the aircraft in flight. This is different from the Pilot in Command who is responsible for the flight and is always the Captain by virtue of positional authority. The FP manipulates the control yoke, thrust levers, and MCP/FMC settings. *See also* Monitoring Pilot.

Glideslope: ground-based system of vertical guidance indicating the vertical deviation of the aircraft from its optimum path of descent towards the runway.

Ground Proximity Warning System: provides warnings and/or alerts to the flight crew when certain conditions that signify dangerous proximity of the aircraft to the ground are met (e.g., excessive terrain closure, altitude loss after takeoff, descent below specific altitude). The various modes are associated with different lights and aural warnings (e.g., "pull up" and "sink rate").

Holding pattern: track of an aircraft that, following instructions from Air Traffic Control is forced to maintain its position by circling within a defined airspace.

Jumpseat: supplementary seats in a cockpit primarily for the use of instructors, check airmen, inspectors, and other persons visiting the cockpit. A Boeing 737 aircraft will typically have up to two cockpit jumpseats.

Localizer: lateral guidance provided by an ILS indicating the horizontal deviation of the aircraft from alignment along the centerline of the runway.

LOSA (Line Operations Safety Audit): method for collection of data on crew, organization, and system performance. The LOSA methodology was developed in the late 1990s by the University of Texas Human Factors Research project in conjunction with major US airlines. Using observations from routine flights and structured interviews of crewmembers, it enables the systematic assessment of operational threats and cockpit crew errors and their management.

Master caution: amber indication that illuminates whenever a caution indication on the annunciator panel is activated, thus directing pilots' attention to it.

MEL (Minimum Equipment List): FAA-approved document that authorizes dispatch of a flight with specified equipment inoperative, including the required maintenance actions and any operational conditions that are required to ensure safety.

Mode Control Panel (MCP): pilots' primary interface to the Automated Flight System. Located centrally, just below the glare shield, it allows either pilot to manipulate key flight parameters (e.g., altitude, rate of climb, heading) for the autopilot and autothrottles to follow, or to turn over lateral and/or vertical navigation to the paths programmed in the Flight Management Computer (FMC). *See* Automated Flight System.

Monitoring Pilot (MP): sometimes also referred to as Non-Flying Pilot. Responsible for monitoring the FP actions, aircraft dynamics, radio communications, and aircraft systems. In most cases the monitoring pilot is responsible for performing checklists, either alone or in cooperation with the flying pilot. *See also* Flying Pilot.

Norms: practices that are not written and required but are common practice. Norms may deviate from formal procedures when the latter do not allow human operators to perform their jobs efficiently and/or safely, or are not enforced. Routine deviation from formal procedures may occur repeatedly without mishap and come to be perceived (often incorrectly) by operators to involve little risk and in time become common practice.

Quick Reference Handbook (QRH): volume of the Flight Operations Manual (FOM) containing all normal checklists, in-flight performance data, non-normal checklists, and non-normal maneuvers.

Safety Management System (SMS): an organized approach to managing safety, including the necessary organizational structures, accountabilities, policies and procedures. A SMS provides the means for safety oversight in an organization, based on proactive identification of hazards, and analyses of their risk. Organizations functioning under the European Aviation Safety Agency (EASA) are required to have an SMS in place by January, 2009. In the United States, the implementation of an SMS is encouraged by the FAA but remains optional.

Speeds: monitoring the aircraft speed either on the ground or in the air is particularly critical during certain phases of flight, such as takeoff, the final stages of the approach, and landing.

- V_1 (takeoff decision speed): speed below which a pilot can reject the takeoff and still be able to stop the aircraft on the runway remaining. At and beyond this speed, the aircraft can successfully climb to clear all obstacles despite an engine failure and crews are trained to continue the takeoff.
- V_R (takeoff rotation speed): speed at which the flying pilot applies control column back pressure to rotate the aircraft.
- V_2 (minimum takeoff safety speed): speed that will allow an aircraft that experiences an engine failure to remain fully controllable and maintain an FAA-required climb gradient.
- V_{ref} (landing reference speed): Speed to be flown on final approach with the aircraft established in the final landing gear and flap configuration; adjusted with additives for steady wind and gust conditions.
- Vmo (max operating): maximum certified operating airspeed.
- Maneuvering speed: maximum speed at which the pitch control (control column) can be rapidly manipulated without overloading the structure of the aircraft.
- Speed bugs: rather than rely on memory for a number of different critical speed settings (e.g., V_1) small plastic tabs around the indicator can be placed to mark the desired settings. Once the airspeed indicator needle points to the tab, the pilot can immediately recognize that the particular speed has been attained. On aircraft with electronic flight instrumentation, the speed bugs may be part of the video display rather than mechanical devices.

Takeoff Configuration Warning System: monitors parameters essential for a safe takeoff and provides an aural warning, such as a loud, intermittent horn, to alert pilots when the aircraft is not properly configured for takeoff. In older variants of the Boeing 737, the warning horn sounds as a function of flaps not having been set for takeoff and EPR (exhaust pressure ratio) reaching a certain setting. In newer variants, the warning horn sounds if the throttles are advanced when the aircraft is on the ground and not properly configured for takeoff.

Traffic Collision Avoidance System (TCAS): identifies the location and tracks the progress of aircraft equipped with transponders, and indicates approximate bearing and relative altitude of all aircraft within a selected range. To alert the flight crew to potential or imminent collisions with aircraft in the area, the TCAS displays color-coded dots and issues a Traffic Advisory (TA) or Resolution

Advisory (RA). All commercial air carriers in the United States are expected to be equipped with TCAS.

Thrust reversers: mechanism by which engine thrust is directed forward to help bring the aircraft to a stop.

Trim: control capability provided to pilots for balancing the aircraft's pitch, roll, or yaw. Trim may be accomplished by repositioning the center positions of the rudder and ailerons, and by repositioning the entire horizontal stabilizer; in other applications trim surfaces are hinged sections of the ailerons, rudder, and elevator. Pilots trim the aircraft using electric trim switches or manual controls to relieve the pressure necessary on the control wheel and rudders while keeping the aircraft in the desired position. Setting the trim tabs to positions calculated prior to takeoff based on load and performance data redefines the corresponding flight control surface to a neutral position relative for the takeoff climb. In transport aircraft designs, autopilots also have the capability to trim one or more control surfaces.

Wing contamination inspection/check: action required of flight crews before attempting to take off in certain winter weather conditions; involves a direct examination of the critical aircraft surfaces within five minutes of takeoff by a crewmember (or qualified personnel outside the aircraft) to ascertain that snow or ice is not adhering to the aircraft's surfaces.

Working memory: a system in which memory items are temporarily retained in a state of high availability to facilitate performance of tasks at hand. Items not in current use revert to long-term memory, from which access is generally slower and more effortful.

References

Allport, D. A., Antonis, B. and Reynolds, P. (1972). On the division of attention: A disproof of the single channel hypothesis. *Quarterly Journal of Experimental Psychology*, 24, pp. 225–235.

Alvarez, G., and Coiera, E. (2005). Interruptive communication patterns in the intensive care unit ward round. *International Journal of Medical Informatics*, 74(10), pp. 791–96.

American Petroleum Institute. (2005). Facilities piping and equipment: Focus on items involved and causes of incidents. *PPTS Operator Advisory 2005–4*. Retrieved 10 October, 2007 from http://committees.api.org/pipeline/ppts/docs/Advisories/2005-4AdvisoryFacilitiesSubset.pdf

Anderson, J. R. (1974). Retrieval of prepositional information from long-term memory. *Cognitive Psychology*, 6, pp. 451–474.

Andrews, G., and Murphy, K. (2006) Does video game playing improve executive functioning? In Michael A. Vanchevsky (Ed.), *Frontiers in Cognitive Psychology* (pp. 145–161). Hauppauge, NY: Nova Science Publishers.

Austen, E. L., and Enns, J. T. (2003). Change detection in an attended face depends on the expectation of the observer. *Journal of Vision*, 3(1), pp. 64–74, http://journalofvision.org/3/1/7/

Aviation Safety Reporting System. (2008). Program briefing. Retrieved 6 August, 2008 from http://asrs.arc.nasa.gov/overview/summary.html

Aviation Safety Reporting System. (2007, November). Air Carrier In-Close Approach Change (ICAC) Events. *Callback*, Monthly Safety Bulletin, No. 335. Retrieved 18 January, 2008 from http://asrs.arc.nasa.gov/publications/callback/cb_335.htm

Barshi, I., and Healy, A. F. (2002). The effects of mental representation on performance in a navigation task. *Memory and Cognition*, 30, pp. 1189–1203.

Barshi, I., and Healy, A. F. (1993). Checklist procedures and the cost of automaticity. *Memory and Cognition*, 21 (4), pp. 496–505.

Barshi, I., Mauro, R., and Loukopoulos, L. D. (in preparation). Revision of normal procedures: A U.S. airline experience.

Bellenkes, A. H., Wickens, C. D., and Kramer, A. F. (1997). Visual scanning and pilot expertise: The role of attentional flexibility and mental model development. *Aviation, Space, and Environmental Medicine*, 68(7), pp. 569–579.

Betsch, T., Haberstroh, S., Molter, B., and Glöckner, A. (2003). Oops, I did it again – relapse errors in routinized decision making. *Organizational Behavior and Human Decision Processes*, 93 (1), pp. 62–74.

Boeing. (2007). *Statistical Summary of Commercial Jet Airplane Accidents: Worldwide Operations 1959–2006.* Retrieved January 13, 2008, from http://www.boeing.com/news/techissues/pdf/statsum.pdf

Boeing (1993). *Accident Prevention Strategies: Commercial Jet Aircraft Accidents World Wide Operations 1982–1991.*

Brandimonte, M., Einstein, G. O. and McDaniel, M. A. (1996). *Prospective Memory: Theory and Applications.* Mahwah, NJ: Lawrence Erlbaum.

Brandimonte, M. and Passolunghi, M. C. (1994). Effect of cue familiarity, cue distinctiveness, and retention interval on prospective memory. *The Quarterly Journal of Experimental Psychology,* 47A(3), pp. 565–587.

Broadbent, D. (1958). *Perception and Communications.* New York: Pergamon Press.

Chappell, S. L. (1996). Using voluntary incident reports for human factors evaluations. In Proceedings of the *1996 International Society of Air Safety Investigators Seminar*, pp. 11–16. Retrieved 6 August, 2008 from http://www.aviationnow.com/media/pdf/Safety_proceed1.pdf

Chisholm, C. D., Collison, E. K., Nelson, D. R., Cordell, W. H. (2000). Emergency department workplace interruptions: are emergency physicians "interrupt-driven" and "multitasking"? *Acad Emerg Med,* 7, pp. 1239–43.

Chou, C. D., Madhavan, D., and Funk, K. (1996). Studies of cockpit task management errors. *International Journal of Aviation Psychology*, 6(4), pp. 307–320.

Cicogna, P. C., Nigro, G., Occhionero, M., and Esposito, M. J. (2005). Time-based prospective remembering: Interference and facilitation in a dual task. *European Journal of Cognitive Psychology,* 17(2), pp. 221–240.

Cook, R. I., and Woods, D. D. (1994). Operating at the sharp end: The complexity of human error. In S. Bogner (Ed.), *Human Error in Medicine* (pp. 255–310). Hillsdale, NJ: Erlbaum.

Crowder, R. G., and Greene, R. L. (2000). Serial learning: cognition and behavior. In E. Tulving, and F.I.M. Craik (Eds.), *The Oxford Handbook of Memory* (pp. 125-135). New York: Oxford University Press.

Damos, D. L. (Ed.). (1991). *Multiple-Task Performance.* Washington, DC: Taylor and Francis.

Davey, E. (2003). Operational procedures: Industry observations and opportunities for improvement. *Canadian Nuclear Society Conference, Toronto, Ontario, 2003 June 08–11.* Retrieved 10 October, 2007, from http://www.crew-ss.com/portfolio/download/ CNS03_Op_Procedures.pdf

De Carvalho, E., Rixey, R. A., Shepley, J. P., Gomes, J. O., and Guerlain, S. (2006). Design of a Nuclear Power Plant Supervisory Control System. *2006 IEEE Systems and Information Engineering Design Symposium*, pp. 251–256.

Degani, A., and Wiener, E. L. (1990). *Human Factors of Flight-deck Checklists: The Normal Checklist.* NASA Report No. 177549. Moffett Field, CA: NASA Ames Research Center.

Dekker, S. (2002). *The Field Guide to Human Error Investigations*. Aldershot, UK: Ashgate Publishing Limited.

Dismukes, R. K. (2007). Prospective memory in aviation and everyday settings. In Kliegel, M., McDaniel, M. A. and Einstein, G. O. (Eds.), *Prospective Memory: Cognitive, Neuroscience, Developmental, and Applied Perspectives*. Mahwah: Erlbaum.

Dismukes, R. K. (2006). Concurrent task management and prospective memory: pilot error as a model for the vulnerability of experts. Proceedings of the *Human Factors and Ergonomics Society 50th Annual Meeting.*

Dismukes, R. K., Berman, B., and Loukopoulos, L. D. (2007). *The Limits of Expertise: Rethinking Pilot Error and the Causes of Airline Accidents.* Aldershot, UK: Ashgate Publishing Limited.

Dismukes, R. K., Berman, B., and Loukopoulos, L. D. (2005, March). The limits of expertise: The misunderstood role of pilot error in airline accidents. Presented at the *ASPA/ICAO Regional Seminar on Cross-Cultural Issues in Aviation Safety. Mexico City, 10–11 March 2005.* Retrieved 17 January, 2008 from http://human-factors.arc.nasa.gov/flightcognition/Publications/KD_ICAO3_05.ppt

Dismukes, R. K. and Nowinski, J. L. (2006). Prospective memory, concurrent task management, and pilot error. In A. Kramer, D. Wiegmann, and A. Kirlik (Eds.) *Attention: From Theory to Practice*. New York: Oxford University Press. Retrieved 5 January, 2008 from http://human-factors.arc.nasa.gov/flightcognition/download/promem_concurrenttask.pdf

Dismukes, R. K. and Tullo, F. (2000, July 17). Aerospace forum: rethinking crew error. *Aviation Week and Space Technology*, 153(3) p. 63.

Dismukes, R. K., Young, G., and Sumwalt, R. (1998). Cockpit interruptions and distractions: effective management requires a careful balancing act. *ASRS Directline*, 10, pp. 4–9. Retrieved January 4, 2005 from http://asrs.arc.nasa.gov/directline_nf.htm

Dodhia R. M., and Dismukes, R. K. (2008). Interruptions create prospective memory tasks. *Applied Cognitive Psychology*, 22, pp. 1–17.

Einstein, G. O. and McDaniel, M. A. (1996). *Prospective Memory: Theory and Applications*. Mahwah, N.J.: Lawrence Erlbaum.

Ellis J. and Kvavilashvili, L. (2000). Prospective memory in 2000: Past, present and future directions. *Applied Cognitive Psychology*, 14, pp. 1–9.

Emerson, R. M. (Ed.). (2001). *Contemporary Field Research: Perspectives and Formulations* (2nd ed.). Prospect Heights, IL: Waveland Press, Inc.

Eurocontrol. (2004). *A Method for Predicting Human Error in ATM (HERA-PREDICT).* Document Identifier Edition Number: HRS/HSP-002-REP-07. Retrieved 10 October, 2007, from http://www.eurocontrol.int/humanfactors/gallery/content/public/docs/DELIVERABLES/HF40%20(HRS-HSP-002-REP-07)%20Released-withsig.pdf

Eyrolle, H., and Cellier, J.-M. (2000). The effects of interruptions in work activity: Field and laboratory results. *Applied Ergonomics,* 31, pp. 537–43.

Eysenck, M. W. (Ed.). (1994). *The Blackwell Dictionary of Cognitive Psychology*. Malden, MA: Blackwell Publishers.

Federal Aviation Administration. (2008). *Aeronautical Information Manual: Official Guide to Basic Flight Information and ATC Procedures*. Retrieved 6 August, 2008 from http://www.faa.gov/airports_airtraffic/air_traffic/publications/ATpubs/AIM/

Federal Aviation Administration. (2007). *Runway Safety Report*. Retrieved 20 January, 2008 from http://www.faa.gov/runwaysafety/pdf/rireport06.pdf

Federal Aviation Administration. (2006a). *Introduction to Safety Management Systems for Air Operators*. Advisory Circular No. 120-92. Retrieved 5 January, 2008 from http://www.airweb.faa.gov/Regulatory_and_Guidance_Library/rgAdvisoryCircular.nsf/0/6485143d5ec81aae8625719b0055c9e5/$FILE/AC%20120-92.pdf

Federal Aviation Administration. (2006b). *Advanced Qualification Program*. Advisory Circular No. 120-54A. Retrieved 5 January, 2008 from http://www.airweb.faa.gov/Regulatory_and_Guidance_Library/rgAdvisoryCircular.nsf/0/1ef8eee828670517862571a20064a40b/$FILE/AC%20120-54a.pdf

Federal Aviation Administration. (2003). *Part 91, 121, 125, and 135 Flightcrew Procedures During Taxi Operations*. Advisory Circular No. 120-74A. Retrieved 6 August, 2008 from http://www.airweb.faa.gov/Regulatory_and_Guidance_Library/rgAdvisoryCircular.nsf/0/331ca20530e3d4b086256dc000565d82/$FILE/AC120-74A.pdf

Flight Safety Foundation (2005, February). Line Operations Safety Audit (LOSA) provides data on threats and errors. *Flight Safety Digest,* .Retrieved March 2, 2005 from http://www.flightsafety.org/pubs/fsd_2005.html

Foerde, K., Knowlton, B. J., and Poldrack, R. A. (2006) Modulation of competing memory systems by distraction. *Proc Natl Acad Sci*, 103(31), pp. 11778–83. Retrieved 5 January, 2008 from http://www.pnas.org/cgi/content/full/103/31/11778

Gawande, A. A., Studdert, D. M., Orav, E. J., Brennan, T. A., and Zinner, M. J. (2003) Risk factors for retained instruments and sponges after surgery. *The New England Journal of Medicine*. 348(3), pp. 229–235.

Gillie, T. Broadbent, D. (1989). What makes interruptions disruptive? A study of length, similarity, and complexity. *Psychological Research*, 50, pp. 243–50.

Glassbrenner, D. (2005). *Driver Cell Phone Use in 2005 — Overall Results. Traffic Safety Facts – Research Note*, Department of Transportation, National Highway Traffic Safety Administration Report No. DOT HS 809 967. Retrieved 5 January 2008 from http://www-nrd.nhtsa.dot.gov/pdf/nrd-30/NCSA/RNotes/2005/809967.pdf

Gollwitzer, P. M. (1999). Implementation intentions: Strong effects of simple plans. *American Psychologist*, 54(7), pp. 493–503.

Gopher, D. (1992). The skill of attention control: Acquisition and execution of attention strategies. In D. Meyer and S. Kornblum (Eds.) *Attention and Performance XIV*. Hillsdale, NJ: Erlbaum.

Gray-Eurom, K. (2006). Creating conflict resolution in the emergency department. *Emergency Medicine and Critical Care Review*, pp. 12–13. Retrieved 8 October, 2007 from http://www.touchbriefings.com/pdf/2459/Gray-Eurom.pdf

Green, C. S., and Bavelier, D. (2006). Enumeration versus multiple object tracking: the case of action video game players. *Cognition,* 101, pp. 217–245

Groeger, J. A. and Clegg, B. A. (1997). Automaticity and driving: time to change gear? In T. Rothengatter and E. Carbonell Vaya (Eds.), *Traffic and Transportation Psychology: Theory and Application* (pp. 137–146). Oxford: Pergamon.

Gunther, D. (2004). Threat and error management (TEM) workshop. Presentation at the *Second ICAO/IATA LOSA/TEM Conference, November 3–4, Boeing Training Center, Seattle, WA.* Retrieved February 23, 2005 from http://www.icao.int/icao/en/anb/peltrg/conf/LOSA_Seattle_2004.pdf

Guynn, McDaniel, and Einstein, 2001

Healy, A. F., Shea, K. M., Kole, J. A., and Cunningham, T. F. (2008). Position distinctiveness, item familiarity, and presentation frequency affect reconstruction of order in immediate episodic memory. *Journal of Memory and Language*, 58(3), pp. 746–764.

Helmreich, R., Klinect, J., and Merritt, A. (2004). Line operations safety audit: LOSA data from US airlines. Presentation at the *Second ICAO/IATA LOSA/ TEM Conference (November 3–4, 2004), Boeing Training Center, Seattle, WA.* Retrieved February 23, 2005 from http://www.icao.int/icao/en/anb/peltrg/conf/ LOSA_Seattle_2004.pdf

Hickam, D. H., Severance, S., Feldstein, A., et al. (2003). *The Effect of Health Care Working Conditions on Patient Safety. Evidence Report/Technology Assessment Number 74.* (Prepared by Oregon Health and Science University under Contract No. 290-97-0018.) AHRQ Publication No. 03-E031. Rockville, MD: Agency for Healthcare Research and Quality. Retrieved 7 January, 2008 from http://www.ncbi.nlm.nih.gov/books/bv.fcgi?rid=hstat1a.table.10182

Hobbs, A. N., and Williamson, A. (2003). Associations between errors and contributing factors in aircraft maintenance. *Human Factors*, 45, pp. 186–201.

Huey, and Wickens, C. D. (Eds.). (1993). *Workload Transition: Implications for Individual and Team Performance* (Chapter 9: Strategic Task Management). Accessed on August 6, 2008 from http://books.nap.edu/openbook.php?record_ id=2045&page=214

Institute of Medicine. (2007). *Preventing Medication Errors.* Accessed on August 6, 2008 from http://www.nap.edu/catalog.php?record_id=11623

Institute of Medicine. (2004). *Keeping Patients Safe: Transforming the Work Environment of Nurses.* Washington, D.C.: National Academies Press. Accessed on August 6, 2008 from http://books.nap.edu/catalog.php?record_id=10851

Jett, Q. R., and George, J. M. (2003). Work interrupted: A closer look at the role of interruptions in organizational life. *Academy of Management Review*, 28(3), pp. 494–507.

Johnson, M. K., Hashtroudi, S., and Lindsay, D. S. (1993). Source monitoring. *Psychological Bulletin*, 114, pp. 3–28.

Joint Commission. (2006, January). Using medication reconciliation to prevent errors. *Sentinel Event Alert*, 35. Retrieved 10 October, 2007 from http://www.jointcommission.org/ SentinelEvents/SentinelEventAlert/sea_35.htm

Kastchiev, G., Kromp, W., Kurth, S., Lochbaum, D., Lyman, E., Sailer, M., and Schneider, M. (2006). *Residual risk: An Account of Events in Nuclear Power Plants Since the Chernobyl Accident in 1986*. Retrieved 10 October, 2007, from http://www.greens-efa.org/cms/topics/dokbin/181/181995.residual_risk@en.pdf

Kirmeyer, S. L. (1988a). Coping with competing demands: Interruption and the Type A pattern. *Journal of Applied Psychology*, 73(4): pp. 621–629.

Kirmeyer, S. L. (1988b). Observed communication in the workplace: Content, source, and direction. *Journal of Communication Psychology,* 16, pp. 175–187.

Klauer, S. G., Dingus, T. A., Neale, V. L., Sudweeks, J. D., and Ramsey, D. J. (2006). *The Impact of Driver Inattention on Near-crash/Crash Risk: An Analysis using the 100-car Naturalistic Driving Study Data*. Department of Transportation Report HS810 594. Retrieved 7 January, 2008 from http://www-nrd.nhtsa.dot.gov/departments/nrd-13/810594/images/810594.pdf

Kliegel, M., Martin, M., McDaniel, M. A., Einstein, G. O. (Eds.). (2004). *Prospective Memory: Cognitive, Neuroscience, Developmental, and Applied Perspectives*. Mahwah: Erlbaum.

Lacagnina, M. (2007, May). Defusing the ramp. *Flight Safety Digest.* Retrieved March 2, 2005 from http://www.flightsafety.org/asw/may07/asw_may07_p20-24.pdf

Latorella, K. (1999) *Investigating Interruptions: Implications for Flightdeck Performance*. NASA TM-1999-209707. Retrieved January 27, 2006 from http://techreports.larc.nasa.gov/ltrs/PDF/1999/tm/NASA-99-tm209707.pdf

Loukopoulos, L. D., Dismukes, R. K., and Barshi, I. (2003). Concurrent task demands in the cockpit: Challenges and vulnerabilities in routine flight operations. In R. Jensen (Ed.), Proceedings of the *12th International Symposium on Aviation Psychology* (pp. 737–742). Dayton, OH: The Wright State University.

Loukopoulos, L. D., Dismukes, R. K., and Barshi, I. (2001). Cockpit interruptions and distractions: A line observation study. *Proceedings of the 11th International Symposium on Aviation Psychology*, Columbus, Ohio, USA.

Luong, A., and Rogelberg, S. G. (2005). Meetings and more meetings: The relationship between meeting load and the daily well-being of employees. *Group Dynamics: Theory, Research, and Practice*, 9 (1), pp. 58–67.

McDaniel, M. A., and Einstein, G. O. (2007). *Prospective Memory: An Overview and Synthesis of an Emerging Field*. Thousand Oaks, CA: Sage.

McDaniel, M. A., Guynn, M. J., Einstein, G. O., Breneiser, J. (2004). Cue-focused and reflexive-associative processes in prospective memory retrieval. *Journal of Experimental Psychology: Learning, Memory, and Cognition*, 30, pp. 605–614.

Miyake, A., and Shah, P. (1999). *Models of Working Memory*. Cambridge, UK: Cambridge University Press.

Monk, C. A., Boehm-Davis, D. A., and Trafton, J. G. (2004). Recovering from interruptions: Implications for driver distraction research. *Human Factors*, 46(4), pp. 650–663.

Mumaw, R. J., Sarter, N., Wickens, C., Kimball, S., Nikolic, M., Marsh, R., Xu, W., and Xu, X. (2000). *Analysis of Pilots' Monitoring and Performance on Highly Automated Flight Decks*. Final project report: NASA Ames Contract NAS2-99074. Seattle, WA: Boeing Commercial Aviation.

Mycielska, K., and Reason, J. (1982) *Absent Minded? The Psychology of Mental Lapses, Little Slips, and Everyday Errors*. Englewood Cliffs, NJ: Prentice Hall.

National Transportation Safety Board. (2002). *Southwest Airlines Flight 1455, Boeing 737-300, N668SW, Burbank, California, March 5, 2000*. (Aircraft accident brief No. DCA00MA030). Retrieved October 24, 2005 from http://www.ntsb.gov/publictn/2002/ AAB0204.pdf

National Transportation Safety Board. (2001). *Runway Overrun During Landing, American Airlines flight 1420, McDonnell Douglas MD-82, N215AA, Little Rock, Arkansas, June 1, 1999.* (Report No. NTSB/AAR-01/02, DCA99MA060). Washington, DC. Retrieved January 27, 2006 from http://amelia.db.erau.edu/ reports/ntsb/aar/AAR01-02.pdf

National Transportation Safety Board. (1997). *Continental Airlines Flight 1943, Douglas DC-9, N10556, Wheels-Up Landing, Houston, Texas, February 19, 1996*. (Report No. NTSB/AAR-97/01, PB97-910401). Retrieved January 27, 2006 from http://amelia.db.erau.edu/reports/ntsb/aar/AAR97-01.pdf

National Transportation Safety Board. (1995). *Runway Overrun Following Rejected Takeoff. Continental Airlines flight 795, McDonnell-Douglas MD-82, N18835, LaGuardia Airport, Flushing, New York, March 2, 1994.* (Report No. NTSB/AAR-95/01). Retrieved 10 October, 2007, from http://amelia.db.erau. edu/reports/ntsb/aar/AAR95-01.pdf

National Transportation Safety Board. (1994a). *A Review of Flightcrew-involved Major Accidents of U.S. Air Carriers, 1978 through 1990*. (Report No. PB94-917001, NTSB/SS-94/01). Retrieved January 4, 2005, from http://amelia. db.erau.edu/cdl/ntsbss.htm

National Transportation Safety Board. (1994b). *Uncontrolled Collision with Terrain, American International Airways Flight 808, Douglas DC-8-61, N814CK, U.S. Naval Air Station Guantanamo Bay, Cuba, August 18, 1993*. (Report No. PB94-910406, NTSB/AAR-94/04). Retrieved January 27, 2006 from http://amelia.db.erau.edu/reports/ntsb/aar/AAR94-04.pdf

National Transportation Safety Board. (1991). *Runway Collision of USAir Flight 1493, Boeing 737 and Skywest Flight 5569 Fairchild Metroliner, Los Angeles International Airport, Los Angeles, California, February 1, 1991*. (Report No. NTSB/AAR-91/08). Retrieved 5 January, 2008 from http://amelia.db.erau. edu/reports/ntsb/aar/AAR91-08.pdf

National Transportation Safety Board. (1989). *Delta Airlines, Inc., Boeing 727-232, N473DA, Dallas-Fort Worth International Airport, Texas, August 31, 1988.* (Report No. PB89-910406, NTSB/AAR-89-04). Retrieved February 5, 2005 from http://amelia.db.erau.edu/reports/ntsb/aar/AAR89-04.pdf

National Transportation Safety Board. (1988). *Northwest Airlines, Inc., McDonnell Douglas DC-9-82, N312RC, Detroit Metropolitan Wayne County Airport, Romulus, Michigan, August 16, 1987.* (Report No. PB88-910406, NTSB/AAR-88-05). Retrieved February 5,2005 from http://amelia.db.erau.edu/reports/ntsb/aar/AAR88-05.pdf

National Transportation Safety Board. (1969). *Pan American World Airways, Inc., Boeing 707-321C, N799PA Elmendorf Air Force Base, Anchorage, Alaska, December 26, 1968.* (NTSB/AAR-88-05). Retrieved August 6, 2008 from http://amelia.db.erau.edu/reports/ntsb/aar/AAR69-08.pdf

Norman, D. A., and Shallice, T. (1986). Attention to action: willed and automatic control of behavior, In R. J. Davidson, G. E. Schwartz, and D. Shapiro (Eds.) (1986) *Consciousness and Self-regulation*, Vol. 4 (pp. 1–18), New York: Plenum Press. (Original work published 1980).

Loft, S., Humphreys, M., and Neal, A. (2004). The influence of memory for prior instances on performance in a conflict detection task. *Journal of Experimental Psychology: Applied,* 10, pp. 173–187.

O'Shea, E. (1999). Factors contributing to medication errors: a literature review. *Journal of Clinical Nursing* 8, pp. 49–504.

Oberauer, K., and Kliegl, R. (2004). Simultaneous cognitive operations in working memory after dual-task practice. *Journal of Experimental Psychology:Human Perception and Performance*, 30(40), pp. 689–707.

Pape, T. M. (2003). Applying airline safety practices to medication administration. *MEDSURG Nursing,* 12(2), pp. 77–93.

Pashler, H., Johnson, J. C. and Ruthruff, E. (2001). Attention and performance. *Annual Review of Psychology*, 52, pp. 629–651.

Patient Safety Authority (2005). Forgotten but not gone: tourniquets left on patients. PA-PSRS, *Patient Safety Advisory*, 2 (2), pp. 19–21.

Raby, M., and Wickens, C. D. (1994). Strategic workload management and decision biases in aviation. *International Journal of Aviation Psychology*, 4(3), pp. 211–240.

Rasmussen, J. (1980). The human as a systems component. In: Smith, H.T. and Green, T. R. G. (Eds), *Human Interaction with Computers*. London: Academic Press.

Reason, J. T. (2002). Combating omission erorrs through task analysis and good reminders. *Quality and Safety in Health Care*, 11, pp. 40–44. Retrieved 28 June, 2007 from qshc.bmj.com.

Reason, J. T. (1997). *Managing the Risks of Organizational Accidents.* Aldershot, UK: Ashgate Publishing Limited.

Reason, J. T. (1992). Cognitive underspecification: Its variety and consequences. In B.J. Baars (Ed.), *Experimental Slips and Human Error; Exploring the Architecture of Volition* (pp. 71–91). Plenum Press: New York.

Reason, J. T. (1990). *Human Error*. New York: Cambridge University Press.

Redelmeier, D. A., and Tibshirani, R. J. (1997). Association between celllular-telephone calls and motor vehicle collisions. *The New England Journal of Medicine*, 336, pp. 453–458.

Roberts, D. F., Foehr, U. G., and Rideout, V. (2005). *Generation M: Media in the Lives of 8–18 year-olds.* Kaiser Family Foundation. Retrieved 6 January, 2008 from http://kff.org/entmedia/upload/Generation-M-Media-in-the-Lives-of-8-18-Year-olds-Report-Introduction.pdf

Rogers, M. L., Cook, R. I., Bower, R., Molloy, M., and Render, M. L. (2004). Barriers to implementing wrong site surgery guidelines: A cognitive work analysis. *IEEE Transactions on Systems, Man, and Cybernetics, Part A: Systems and Humans,* 34(6), pp. 757–763.

Rubenstein, J. S., Meyer, D. E., and Evans, J. E. (2001). Executive control of cognitive processes in task switching. *Journal of Experimental Psychology: Human Perception and Performance*, 27(4), pp. 763–797.

Rukab, J. A., Johnson-Throopa, K. A., Malinb, J., and Zhang, J. (2004). A Framework of Interruptions in Distributed Team Environments. In M. Fieschi et al. (Eds.), *MEDINFO*, Amsterdam: IOS Press, pp. 1282–88.

Sarter, N. B. and Alexander, H. M. (2000). Error types and related error detection mechanisms in the aviation domain: An analysis of ASRS incident reports. *International Journal of Aviation Psychology*, 10(2), pp. 189–206.

Schneider, W., Dumais, S. T., and Shiffrin, R.M. (1984). Automatic and control processing and attention. In R. Parasuraman and D. R. Davies (Eds.), *Varieties of Attention* (pp. 1–27). Orlando,FL: Academic Press.

Shakeri S., and Funk, K. (2007). A comparison of human and near-optimal task management behavior. *Human Factors,* 49(3), pp. 400–416.

Shebilske, W., Goettl, B., and Regian, J.W. (1999). Executive control and automatic processes as complex skills develop in laboratory and applied settings. In D. Gopher and A. Koriat (Eds.), *Attention and Performance XVII: Cognitive Regulation of Performance: Interaction of Theory and Application.* Chapter 14. Cambridge, MA: MIT Press.

Shiffrin, R. M. and Schneider, W. (1977). Controlled and automatic human information processing: II. Perceptual learning, automatic attending, and a general theory. *Psychological Theory*, 84, pp. 127–190.

Simons, D. J., and Rensink, R. A. (2003). Induced failures of visual awareness. *Journal of Vision*, 3(1), http://journalofvision.org/3/1/i/

Speier, C., Vessey, I., and Valacich, J. S. (2003). The effects of interruptions, task complexity, and information presentation on computer-supported decision-making performance. *Decision Sciences*, 34(4), pp. 771–797.

Stone, M., Dismukes, R. K., and Remington, R. (2001). Prospective memory in dynamic environments: Effects of load, delay, and phonological rehearsal. *Memory*, 9(3), pp. 165–176.

Strayer, D. L., Crouch, D. J., and Drews, F. A. (2004). A comparison of the cell phone driver and the drunk driver. *AEI-Brookings Joint Center*, Working Paper No. 04-13. Retrieved 9 January, 2008 from http://ssrn.com/abstract=570222

Strayer, D. L., Drews, F. A., and Johnston, W. A. (2003). Cell phone-induced failures of visual attention during simulated driving. *Journal of Experimental Psychology: Applied*, 9(1), pp. 23–32.

Sumwalt, R. L. III, Thomas, R. J., and Dismukes, R. K. (2003). The new last line of defense against aviation accidents. *Aviation Week and Space Technology*, 159(8), p. 66.

Sumwalt, R. L. III, Thomas, R. J., and Dismukes, R. K. (2002). Enhancing flight-crew monitoring skills can increase flight safety. In *Proceedings of the 55th International Air Safety Seminar, Flight Safety Foundation* (pp. 175–206), Dublin, Ireland, November 4–7. Retrieved 7 January, 2008 from http://human-factors.arc.nasa.gov/flightcognition/Publications/FSF_Monitoring_FINAL.pdf

Theureau, J., Filippi, G., Saliou, G., Le Guilcher, B., and Vermersch, P. (2002). Cultural issues of nuclear power plant collective control in accidental situations and their impact upon design issues. *Eleventh European Conference on Cognitive Ergonomics ECCE-11, 8–11 Sept., Catania, Italy*.

Trafton, J. G., Altmann, E. M., Brock, D. P. and Mintz, F. E. (2003). Preparing to resume an interrupted task: effects of prospective goal encoding and retrospective rehearsal. *Int. J. Human-Computer Studies*, 58, pp. 583–603.

Tucker, A. L., and Spear, S. J. (2006). Operational failures and interruptions in hospital nursing. *HSR: Health Services Research* 41(3), pp. 643–662.

United States Government Accountability Office. (2007). *Aviation Runway and Ramp Safety: Sustained Efforts to Address Leadership, Technology, and Other Challenges Needed to Reduce Accidents and Incidents*. Report to Congressional Requesters. Retrieved 13 January, 2008 from http://www.gao.gov/new.items/d0829.pdf

US DOT, Federal Rail Administration (2001). *DOT/FRA/ORD-01/02, Final Report May 2001: Understanding How Train Dispatchers Manage and Control Trains: Results of a Cognitive Task Analysis*. Retrieved 6 August, 2008 from http://www.fra.dot.gov/downloads/Research/ord0102.pdf

Veillette, P. R. (2005). Threat and error management. *Aviation Week's Business and Commercial Aviation*, 9 February.

Welford, A. T. (1967). Single channel operation in the brain. *Acta Psychologica*, 27, pp. 5–21.

Wickens, C. D. (2005). Attentional tunneling and task management. In R. Jensen (Ed.) *Proceedings, 13th International Symposium of Aviation Psychology*. Oklahoma City.

Wickens, C. D. and Hollands, J. G. (Eds.) (2000). *Engineering Psychology and Human Performance* (3rd Ed). Upper Saddle River, NJ: Prentice-Hall.

Wickens, C. D., and Seidler, K. S. (1997). Information access in a dual-task context: Testing a model of optimal strategy selection. *Journal of Experimental Psychology: Applied*, 3(3), pp. 196–215.

Zohar, D. (1999). When things go wrong: The effect of daily work hassles on effort, exertion and negative mood. *Journal of Occupational and Organizational Psychology*, 72, pp. 265–283.

Index